BAT
WORKERS'
MANUAL

3RD EDITION 2004

Edited by
A. J. Mitchell-Jones & A. P. McLeish

Illustrated by T. P. McOwat

JOINT
NATURE
CONSERVATION
COMMITTEE

Contents

Foreword

It is now 15 years since the first edition of the *Bat Workers' Manual* was produced and almost 5 years since the second edition appeared. During the last 15 years the bat conservation movement has gone from strength to strength, with a continuing expansion of local bat groups and the development of the Bat Conservation Trust to provide a national focus. At the same time, there have been fundamental changes in the organisation of the statutory conservation bodies, with the split of the Nature Conservancy Council into three separate country agencies and the Joint Nature Conservation Committee, followed by internal reorganisations in each agency. Despite these changes, close working relationships between government and non-government organisations have persisted and, happily, the movement can be characterised as co-operative rather than confrontational.

A major change in the second edition was the development of a chapter on safety in bat work, which drew together and expanded information from the first edition. Although bat-workers have a good safety record, recent litigation has shown clearly that organisations have a responsibility to ensure that people working under their direction, whether paid or not, are able to work in safety. This is a responsibility we must all share and so safety has now been incorporated explicitly into the training syllabus.

The third edition has been produced only 5 years after the second edition because the tragic death of a batworker in Scotland from European Bat Lyssavirus (EBLV) infection at the end of 2002 signalled a fundamental change in the way organisations and individuals approach bat work. This death, together with two records of EBLV in Daubenton's bats in England, means that it must now be assumed that the virus is present in bats in the UK and that bat-handling practices, and health and safety advice must change. This third edition of the manual incorporates those changes and updates some other information and advice.

In other respects very little has changed. A great deal of the original material in the first edition remains as relevant now as it did 15 years ago. The internal reorganisation carried out in the second edition, with the addition of new material to reflect new concerns and the development of new areas of interest, has been retained in the third edition. The excellent drawings by Tom McOwat have almost all been retained with some updated diagrams where necessary to reflect the changes in health and safety practices.

The third edition has retained a number of case studies on a variety of subjects, which were new to the second edition. These provide a useful perspective on the practical problems that confront bat-workers from time to time and suggest solutions that could be adapted to other circumstances. Good case studies have proved hard to find and we are very grateful to those individuals or organisations who have contributed.

In 1987, the original manual was one of the few publications available to guide practical bat work in the UK. We are now in the fortunate position of having a much greater range of publications available on a variety of topics, such as the use of bat-detectors, habitat conservation, survey work or the construction or modification of roosts of various types. Clearly a manual cannot, and should not, duplicate these, but we have tried to give a brief introduction to these subjects and to suggest sources of further information. An example is the expanding use of bat-detectors, which were barely mentioned in the first edition. Since then the development of technology and fieldcraft have led to a great advance in their use.

Overall, the change in balance of the manual reflects some of the changes that have happened in bat conservation over the last 15 years. For example, there has been less focus on the impact of remedial timber treatment, following the adoption of safer chemicals, whereas the importance of field survey work away from roosts has increased. The importance of public relations and problem-solving for a group of species that depend so heavily on buildings has remained a central theme.

The manual is the product of extensive consultation with many individuals involved in bat conservation and has benefited greatly from their input. It has been impossible to include all the suggestions we have received, but we hope this expanded publication will continue to serve the needs of bat conservationists.

Tony Mitchell-Jones
Andrew McLeish

Acknowledgements

As with the first edition, many people helped with the revision and improvement of the second edition, either through general comments and discussion or by contributing sections to particular chapters.

General help was provided by David Bullock and Miriam Glendell (National Trust), Amy Coyte, Tony Hutson, Shirley Thompson and Phil Richardson (Bat Conservation Trust), Rob Raynor (Scottish Natural Heritage), Ruth Warren (Countryside Council for Wales), Gloucester Bat Group, Patty Briggs, Stuart Corbett, Tom McOwat, Louise Oliver and Gill Hinchcliffe.

Chapter 11 benefited greatly from additional information from Frank Greenaway (caves and mines), Geoff Billington (bridges) and Mike Holmes (trees). Peter Smith updated the information about radio-tracking in Chapter 6, Maggie Brown and Andrew Routh helped to update Chapter 7 and Mike Worsfold provided additional information for Appendix 2.

The swift revision of this third edition was helped greatly by comments from Stewart Pritchard (SNH), Jessa Battersby (JNCC), Liz Halliwell (CCW), staff at the Bat Conservation Trust (Colin Catto, Ali Rasey) and Tony Hutson. Tom McOwat obligingly redrew some of the illustrations.

It is with sadness that we record the untimely death of Gill Hinchcliffe (1958–2002), who contributed so much to bat conservation and the development of bat groups.

Pipistrelle bat. © Frank Greenaway

Bechstein's bat. © Frank Greenaway

Bats and the law

A J Mitchell-Jones & C J Robertson

1.1 Legislation in the United Kingdom

In England, Scotland and Wales all bat species are fully protected under the Wildlife and Countryside Act 1981 (WCA) (as amended) through inclusion in Schedule 5. In England and Wales, this Act has been amended by the Countryside and Rights of Way Act 2000 (CRoW), which adds an extra offence, makes species offences arrestable, increases the time limits for some prosecutions and increases penalties. In Scotland, the Criminal Justice (Scotland) Act 2003 has amended the WCA to widen the powers of arrest, increase the time limits for some prosecutions, increase penalties and extend the use of search warrants. It does not, however, introduce any new offences. The Nature Conservation (Scotland) Bill will introduce further amendments to the WCA in Scotland in 2004.

In Northern Ireland all bats are fully protected by the Wildlife (Northern Ireland) Order 1985 (as amended) through inclusion in Schedule 5.

All bats are also included in Schedule 2 of the Conservation (Natural Habitats, &c.) Regulations 1994, (or Northern Ireland, 1995) (the Habitats Regulations), which defines 'European protected species of animals'.

These various pieces of legislation almost parallel each other, with a few small differences in wording. The legal significance of these differences has not yet been fully established and so the following account attempts to combine them to provide a simplified summary.

Taken together, the Act, Order and Regulations make it illegal to:
*   intentionally or deliberately kill, injure or capture (or take) bats;
*   deliberately disturb bats (whether in a roost or not);
*   recklessly disturb roosting bats or obstruct access to their roosts (England & Wales only; proposed for Scotland in 2004);
*   damage or destroy bat roosts;
*   possess or transport a bat or any part of a bat, unless acquired legally;
*   sell (or offer for sale) or exchange bats, or parts of bats.

The word 'roost' is not used in the legislation, but is used here for simplicity. The actual wording in

Brown long-eared bat. © Frank Greenaway

the legislation is 'any structure or place which any wild animal…uses for shelter or protection' (WCA) or 'breeding site or resting place' (Habitats Regulations). Because bats tend to re-use the same roosts after periods of vacancy, legal opinion is that the roost is protected whether or not the bats are present at the time.

Intentionally can be interpreted directly as 'a result is intended when it is the actor's purpose' or it can be inferred by a court when the result is a virtually certain consequence of the act and the actor knows that it is a virtually certain consequence. Deliberately is not well defined in law, although the House of Lords has equated it with 'wilfully'. A person acts recklessly if he deliberately takes an unacceptable risk (recognises the risk but takes it anyway) or fails to notice or consider an obvious risk (does not consider whether there is a risk).

There are three defences in the law, which allow what would otherwise be prohibited acts.
1   Injured or disabled animals may be taken and possessed solely for the purpose of looking after them and releasing them once they are no longer disabled; similarly, badly injured animals may be killed legally.
2   Within dwelling-houses, bats may be disturbed and bat roosts may be damaged, destroyed or obstructed. However, bats may not be killed, injured or taken.

3   Killing, injuring, taking or disturbing bats, or damaging, destroying or obstructing roosts are not offences if these were the incidental result of a lawful operation and could not reasonably have been avoided.

The above statements apply to any species on Schedule 5 of the Wildlife & Countryside Act 1981 (the Wildlife [Northern Ireland] Order 1985) or any 'European protected species', but there is one special provision, which applies only to bats. This states that defences 2 and 3 above cannot be relied on (except within the living area of a dwelling house) unless the appropriate Statutory Nature Conservation Organisation (SNCO) had been notified and allowed a reasonable time to advise on whether the proposed action should be carried out and, if so, the method to be used. The SNCOs are English Nature, Scottish Natural Heritage, the Countryside Council for Wales and the Environment and Heritage Service in Northern Ireland.

The police are the primary law enforcement agency, so if you think the law has been broken, contact your local police wildlife liaison officer (WLO) or police force. A list of WLOs is available from the RSPB Investigations Section (tel: 01767 680551). Prosecutions for offences under the legislation in all countries must be brought within 6 months of the date on which sufficient evidence became available to the prosecutor, subject to a time limit of 2 years after the commission of the offence. Penalties for most offences are up to level 5 on the standard scale per offence (£5000 per offence in 2003) and/or a custodial sentence of up to 6 months. Further details are given in Childs (2003), which is updated whenever the legislation changes.

The SNCOs can issue licences to allow otherwise prohibited actions, such as catching and handling bats, for scientific or educational reasons, ringing and marking, conservation, photography or protecting zoological collections. Applications should be made to the Licensing Section of the appropriate SNCO.

Licences in connection with public health or safety, prevention of the spread of disease or the prevention of serious damage to livestock, crops or other property may be issued, as appropriate, by the Department for Environment, Food and Rural Affairs (Defra), the Scottish Executive, the National Assembly for Wales Countryside Division or the Environment & Heritage Service (Northern Ireland). These departments also issue licences under the Habitats Regulations to permit otherwise prohibited acts where this is considered to be for imperative reasons of overriding public interest (primarily development). Licences can only be issued when there is no satisfactory alternative and when the action authorised will not be detrimental to the maintenance of the populations of the species concerned at favourable conservation status in their natural range. Note that these arrangements are subject to change.

Acts or operations that take place on a Site of Special Scientific Interest (SSSI) (Areas of Special Scientific Interest (ASSI [in Northern Ireland]) are covered by Part II of the Wildlife & Countryside Act. The SNCOs have a particular role in the enforcement of this part of the legislation and should be contacted if you believe something illegal is taking place.

This is only a general and simplified guide to the main provisions of the law. The Wildlife and Countryside Act 1981 (and its amendments), the Environmental Protection Act 1990, the Conservation (Natural Habitats, &c.) Regulations 1994, the Countryside and Rights of Way Act 2000, the Criminal Justice (Scotland) Act 2003 or the equivalent legislation in Northern Ireland should be consulted for further details.

Bats are similarly protected in all other parts of the British Isles. Information on bat protection in the Republic of Ireland can be obtained from National Parks & Wildlife, Department of Environment, Heritage and Local Government, 7 Ely Place, Dublin 2 and in the Isle of Man from DAFF, Knockaloe Farm, Peel, Isle of Man IM5 3AJ.

Information on bat protection and the law in the UK is contained in various leaflets, which are available from the SNCOs: English Nature – *Focus on bats* and *Bats in roofs: a guide for surveyors*; Scottish Natural Heritage – *Bats and people*; Countryside Council for Wales – *Ystlumod, Bats*; The Environment and Heritage Service (Northern Ireland) – *Focus on Bats*.

Law enforcement – gathering evidence

There may come a time when, in the course of your bat work, you witness, or find evidence of, the law being broken. It is essential in such a case that a careful and detailed record of events and evidence is kept if there is to be any hope of a subsequent prosecution being successful. Normally it would be best to ask a police WLO to gather the evidence, but if you are the first on the scene of a crime you can follow these best practice guidelines to gather admissible evidence.

The following notes explain what is required by a court and give some idea of what you can expect if you are asked to give evidence:

- It is vital that you make written notes of any incident. If possible make the notes as the incident occurs, but if this is not possible then make them as soon as possible after the event. If made too late after the event, a court may decide they are inadmissible. If you are making notes at the time, record as many details as you can as they happen. You can follow up these notes after the event with a more methodical appraisal of the situation as you remember it, including anything you did not have time to record.
- Important details to note: date, time, location (including grid reference if possible), descriptions of people, names, addresses and telephone numbers if you know them, vehicle registration numbers and descriptions, exactly what you saw and heard. You can include in your notes things that you overheard somebody else say (e.g. "Mr X told me that Mr Y said..."), but this is called hearsay and it will probably be inadmissible as evidence in court. However, by including it in your notes you may assist the investigating officer with his/her inquiries.
- When writing notes try not to leave any blank spaces and fill in any blank spaces with a line. This shows the court that no changes could have been made after the event. If you do need to make a change, cross out the incorrect section lightly so that it can still be read and add the corrected statement. You must initial and date/time this entry.

- When you have written your notes, sign and date/time them. Make sure any other witnesses read and sign and date/time them too (assuming they agree). Make sure you have their contact details. You must also give the suspect, if present, the opportunity to read and sign your notes. If they refuse, add a note that you gave them this opportunity.
- A statement may be necessary at some stage. A police officer or other investigating officer will take this for you and advise you how it needs to be done.
- If you are asked to appear in court as a witness or expert witness do not worry. It is not you who is on trial. You will be asked to stand in the witness box and swear an oath to tell the truth. You will first be guided through your statement by the prosecution solicitor, after which you will be asked questions by the defence solicitor. You should address your answers to the Magistrates. If you do not know or cannot remember the answer to a question, just say so. Take your original notes along with you. If you wish to refer to them to assist your memory while in the witness box (a prosecution may be many months after the event), ask for permission. There will be a discussion about the admissibility of your notes, so you will need to tell the court how soon after the event you wrote them. In court, you will not be allowed to give hearsay, but do not worry if you are not too sure what that means because you will simply be stopped if the evidence you give is inadmissible.
- Make sure that you report the incident as soon as possible. It makes sense to find out who your local police Wildlife Liaison Officer is and to make contact with them if you suspect you may need their services during your bat work. You can also get help from the SNCO, the Bat Conservation Trust or any police officer.

Source: English Nature/RSPB.

1.2 International protection

As well as domestic legislation, bats are also protected under several international Conventions, Directives or Agreements. Where these place obligations on the UK government, they have been translated into the domestic legislation described in Section 1.1.

European Union Directive on the Conservation of Natural Habitats and of Wild Fauna and Flora (Habitats and Species Directive)

This Directive places a legal requirement on all Member States of the European Union to protect specified habitats and species through their own domestic legislation. In the UK this has been implemented by the Conservation (Natural Habitats, &c.) Regulations 1994. All species of bats are on Annex IV ('European protected species of animal'), which requires that they are given full protection. Five species (greater horseshoe, lesser horseshoe, Bechstein's, barbastelle and greater mouse-eared (believed extinct)) are also on Annex II, which requires the designation of Special Areas of Conservation (SAC) to ensure that the species is maintained at a favourable conservation status. In the UK this is being done through the designation of certain selected SSSIs. This international network of sites is known as the Natura 2000 series.

Convention on the Conservation of European Wildlife and Natural Habitats (Bern Convention)

This convention, to which the UK is a signatory, places obligations on member states to protect threatened or endangered species and their habitats and to ban the use of many unselective methods of capture. It is translated into domestic legislation as the Wildlife & Countryside Act 1981.

All species of bats, except the pipistrelle *Pipistrellus pipistrellus*, are on Appendix II, which requires that they are given special protection. The pipistrelle is on Appendix III, which requires the regulation of its exploitation.

Convention on the Conservation of Migratory Species of Wild Animals (Bonn Convention)

This global Convention is intended to encourage co-operation between member parties in the conservation of species that move between range states. It provides for the protection of some migratory species, but its main intended method of operation is to encourage range states to set up Agreements to benefit species listed on Appendix II, which includes all European bats.

One such Agreement is the 'Agreement on the Conservation of Populations of European Bats', known as 'Eurobats', which came into force in 1994. Its main provisions are: to restrict the killing or capture of bats; the protection of key bat habitats; the co-ordination of research and conservation experience; and increasing public awareness of bat conservation. These requirements do not appear to need any changes to current UK domestic legislation.

1.3 Bat workers and the law

Perhaps the most significant element of legal protection from the bat worker's point of view is the requirement that householders with bats in their houses, other than in the living area, must notify the appropriate Statutory Nature Conservation Organisation (SNCO) before taking any action against the bats or their roost. Similarly, the SNCO must be notified before any activities that could incidentally affect bats or their roosts are started. This could include building and re-roofing operations, pest control, remedial timber treatment or cavity-wall insulation. The need for the SNCO to be given an opportunity to advise an owner provides great scope for the prevention of damage to roosts and for education. Most licensable bat work carried out by licensed bat workers relates to the provision of this advice.

1.4 Bat work without a licence

Much research and survey work can be done without a licence, for example searching for new roosts, observing or counting bats outside roosts, discovering feeding areas, analysing food from bat droppings, or building and erecting bat boxes. Much can be learnt through the literature, by talking to other bat workers and by joining a local bat group. Similarly, public relations and publicity work, such as general advice, talks, walks or disseminating information, which forms the core of much conservation activity, does not require a licence. However, if you wish to enter known roosts (including bat boxes that have been or are being used by bats) or disturb, catch or handle bats, you must be covered by an appropriate licence.

1.5 The licensing system

It is important to ensure that you have the licence you need and that you fulfil its conditions. A casual approach to the question of licences may not only jeopardise your own ability to work with bats, but may undermine all our efforts to persuade people who feel seriously inconvenienced by the law to abide by it.

The SNCOs are responsible for issuing licences to enable otherwise prohibited activities to be carried out for scientific, educational or conservation purposes. For most protected species, licence applicants have traditionally been asked to provide references (to establish bona fides) and to justify fully the need to carry out the requested activity. However, for bat work a special training scheme has been set up, which provides training and obviates the need for two references (see Section 1.6).

Special licences can be issued to cover particular circumstances, non-standard techniques, particular liaison requirements and so on, but one standard licence covers the majority of licensees, who are mainly involved in bat-roost visiting.

Licences are not considered necessary for examining single bat boxes because they are unlikely to contain bats. Only if a bat is found in a bat box and further examinations are proposed should a licence be obtained. Similarly, visits to lofts or caves and mines are not licensable unless it is known that bats are likely to be present.

Although the way in which licences are assessed and processed differs between the SNCOs, the following sections describe the licences most commonly issued, together with an indication of the level of knowledge or experience required. Further details will be found in Appendix 7.

1.5.1 Bat-roost visitor (conservation) licences

Bat-roost visiting, either in response to a direct enquiry or at the request of the SNCO, is one of the most important activities carried out by local bat-group members because it makes an enormous direct contribution to bat conservation, benefiting many thousands of bats each year.

The standard licence should meet all the legal requirements of a roost visitor, who may need to examine and handle bats in their roosts. The taking of bats by hand or static hand-net can be useful for identification and for public relations, to show a householder how interesting and attractive bats are, so it is included in the standard licence. Occasionally, where a licensee has little or no experience of handling bats, it may be deleted.

Normally only one or two bats should be taken for identification or to show to householders and these should be released as soon as possible. If resting bats cannot be taken by hand, a hand-net may be held in a stationary position beneath the exit hole so that one or two bats are caught as they drop from the exit. It should never be necessary to catch horseshoe bats because these can easily be identified in roosts. Obviously, hibernating bats should be disturbed as little as possible and should not normally be handled.

A basic knowledge of the biology and ecology of bats, plus an ability to catch, identify, handle and present them to people are required to obtain a licence to visit roosts in dwelling houses from April to September. Endorsements to this basic licence may be subject to further conditions.

1.5.2 Licences to disturb, take or possess bats for scientific purposes

Licences can be issued to disturb, take or possess bats for research or survey purposes. These include licences to visit known hibernacula, licences to use mist-nets, harp traps or other methods of catching bats in free flight, and licences to possess bats in captivity for research purposes. Licences to disturb or take bats in hibernacula for survey purposes can be viewed as a logical extension of the basic batworker licence, but most other licences are only issued once a project plan has been agreed with the appropriate SNCO.

i) To disturb or take bats in hibernacula for survey purposes

Visits to caves, mines, tunnels or other areas known to be regularly used for hibernation can cause disturbance to the bats that hibernate there. Such visits need to be regulated, and licences to disturb hibernating bats will be issued only to applicants who have demonstrated an understanding of the dangers involved and shown themselves to be careful workers. Survey of caves or mines for previously unknown hibernation sites does not require a licence, provided that the visit is abandoned once bats are discovered.

Experienced workers monitoring hibernacula for scientific or survey purposes may wish to be able to handle bats from time to time, for example to monitor their physiological condition or to check the identity of unusual specimens. In practice, experienced surveyors rarely touch bats.

The standard survey licence is usually valid for all species of bat, but exceptions can be made for very sensitive species in particular areas, such as disturbance or handling of horseshoe bats in those areas where they occur. However, members of bat groups who have shown themselves to be valuable and responsible licence holders will not normally be excluded from dealing with any species of bat, on the basis that they will know very well which are the most sensitive species for their area and will not wish to cause disturbance if this can be avoided. It is rarely necessary to take hibernating bats under licence for conservation purposes, as rescuing bats in an emergency can be done without a licence.

The licence, which may be valid for between 1 and 3 years, carries a number of conditions including, most importantly, a general liaison clause to prevent conflict between workers in adjacent areas.

ii) To disturb, take or possess bats for scientific purposes

This allows endorsements of special techniques or types of activity not otherwise covered. However it does not cover ringing, marking or disturbance for photography, which are licensed separately.

The types of projects that might be covered include:
*   use of mist-nets or harp traps for surveys or scientific research;
*   taking bats for genetic sampling;
*   taking bats for radio-tracking studies (combined with a marking licence);
*   possessing bats for flight or echolocation studies in the laboratory.

iii) To disturb bats for the purpose of photography

Licences may be issued specifically for bat photography but only where there is a special case for doing so. This will normally only be where the results contribute directly to public awareness about bats, as with some filming for television. The welfare of the bats must be the prime consideration at all times.

In England, Scotland and Wales, the standard licence includes a note about photography, which is permissible as an incidental part of licensed conservation or scientific work where no additional disturbance is caused thereby. This does not require a separate licence, but care must be taken not to cross the boundary between what is genuinely incidental and what is designed to get a good photograph. If you are in doubt, it is better to consult the SNCO's Licensing Section and obtain a licence if necessary. In Northern Ireland incidental photography (without a flash) is considered to be included in the basic roost visitors licence. Where you have a valid licence to disturb, take or possess bats, the camera can be a useful device to record the activities undertaken without intruding on them. Flash photography in roosts or hibernacula does not come into this category and requires separate licensing, as does the taking of bats into captivity for filming or photography. Flash photography of

hibernating bats should generally be limited as the noise and light could disturb them.

In order to gain a scientific or photographic licence, applicants need to demonstrate a serious interest in bat work and an understanding of how and when particular techniques should be employed.

Licences for netting, trapping or other techniques for catching bats in flight will require the applicant to demonstrate experience and competence in the use of the particular catching technique, as witnessed by a trainer, and appreciation of its appropriate application. Licences will be issued only for projects that have been agreed with the appropriate SNCO.

1.5.3 Licences to ring or mark bats for scientific purposes

These licences are only granted for research projects with clear objectives. Techniques such as fur clipping or the attachment of radio transmitters or passive integrated transponder (PIT) tags are also covered by these licences.

Ringing and marking, or the disturbance associated with these activities, can be harmful to bats so that ringing has been stopped or severely curtailed in several countries. In the UK, the value of ringing and marking techniques is recognised, but licences are issued only for clearly defined projects which will be subject to the approval of the licensing authority. Details of approved ringing and marking methods are given in Chapter 6.

1.6 Trainers and training

Trainers receive licences allowing them to train unlicensed bat workers in some or all the activities covered by the standard licence. Conservation licences are of most direct relevance to the work of bat groups, and every bat group should have at least one authorised conservation licence trainer. Initially, each trainer should be able to take on four or five students, but this will obviously vary according to circumstances and should decrease as the number of trainers increases.

The training system allows bat workers without any experience of a particular aspect of bat work, such as handling or the use of hand-nets, to train under their trainer's licence in order to gain the necessary experience to obtain their own licences. It also helps to ensure that conservation activities are carried out to a high standard and that appropriate conservation advice is given when responding to enquiries.

The knowledge and skills required for each type of licence are set out in the training syllabus (Appendix 7). Both knowledge and skills can be gained in a variety of ways, such as attending talks, conferences or training days, background reading, participation in bat group projects or roost visits under the supervision of a trainer or other licensed bat worker.

1.7 Applications, returns, reports and renewals

Application forms need to be completed for the various types of licence and for licence extensions. If you have already had a licence, this can be renewed periodically, provided that you have observed its conditions and reported on your activities.

Application forms for standard licences are available from the SNCO's Licensing Section. They should be completed by the applicant and countersigned by a trainer. However, if an applicant is unable to contact a licensed trainer, the names and addresses of two experienced bat-licence holders who are prepared to act as referees may be provided instead.

It is a condition of all licences that appropriate returns are made stating what licensed activities have been carried out. Where separate reports of bat roost visits have been submitted, this information should not be duplicated on licence returns. A statement of licensed activities carried out is required, so that some assessment of licensed disturbance can be made and the data can be used to further the conservation of bats. Numbers of bats recorded or other information on return forms may be used by the conservation organisations to monitor the status of bats or the value of individual sites.

If an exact renewal of a licence is required on its expiry, this should be requested on the licence return form. If a licence, which is not an exact renewal of a previous licence but includes some additional features, is required, a licence application form should be submitted. This should be accompanied where appropriate by a statement of

the training received or experience gained in the previous year and should be signed by a trainer.

Advice on all aspects of licensing can be obtained from the appropriate SNCO Licensing Section.

1.8 Planning Policy

1.8.1 Planning Issues

British and international wildlife legislation is central to protecting and conserving our wildlife heritage. However, conflicts frequently arise between the needs of wildlife and the needs of development, either of a specific site or in the wider context of local, regional or national planning.

The requirements for a bat survey in the case of a proposed development will vary according to the type of development, time of year and the type of site to be surveyed. Where an environmental assessment is required, a scoping study would normally be carried out at the outset to determine the likely impacts of any development and the investigations which should be carried out to ensure that the needs of bats are fully met.

1.8.2 Planning applications

The majority of development proposals do not require full environmental assessment. Barn conversions, small-scale new housing projects and building alterations are all decided through the local authority planning process. The Local Planning Authority (LPA), when considering an application for development that would be likely, if carried out, to result in a breach of The Wildlife and Countryside Act 1981 or the Conservation (Natural Habitats, &c.) Regulations 1994, should consider what precautions could be taken to prevent such a breach occurring in the event of the development going ahead. The presence of a protected species is therefore a material consideration when a LPA is considering a development proposal. The LPA may impose a planning condition or draw up an agreement under Section 106 of the Town & Country Planning Act 1990 (or S 75 of the Town & Country Planning (Scotland) Act 1997) with the developer to ensure that the needs of bats are fully met.

The LPA should consult with the SNCO, prior to granting planning permission if it appears that a licence may be required with respect to the development proposal (i.e. if evidence of bats has been found). Note that the destruction of a bat roost is an absolute offence under the Conservation (Natural Habitats &c.) Regulations, so the onus lies with the applicant to satisfy himself that no offences will be committed if the development goes ahead.

In all circumstances it is essential that sufficient information is gathered both about the proposed development and the presence of bats to ensure that an accurate and reasonable opinion can be reached over both the nature and importance of the bat site and the likely impacts should the development go ahead. Proposals for mitigation should be considered at an early stage.

The bat survey work should always be carried out by a consultant with adequate experience and, if necessary, an appropriate licence. If a bat group is to carry out the survey it would be wise to ensure that the group is covered by both appropriate public liability insurance and professional indemnity insurance (the Bat Conservation Trust can provide advice on this).

In many cases the LPA, developer and consultant can work together to find a solution that will be agreeable to all parties. The LPA has the final word in deciding whether an application will be approved. Where planning permission is refused an applicant has a right of appeal. This may be by way of a written procedure or, in about 5% of cases, by way of Public Inquiry. In either case, evidence from expert witnesses may be presented. At public inquiries witnesses are subject to cross-examination by the appellants and possibly by the Inspector.

Once planning permission for a development has been granted, it will still be necessary to obtain a licence from the appropriate authority (see Section 1.1) to permit the disturbance of bats or the destruction of a bat roost. Awareness of planning law and issues in relation to nature conservation varies from authority to authority. In England, *Policy Planning Guidance: Nature Conservation (PPG9)* published by the Department of the Environment, Transport and the Regions (now Defra), sets out the Government's policies on different aspects of planning and gives guidance on how policies for the conservation of our natural heritage are to be reflected in land-use planning. In Scotland, *National Planning Policy Guideline (NPPG) 14:* Natural Heritage, published by the

Scottish Office (now the Scottish Executive) performs a similar function, providing the definitive statement of national planning policy in relation to Scotland's natural heritage. In Wales, TAN(W)5 – a technical advice note – provides information about nature conservation and planning. In Northern Ireland, the Environment and Heritage Service has produced *Planning Conservation Guidelines – Nature Conservation and Planning.*

A personal approach by a bat worker/group may help the LPA gain a better understanding of bat related issues and consequently act on planning applications with more precision and understanding.

1.8.3 Environmental Assessment

The definition of an Environmental Assessment (EA) states 'EA is the process by which information about the environmental effects of a project is collected, assessed and taken into account by the planning authority in reaching a decision on whether the proposed development should go ahead'.

Only certain types of development require that an Environmental Assessment (EA) be carried out. Projects are categorised into two schedules depending on their likely environmental affects. Environmental assessment is mandatory for Schedule 1 projects where an EA may be appropriate, which includes oil refineries and major road schemes. Schedule 2 projects are those such as mining or industrial installation where there may be significant effects by virtue of their size, nature or location. The proximity to Sites of Special Scientific Interest or other designated sites is a case in point. Government advice as to the likely need for EA is given in circulars, which are updated at intervals when new information is available.

The information required for an EA can be collated from published documents, consultation exercises and survey work but should be sufficient for a reasonable judgement to be made on the project, whether it is a major road scheme or the development of a new housing estate. The final decision may, for example result in the scheme being turned down, the re-routing of the road link or alteration of the housing-estate design.

The Environmental Statement (ES) is the document produced at the end of this data collation process and should include the following information to

meet current guidelines:
- a description of the development;
- data necessary to identify the main effects of the development;
- an assessment of the likely significant effects on the environment (including fauna);
- measures to avoid, reduce or remedy the impacts of adverse effects.

The needs of bats must be taken into account if they are present on the site of a proposed development that is subject to an EA.

1.8.4 Local plans and unitary development plans

There is one other area in which bat workers/groups may take an interest in planning issues. Local plans and unitary development plans should identify relevant international, national and local nature conservation interests. They should ensure that the protection and enhancement of those interests is properly provided for in development and land-use policies, and place particular emphasis on the strength of protection afforded to international designations. Plans should offer reasonable certainty to developers, landowners and residents about the weight that will be given to nature conservation interests in reaching planning decisions. Nature conservation issues should be included in the surveys of local authority areas as required by sections 11 and 30 of the Town and Country Planning Act 1990 (S. 4 of the Town & Country Planning [Scotland] Act 1997), to ensure that plans are based on sufficient information about local species, habitats, geology and landform. Plans should be concerned not only with designated areas but also with other land of conservation value and, possibly, provision of new habitats.

All local authorities will maintain a record of important nature conservation sites in their area. In many cases the authority will work with the local wildlife trust to achieve this. Recently some authorities have started to store this data on Geographic Information Systems (GIS). The advantage of this method is that planners can refer directly to a computerised map and database to see if there is a nature conservation issue connected with a planning proposal. Important bat sites can be included on the GIS and bat groups should encourage authorities to record these sites on their systems (subject to an appropriate confidentiality agreement).

1.9 Biodiversity

In 1994 the government published Biodiversity: The UK Action Plan. This was the British response to the Biodiversity Convention held in Rio de Janeiro, which the government signed in 1992. The overall goal of the UK Action Plan is 'to conserve and enhance biological diversity within the UK, and to contribute to the conservation of global diversity through all appropriate mechanisms'.

Following the publication of the Action Plan, a Biodiversity Steering Group was established, which developed costed action plans for priority species and habitats. Action plans now exist for the greater mouse-eared, pipistrelle, greater horseshoe, lesser horseshoe, barbastelle and Bechstein's bats (Biodiversity: The UK Steering Group Report).

These action plans contain targets for maintaining or increasing populations and proposed actions for achieving those targets.

If the UK Action Plan is to be implemented successfully, it is important that national targets are translated into effective action at a local level. Local Biodiversity Action Plans (LBAPs) are the means by which practical actions can be achieved. The development of Local Biodiversity Action Plans is dependent upon partnership between many organisations, although local authorities are well placed to take the lead in promoting plans, particularly at the county/council area level.

Many LBAPs have now been developed and these will include action plans for individual species of bat and also habitats that are important to bats. Bat groups are well placed to become involved in both developing and implementing LBAPs. Information on developing LBAPs in each country can be obtained through the appropriate Biodiversity Group (see http://www.ukbap.org.uk/contacts_links.htm for details). The Countryside and Rights of Way Act 2000 (S74) places some obligation on Ministers and government departments in England and Wales to have regard to the conservation of biological diversity and to publish lists of habitats and species that are of principal importance for this. The Nature Conservation (Scotland) Bill, to be enacted in 2004, contains similar obligations.

Public Inquiry confirms importance of lesser horseshoe bat roost

In the autumn of 1991, a breeding roost of lesser horseshoe bats *Rhinolophus hipposideros* in an old coach house near Welshpool, Powys (formerly Montgomeryshire), Wales, came under threat from development proposals. The owner was seeking planning permission to convert the buildings into six flats. This would have considerably reduced the extent of roosting space used by the bats. While space in the small clock turret would have remained, this would not have been adequate to ensure the survival of the breeding colony of up to 70 lesser horseshoe bats; the colony was one of only five in the former county of Montgomeryshire.

The Countryside Council for Wales (CCW) and the Montgomeryshire Wildlife Trust (MWT) assessed the requirements for the roost and advised that if the proposed scheme were reduced to five dwelling units the lesser horseshoe bats would not be threatened.

However, no significant changes to the plans were made and the district council planning committee resolved that planning permission should be granted despite contrary

advice submitted by CCW and MWT. The district council said that legal protection of bats was not as important as the local issues of housing and providing job opportunities. Faced with the impending loss of the breeding colony, CCW and MWT asked the Welsh Office to call the planning application in for decision by the Secretary of State for Wales. This was done, just in time, before the decision of the local planning committee had become operative.

A public inquiry lasting 3 days was held in September 1992, where evidence was given concerning the needs of the lesser horseshoe bats. The outcome was announced almost a year later, in August 1993, when the Secretary of State for Wales decided that planning permission should be refused. In reaching the decision it was recognised that more than local issues were at stake and that the government had a duty to respect both national legislation and the obligation to international agreements relating to bats. This was the first ever public inquiry at which bats were the key issue.

Source: Bat News No 31, October 1993.

Lesser horseshoe bat. © Frank Greenaway

References and further reading

ANON. 1979. *Convention on the Conservation of European Wildlife and Natural Habitats.* European Treaty Series No. 104. (Bern Convention, 1982.)

ANON. 1980. *Convention on the Conservation of Migratory Species of Wild Animals.* Treaty Series No. 87. (Bonn Convention, 1982.)

ANON. 1981. *Wildlife and Countryside Act 1981.* HMSO, London. 128 pp. ISBN 0 10 546981 5.

ANON. 1991. *Agreement on the Conservation of Bats in Europe.* (Eurobats.)

ANON. 1994. *Biodiversity: the UK Action Plan.* Cm 2428. HMSO, London.

ANON. 1995. *Biodiversity: the UK Steering Group Report. Vol 1: Meeting the Rio Challenge. Vol 2: Action Plans.* HMSO, London.

ANON. 1996. *Wild Mammals (Protection) Act 1996.* HMSO, London. 2 pp. ISBN 0 10 540396 2.

ANON. 1998 *UK Biodiversity Group Tranche 2 Action Plans. Volume 1 - Vertebrates and Vascular plants.* English Nature, Peterborough. 267 pp. ISBN 1 85716 406 7.

ANON. 2000. *Countryside and Rights of Way Act 2000.* HMSO, London. ISBN 0 10 543700 X.

ANON. 2003. *Criminal Justice (Scotland) Act 2003.* The Stationery Office, London. ISBN 0 10 590049 4.

ANON. 2003. *Nature Conservation (Scotland) Bill.* (As introduced in the Scottish Parliament on 29th September 2003.)

CHILDS, J. 2003. *Bats and the law: what to do when the law is broken.* Bat Conservation Trust & Royal Society for the Protection of Birds. Available on the internet at http://www.bats.org.uk/batlaw.htm

COMMISION OF THE EUROPEAN COMMUNITIES. *Council Directive 92/43/EEC of 21st May 1992 on the Conservation of Natural Habitats and of Wild Flora and Fauna.* Official Journal of the European Communities. No. L206/7, pp. 206–92.

COMMISION OF THE EUROPEAN COMMUNITIES. *Council Directive 85/337/EEC of 27th June 1985 on the Assessment of the Effects of Certain Public and Private Projects on the Environment.* Official Journal of the European Communities. L 175, pp. 40–48.

DEPARTMENT OF THE ENVIRONMENT. 1989. *Environmental Assessment: A guide to the Procedures.* HMSO, London.

DEPARTMENT OF THE ENVIRONMENT. 1994. *Planning Policy Guidance* (PPG 9). Nature Conservation. HMSO, London. 59 pp. ISBN 0 11 752787 4.

DERBYSHIRE COUNTY COUNCIL. 1996. (2nd edn). *Species Protected by Law - guidance note.* Derbyshire County Council, Matlock. 22 pp.

ENGLISH NATURE. 1994. *Roads and Nature Conservation. Guidance on impacts, mitigation and enhancement.* English Nature, Peterborough. 81 pp. ISBN 1 85716 134 3.

ENGLISH NATURE. 1994. *Nature Conservation in Environmental Assessment.* English Nature, Peterborough. 50 pp. ISBN 1 85716 135 1.

ENVIRONMENT AND HERITAGE SERVICE. *Planning Conservation Guidelines – Nature Conservation and Planning.* Department of the Environment (NI). ISBN 0 337 082979.

THE SCOTTISH OFFICE DEVELOPMENT DEPARTMENT. 1999. *National Planning Policy Guideline NPPG 14: Natural Heritage.* ISBN 0 7480 7997 1.

STATUTORY INSTRUMENT NO. 2716. 1994. *The Conservation (Natural Habitats, &c.) Regulations 1994.* HMSO, London. 59 pp. ISBN 0 11 045716 1.

STATUTORY INSTRUMENT NO. 171 (NI 2). 1985. *The Wildlife (Northern Ireland) Order 1985.* HMSO, London. 39 pp. ISBN 011 056171 6.

STATUTORY INSTRUMENT NO. 1160. 1997. *The Hedgerow Regulations 1997.* The Stationery Office Ltd, London. 15 pp. ISBN 0 11 064458 1.

Daubenton's bat. © Frank Greenaway

Health and safety in bat work

A. J. Mitchell-Jones

Bat work may involve visits to sites that are potentially dangerous, particularly for those who have received inadequate or insufficient training and are unaware of the correct safety measures. It cannot be emphasised too strongly that safety is of paramount importance in all situations. No site or colony is worth taking risks over, so if in doubt abort the visit. Always ask yourself whether you could get the information you need without entering a hazardous area.

Risk assessment plays an important part in ensuring that bat group members operate in a safety-conscious way and bat groups can help by ensuring that safety procedures are discussed and reviewed regularly. Appendix 8 includes sample risk assessments for entry into buildings and disused mines.

Employers should be aware that bat work is covered by Health and Safety legislation. A summary of the main requirements can be found in Appendix 8, including relevant references.

2.1 Health and first aid

In Britain, bats rarely transmit diseases to man, but the death of a batworker from the rabies-related European Bat Lyssavirus (EBLV) in 2002 illustrates the need to take steps to avoid being bitten, as it must now be assumed that this virus is present in bats in the UK and this fatal disease can be contracted from a bat bite (see Box: *Advice on bats and rabies* for details). In addition, it is always wise to take simple hygiene precautions when visiting bat roosts. Always cover any open cuts before entering bat roosts and wash your hands after handling bats or their droppings and before eating, smoking or drinking. Anyone working with animals or in dirty areas must ensure that their anti-tetanus immunisation is kept up to date.

Visits to or, more especially, prolonged work in, some sorts of sites may carry a risk of disease. Tick-borne Lyme disease is unlikely to be a hazard to bat workers, but work in sites contaminated by sewage or rats carries a risk of leptospirosis (Weil's disease). A small number of cavers have contracted this disease, indicating that there is a risk wherever there is contact with water. If you work in such sites, make sure you observe the hygiene precautions described above and report any influenza-like symptoms immediately to your doctor together with information about your work.

Greater horseshoe bat colony. © Frank Greenaway

A quick reference guide may be available from your SNCO contact.

Carrying a simple first-aid kit, and knowing how to use it, would be a sensible precaution for all site visits including those underground. Standard kits are widely available and could be kept as a permanent part of your site visit equipment.

2.2 Travel and night or lone working

Travelling to and from bat work and working at dusk or at night carries an element of personal risk which can be minimised by taking a few simple precautions.

- Avoid working alone wherever possible. Never go underground alone.
- Avoid sites with a reputation for incidents. This might apply particularly to night-time fieldwork at urban sites.
- Be aware of what is going on around you and the location of the nearest house or phone box. Remember that when wearing headphones with bat detectors you may be unaware of what is going on around you.
- Consider carrying a personal attack alarm.
- Always tell someone reliable where you are going, what time you expect to return and what to do if you don't turn up. Always keep to these arrangements and phone if you are going to be late.
- Some SNCO offices have well-developed 'buddy' systems or recording systems. These should be used where available.
- Don't rely on a mobile phone as you may be in an area with poor reception.

Advice on bats and rabies
See also 9.1.1 – Transmission of disease.

Vaccination

Following the discovery of European Bat Lyssavirus type 2 in two Daubenton's bats in England and the death of a batworker in Scotland from the same virus, it must now be assumed that this virus is present in bats in the UK. Testing of dead bats by MAFF/Defra over the last decade indicates that the overall incidence of infection is likely to be very low, although limited testing of live Daubenton's bats for antibodies suggests that exposure to EBL2 may be more widespread. Nevertheless, infected bat bites have caused human deaths so appropriate precautions against infection must be taken.

The Department of Health's recommendation is that people regularly handling bats should be vaccinated against rabies. Included in this category are all active bat workers and wardens, and those regularly taking in sick and injured bats. The SNCOs and the Bat Conservation Trust urge all those involved in bat work to ensure that they are fully vaccinated and that they receive regular boosters. Bats should not be handled by anyone who has not received these vaccinations.

Even when fully vaccinated, people should avoid being bitten by wearing appropriate bite-proof gloves when handling bats. Any bat bite should be thoroughly cleansed with soap and water and advice should be sought from your doctor about the need for post-exposure treatment. Further information is available from the SNCOs, the Bat Conservation Trust or the Health Protection Agency (HPA) /Scottish Centre for Infection and Environmental Health (SCIEH). The BCT website http://www.bats.org.uk/batinfo/rabies.htm provides up to date information.

Advice to the public who find grounded bats

Members of the public should be advised not to handle grounded bats. The advice from the Department of Health is that there is no risk to the public provided they do not touch or pick up bats. It may be possible for a bat worker to visit to examine the bat and retrieve it if appropriate. The local Animal Health Divisional Office (or its equivalent in Northern Ireland, Republic of Ireland, Isle of Man and Channel Islands) should be contacted if the bat is behaving abnormally or aggressively and for which no explanation of its behaviour is readily available. It should be remembered that there are hazards to both wild animal and human in inexperienced people handling any wild animal. The bat worker should establish whether the bat has bitten anybody. If so, then the bat worker should consider encouraging the finder to collect the bat (using a box and cardboard slide, bite-proof gloves or a heavy cloth) into a box where it can be examined later.

If a bat has bitten, or may have bitten, a member of the public, they should be advised to seek immediate medical advice. If available, the bat should be retained in captivity for assessment by an experienced person, or euthanasia applied, depending on the assessed risk. Post-exposure treatment, which appears to be highly effective, should be considered after discussions with a doctor or GP. The HPA (tel: 020 8200 4400) or SCIEH

(tel: 0141 300 1100) can provide advice to doctors or the public about the assessment of risk.
The BCT office holds a list of all Animal Health Divisional Offices (AHDOs) and their equivalents elsewhere and has details of appropriate health offices. A list of AHDOs can be found at http://www.defra.gov.uk/corporate/contacts/ahdo.htm

Submission of fresh dead bats to the Veterinary Laboratories Agency (VLA)

To encourage an increase in the rabies surveillance:
1. All dead bats should be sent by first-class mail to VLA as soon as possible (but not on a Friday). If there is to be delay in posting, keep in a refrigerator (4–6°C) until the bat can be collected or posted. Rabies-related virus can be isolated from frozen or decomposing material, but the chances are enhanced in fresh unfrozen specimens.
2. If euthanasia is agreed, this can be carried out by a vet using intraperitoneal injection of a small volume of barbiturate; alternatively, gaseous anaesthesia can be used if facilities exist. Other methods are available but should avoid breaking the skin or skull.
3. Details of date, source and circumstances of finding should accompany samples. If there is reason to be suspicious of the animal call your local Animal Health Divisional Office before dispatching the bat.
4. Packaging must comply with the Post Office regulations for pathological material. Carcasses should be packed in a tightly sealed container and surrounded by absorbent material. This should be securely fastened and placed in a stout envelope or padded bag. The package must be marked 'Pathological specimen: Fragile with Care' and sent by first-class post to VLA. Packages should be clearly marked with a large red 'R' next to the address. Suitable pre-paid envelopes, forms and specimen tubes are available free of charge from the Bat Conservation Trust.
5. The package should be sent to Rabies Diagnostics, Veterinary Laboratories Agency, New Haw, Addlestone, Surrey KT15 3NB. Some bat groups have had an arrangement with the Veterinary Officers of their local Animal Health Divisional Office regarding collection of bats for delivery to VLA.
6. As in other countries, the identification of all bats submitted to VLA is confirmed by an appropriate bat specialist and the material is subsequently passed to one of our national museums (mostly to Liverpool or Edinburgh).

Taking bats into captivity

Bats should be held in captivity in accordance with the Bat Conservation Trust guidelines.

Defra has confirmed that any captive bat that is still alive after any necessary treatment and care can be considered safe to release as soon as it is in a fit state

All bats that die in captivity should be submitted to the VLA as soon as possible.

2.3 Safety in and around buildings

Visits to locate or inspect bat roosts in buildings may involve access to parts of the building that present particular safety hazards. It is important that you are properly equipped for such visits and are aware of the hazards that may exist. Refer to the sample risk assessment in Appendix 8. When you visit a building, the occupier of those premises shares a legal responsibility for your health and safety.

2.3.1 Personal protective equipment (PPE)

If it is necessary to enter a bat roost, proper equipment is essential and appropriate clothing should be worn. Overalls are recommended because they protect clothes from dirt and the body from splinters or irritation caused by fibreglass insulation. Shoes or boots with a thick sole should be worn to give protection against projecting nails; industrial safety boots or safety trainers with nail-resistant soles are ideal. Tough gloves, such as gardening gloves, can give protection against splinters, nails and sharp edges. Their use is a matter of individual preference, although gloves must always be worn for handling bats. Dust masks should be worn if you have any form of respiratory sensitivity and eye protection may be advisable when opening a loft hatch from below.

Hard hats can provide considerable protection against falling objects or projecting nails, but they need a certain amount of care if they are to function properly. The hat must be a good fit, with the inner harness and strap adjusted properly. The gap between the harness and the plastic shell is essential for the proper functioning of the hat, so do not store anything there. The plastic shell is tough, but not indestructible, and you should ensure that it is cared for properly; do not apply solvents to it or modify it in any way. Hats that have received a significant sharp blow or are over 5 years old should be replaced. Hats that are over 2 years old should be tested regularly by squeezing the sides and watching for any cracking, whitening or kinking of the plastic. In an ordinary attic, the use of a hard hat is optional, but they should be worn if there is any risk of being hit by a falling object, such as a roof tile or any debris from old or derelict buildings. Baseball 'bump-caps', which give protection against projecting nails and bumps against roof timbers, are widely available.

Any roost visit requires good lighting. A head torch is preferable because it leaves you with both hands free and provides light in the direction you are looking. Small dry-battery operated head torches are light and convenient for visits to domestic roosts, but rechargeable caving and mining lamps have a much longer life, although they are fairly heavy. Always carry a spare torch as insurance against being stranded in the dark.

2.3.2 Ladders and tower scaffolds

Many accidents are caused every year by the misuse of ladders, with the most common problems being defective ladders, ladders slipping at the top or bottom, or ladders sinking unevenly into soft ground. Always follow this safety code:

- Check the condition of the ladder carefully, particularly if it is borrowed. Do not use ladders that are damaged or incomplete. Avoid borrowing ladders wherever possible.
- Do not use a wooden ladder that has been painted, as this can hide defects.
- Erect the ladder at a 75° angle, 1 metre out for every 4 metres of height.
- Place the ladder on a firm footing and use a non-slip foot on smooth surfaces.
- Ladders should either be tied firmly in place or held at the bottom by an assistant. Tying the ladder at the top is probably the safest method.
- Do not over reach. Your body should not move outside the line of the ladder.
- Use both hands when climbing. Tools or equipment should be carried in a belt or rucksack.
- Watch out for overhead power or telephone cables.
- Erect the ladder taking full account of site conditions, e.g. exposure, weather, movement of persons or vehicles.
- Make certain the ladder reaches at least 1 metre above any landing platform.
- Use the correct ladder for the job. Never lash two short ladders together to make a longer one.
- When using an extension ladder allow a two-rung overlap for sections up to 5 metres each and a four-rung overlap for 6 metres. The Health & Safety Executive (HSE) advise that any ladder reaching a height of more than 9 metres vertically should have safe landing areas and platforms.

Tower scaffolds are widely used, but they are involved in numerous accidents each year and are inappropriate for most bat work. Obtain a copy of HSE Construction Information Sheet No. 10 (Rev 3) (available at http://www.hse.gov.uk) and follow the instructions set out in the sheet.

2.3.3 Access to roofs

If you are considering access on to a roof at any stage, you should bear in mind that in the construction industry falls from and through roofs cause more deaths than almost anything else. Access to single storey flat roofs, such as garages or house extensions needs only basic care at the edge, but access to any other sort of roof needs a careful assessment of the risks involved and the provision of appropriate safety equipment. Access to roofs should not be required for most bat work and must not be attempted unless you have the training and specialist knowledge to do so safely. The roofs of many industrial and farm building are made out of corrugated cement sheet. These are fragile and brittle and must not be walked on without crawl boards.

2.3.4 Building and demolition sites

Building and demolition sites are dangerous places. The site contractor is responsible for your safety and you should make sure that you are always accompanied by a site representative and follow any safety instructions you are given. Normally the wearing of a hard hat is mandatory.

2.3.5 Visits to roof voids

Visits to roof voids always carry a risk of falling through a lath-and-plaster or plasterboard ceiling. These risks are multiplied in older buildings, where rot or woodworm attack may have weakened the timbers. This is a dangerous and expensive mistake to make and can be avoided by moving steadily and methodically and only ever walking on sound joists. A good torch is essential for checking the position and soundness of the joists, and one hand should always be kept free for holding on to the roof trusses to maintain balance. In some roofs, joists may be in such a poor state that the visit should be abandoned or the search confined to sound areas of the roof. Before entering a confined space like this, always ensure you have a safe means of exit in case of emergency.

There are several other potential hazards.

Dust and insulation

Dust and fibreglass or mica insulation particles, which are often stirred up during visits, can be irritating to the skin and lungs and sometimes cause allergies. A simple dust mask, as sold in DIY stores or builders' merchants, can prevent respiratory trouble and is a sensible precaution. Insulation fibres can be difficult to remove from clothing, so wear one-piece overalls to keep fibres off your normal clothing. Wherever possible, avoid disturbing or handling insulation material.

Pesticides

Although aerial levels of pesticides in roofs that received remedial timber treatment several years previously will be so low as to be negligible for a mammal as large as a human, more care is needed in roofs that have received recent treatment. The risks of even mild irritation are extremely low from a single visit to a treated roof but, if there is a strong smell of solvents or if the wood is still wet or glistening, full protective clothing is advisable or the visit should be abandoned. The label guidance on licensed products will give details of any restrictions on post-treatment access. If in any doubt, wear rubber gloves and wash exposed skin after the visit.

Electric wiring

Houses that have been wired or rewired to current safety standards should present no problems, but in older houses wires may be draped across the joists and the insulation may have perished in places. Avoid standing on any wire, even if it looks in good condition. As well as being a potential threat to the bat worker, unsafe wiring is a considerable fire hazard and so should be drawn to the attention of the owner of the property.

Asbestos

The inhalation of asbestos fibres can cause asbestosis, a type of cancer. Asbestos occurs very occasionally as lagging round hot water pipes in old properties. **If the presence of asbestos is suspected, the visit should be abandoned immediately**. Do not poke at insulation to see if it asbestos; it is difficult to differentiate between asbestos and other less harmful mineral fibres and disturbance will only disperse the fibres into the air. Rock wool fibre is often used for loft insulation; this is usually a muddy brown colour rather than silvery white. Fibreglass is often pink.

Woodwork

In many roof voids this is fairly rough and there may be nails sticking out of the trusses, joists or sarking. A hard hat, strong shoes and gloves will avoid the possibility of minor injuries. Sometimes loose bricks or stonework may be encountered, especially around chimneys. Avoid dislodging anything.

Wasp, bee and hornet nests

Wasp nests are the most common. Occupied nests should not be disturbed and if you encounter one you may wish to consider abandoning the visit because being stung (or trying to avoid being stung) could put you at risk of a fall.

2.4 Safety underground

Survey or monitoring work in caves and mines requires particular attention to safety because the potential for a serious accident is probably greater than in buildings. Inexperienced workers must seek advice and practical guidance from an experienced caver, who should have the appropriate equipment and be familiar with good caving practice. Guides to good caving practice and techniques are available from the mining and caving organisations listed in Appendix 6. A glossary of caving and mining terms is given in Appendix 2. A sample risk assessment for entry into disused mines is given in Appendix 8.

Training in underground techniques, with a firm emphasis on safety, is available from a variety of sources. Courses specifically for bat workers are organised at irregular intervals by some bat groups. Caving clubs and outdoor centres often run a range of courses, and videos and books are available on simple and vertical caving. Specialist caving equipment suppliers can also be an excellent source of advice on the type of equipment that will be required.

The following safety rules are expanded from safety codes produced by caving and mine-history organisations.

- Never go alone. Even the simplest accident can immobilise a lone caver and lead ultimately to death from exposure. Don't split up underground and always ensure the party is within shouting distance. A party of four is the minimum recommended size, so that one can stay with an injured person while two go for help.
- Always tell a reliable person where you are going and what time you expect to be back.
- Take spare lights. Although purpose-built mining or caving lights are reliable, accidents and equipment failures do happen. Make sure that there is always at least one spare light in the party and it is preferable that each member carries their own spare. Chemical lights (Cyalume) can be carried for emergencies, though their low light output restricts their usefulness.
- Wear appropriate clothing. Caves and mines are generally between 8 and 10°C (although some sites, e.g. disused railway tunnels, can be cooler [2–9°C]), so for dry caves normal outdoor clothing is appropriate. Wet sites are more of a problem because heat loss through wet clothing is considerably higher. Wet or dry suits are the preferred solution for many keen cavers, but a good combination for bat workers is a waterproof oversuit together with either a fleece undersuit or old clothes and thermal underwear. Wellingtons are often the best footwear.
- Take appropriate equipment and know how to use it. Many levels, adits and caves can be entered without any special equipment, but even apparently straightforward horizontal passages can contain hidden hazards, such as unsafe floors and roofs, shafts covered with rotting timber or deep water. Abandoned mines should always be treated with extreme caution and old timber or metalwork should never be touched, let alone trusted.
- Vertical shafts should be attempted only with adequate safety equipment and never without proper training on the surface beforehand. The use of wire caving ladders (electron ladders) and SRT (single rope technique) should never be attempted underground until full proficiency is achieved above ground.
- Try to obtain a survey map of the site before the visit. These are sometimes available through local caving clubs. In all but the simplest sites it would be prudent to take a guide who knows the system because it is quite easy to get lost underground.

- See English Nature's Health and Safety Information Notices 11/97 *Visiting Working Mines* and 12/97 *Visiting Disused Mines*.

2.5 Safety at tree roosts

Many tree roosts are in trees that would be classified by an arboriculturalist as hazardous because bats tend to use old trees, which have developed hollow limbs, rot holes in the trunk or loose bark. If you wish to examine such trees using a ladder, follow the ladder code and place the ladder against sound trunk wood, never against a branch. Tie the ladder to the tree by means of a rope or strop.

When checking or erecting bat boxes observe the following guidelines:
- wear a safety helmet;
- do not carry loose tools in the hand – put the tools you require in a haversack with a shoulder strap;
- wrapping a piece of cloth or rubber tube around the top rung will help prevent the ladder slipping on the narrower tree trunks;
- make sure you have an assistant firmly holding the ladder at the base;
- ensure the assistant at the base of the ladder wears a safety helmet too;
- do not climb trees without the help of a ladder – tree climbing requires special training.

2.6 Safety at public events

Health and safety considerations should be considered when organising events or talks and attending shows. At major shows the organisers usually circulate Health and Safety requirements to stand-holders. However, one should remain aware of specific risks around the stand, such as free-standing display boards, which can frequently fall over on uneven ground or on windy days. Electrical appliances should be shielded from any exposure to rain.

When organising bat walks involving members of the public, carry out a short risk assessment of the proposed route and have a contingency plan in case of accident. Some landowners may require the submission of a risk assessment before giving permission for the event. BCT can provide risk assessment forms and guidelines for bat walks and events.
- ensure that there is a sufficient number of torches amongst the group and people come wearing suitable clothing and footwear;

- announce some basic safety considerations at the beginning of the walk and highlight any potential hazards along the route;
- have a helper bringing up the rear, particularly with large groups;
- do not let young children attend the walk unaccompanied;
- know the location of the nearest telephone or carry a mobile telephone;
- carry a basic first aid kit.

2.7 Working with others

Working with young people may impose certain legal and ethical requirements related to safety and supervision. This is unlikely to affect most bat group work, but further information can be obtained from the Child Protection in Sport Unit (Tel: 0116 234 7278/7280, website http://www.sportprotects.org.uk).

2.8 Insurance

Matters of insurance for bat workers are not always clear and may vary for different bat groups. Some individuals may be covered for some or all aspects of bat work by their own private insurance but some bat-workers, including those not members of a local bat group, may have no cover at all.

Bat workers carrying out roost visits for the SNCOs are covered in the same way and have the same rights as members of staff. Some of the SNCOs provide additional limited personal accident insurance. Bat workers should check the status of their insurance with the relevant local office if in any doubt.

Bat group members involved in bona fide bat group activities can be covered for public liability insurance (including member to member) under the Bat Conservation Trust's policy, provided the bat group is affiliated to the BCT. The policy has a maximum liability of £5 million. The BCT policy does not provide cover for personal accident or equipment loss.

Some landowners are uncomfortable with letting bat workers on their land or property without proper insurance, particularly if the visit is to an abandoned mine.

When attending shows or hiring rooms check with the organisers or room owner that they have the necessary public liability cover.

Survey and monitoring

A. Walsh & C. Catto

3.1 Introduction

Surveying for bats and their roosts is an important aspect of bat work for both research and conservation purposes. Until recently, bats were probably one of the most under-recorded groups of vertebrates. However, rising interest and the accumulation of data from enquiries and other initiatives have led to a great increase in the number of records and a better idea of the distribution and relative abundance of the various species. Advances in equipment, notably bat detectors, have increased the potential for surveying bats away from roosts and created a doorway to understanding the foraging and habitat needs of bats.

A National Bat Monitoring Programme was initiated in 1996 and is run by the Bat Conservation Trust. This aims to track the population changes of target species on a UK-wide basis. The Agreement on the Conservation of Populations of European Bats also has target species for Europe-wide monitoring.

For the purpose of this chapter, the monitoring of sites and bat populations can be considered as an extension of surveying. Survey includes the discovery of bat sites and the mapping of species distribution, key bat roosting / hibernation sites and feeding areas. Monitoring is the repeated counting of bats either in roosting / hibernation sites or feeding areas over a period of time. Specialised techniques such as ringing and other types of marking are covered in later chapters.

3.2 Purpose and design

All survey and monitoring techniques for bats are to some degree selective and no single technique will give a complete and unbiased picture of the bat population of an area. Surveys in buildings overemphasise the frequency of those species that habitually roost in buildings, bat detector surveys under-record species with weak echolocation calls, hibernacula surveys concentrate on cave hibernators, and mist-nets tend to catch those species that fly low or close to vegetation. All these factors must be borne in mind when organising bat survey work.

The most important factor to consider at the outset is the purpose and scale of your intended study. Appropriate methods for a particular study become more obvious if there is a clear aim, specified in

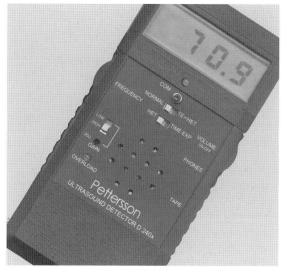

Pettersson D240x Bat Detector. © Alana Ecology.

advance. Three main aims at either a local, regional or national scale are:

3.2.1 Inventory and distribution studies

The simplest aim is to ask what bat species are present or absent in a given area. Knowledge of the distribution of species is important because it can be related to land use and can provide valuable information on the relative value of areas for bats. Such data can be used to assist in the process of Environmental Assessment and for issues of planning and land use.

3.2.2 Location of key sites and feeding areas

A second aim is to ask where bats are roosting, hibernating or feeding in a given area and how many of these sites exist. This has two main purposes: first to improve our knowledge of the ecology of bats and second, to improve the identification of important sites for special protection.

3.2.3 Monitoring the status of sites and populations

An increasingly important aim is to track how sites and bat numbers at sites are changing over time, so that declines and potential threats to populations can be identified at an early stage. Tracking changes in distribution of species over time is also a valuable method in assessing the status of populations.

3.3 Inventory and distribution studies

The great majority of species records are collected at a county level. Records are generally collected on a casual basis over time and are derived from roost visits at the request of householders, reports of dead, trapped, injured or grounded bats, reports from the public, from bat walks or from specific roost, feeding area, bat box or hibernation site surveys. Plotting records collected in this way by some map unit (e.g. 2-km squares), gives an indication of the distribution of species, but care should be taken in interpreting such maps. There are inherent biases in the ability to find some species. House-dwelling species, such as pipistrelles, are more likely to be located than tree-dwelling species, such as noctules. In surveys of free-flying bats, loud echolocators, such as serotines, are more likely to be located than weak echolocators, such as Natterer's bats. If coverage of an area is uneven, maps may show the distribution of observer effort as much as the distribution of bats. A more accurate picture of distribution can be gained if a specific atlas survey is organised, which is designed to ensure a fairly uniform coverage in different areas, and uses standard searching and species identification checking procedures. Failing this, coverage and search effort need to be measured and reported. A good example of an atlas study at a national scale is one completed in the Netherlands (Limpens *et al.*, 1997).

3.4 Location of key sites and feeding areas

3.4.1 Finding roosts in houses, trees or other structures

Promoting reports of roosts

The great majority of records of bat roosts arise from requests for advice from householders. In order to maximise the numbers of reports of bats received by yourself or your bat group, it is useful to develop good relations with the local building professions because they are most likely to come across bats or signs of bats during their work. Other than this, possible roost sites can be found in a number of ways. Placing posters that request details of any known roosts in public places, such as petrol stations, shops and post offices, is a relatively simple and cheap technique. Similarly, appealing

for information through local newspapers, television and radio is a good way to stimulate public interest in bats and produce a list of potential roost sites. Posting questionnaires or leaflets with a returnable slip through letterboxes of every building or a proportion of buildings selected at random in the study area is a slightly more costly method but is probably the most thorough way of locating roosts in buildings. A much higher response rate will be achieved if you provide a stamped addressed envelope, although this will increase costs. With all of these methods, respondents claiming to have roosting bats in their building, or knowledge of a roost elsewhere, should be contacted by telephone and, where possible, the site visited to validate their claim and identify the species concerned. Speakman *et al.* (1991) is a good example of the use of these methods in a survey conducted in Scotland.

Day surveys of potential roost structures

Inspecting every building or structure (e.g. trees, bridges, barns, outhouses) likely to be inhabited by bats during the day is a time-consuming process. However, survey time can be reduced if roost preferences of individual species are taken into account. For instance, long-eared and lesser horseshoe bats show a marked preference for older buildings, while pipistrelles are commonly found in modern buildings. Daubenton's bats are frequently found roosting underneath bridges, and noctule colonies are most frequently found in big trees.

When surveying buildings, ask the householder first whether bats are known to be present. A negative response should be treated with some caution because, often, bats are present without the householder's knowledge, but positive replies should always be followed up. Carefully survey the outside of the building for droppings, paying particular attention to sheltered areas such as window ledges or pipes where droppings can lie undisturbed. Cobwebs can often trap droppings and are always worth a close inspection. Scan the outside of the building for potential access points such as broken ventilation bricks or loose slates and look for droppings under these points (see also Hutson 1987, 1993).

Search the loft space, although check with the householder first about safety and potential hazards (see Chapter 2). Gable ends and chimneys are often roosting points for pipistrelles and serotines, although long-eared bats can be found anywhere along the roof ridge. Look for droppings and listen for squeaking or movement from between the tiles and felt on hot days. Bats have frequently been found drowned in open water tanks, so it is always worthwhile to check them.

It is hard to locate tree roosts by day surveys because there are often no external signs of bat occupancy. One technique is to survey trees in winter when the foliage is not present and look for obvious holes. If large colonies use them in the summer the wood may be smoothed at the entrance. Brown staining from urine, faeces or fur rubbing can be present but often brown stains are connected with rot so their presence is not conclusive. Likely trees can be marked and re-visited in the summer at sunset to watch for emerging bats. On hot days colonies are active and can be quite noisy so it is possible to walk through woods listening for the sounds of colonies. Walking through woodland an hour before sunrise during July and August can also reveal roosts (see Appendix 4).

Case study – Bats in Barns Survey

During a survey of 92 barns in Hertfordshire and Middlesex, carried out over an 18-month period, various criteria emerged that typified barns most likely to be used by bats. These included an age of over 100 years, a floor space of at least 300 sq m, and the presence of thick beams and a roof. The roof could be of any type including corrugated iron. Barns in a poor state of repair were found to be used but those housing grain drying machinery were not, presumably because they were too dirty.

The features found to be most attractive to bats were the crevices in the mortice joints of beams. Most of the barns examined during the survey were constructed with post-and-truss frames, a type typically built in the south and south-east of England between the 12th and 19th centuries. Nails were uncommon before the 19th century, so looking for wooden pegs and wedges can give an indication of the age of a barn.

Forty of the surveyed barns contained evidence of use by bats. The species most often present were Natterer's bats (15 barns) and brown long-eared bats (13 barns). The brown long-eared bats tend to roost along the central ridge beam and, therefore, often leave a line of droppings underneath, which can be a useful clue to their presence. The Natterer's bat roosts were all in listed buildings, close to woodland, with hollow mortice joints, open or absent doors and unimpeded flying space inside. It was found that Natterer's bat colonies were often mobile, regularly moving between joints and making use of all that were available. Signs that joints were being used included staining and lack of cobwebs around the joint gaps. Droppings may be visible but, even in larger roosts, the number easily seen may be relatively small.

Owners were often unaware that their barns were used by bats. This may be, in part, due to the late emergence of these species and the fact that they were only present in significant numbers during the summer breeding period.

Suitable barns are increasingly being converted for residential use and, consequently, their suitability as bat roosts is often lost. It may be possible to reduce this loss by retaining features that are required by bats, such as hollow mortice joints and room within the roofspace for bats to fly in.

Source: Extract from *Bat News*, No. 44, January 1997 (see Briggs, 1995).

Case study – The 'Bats in Churches' Project

The Bats in Churches Project was established by The Bat Conservation Trust in 1991. This 3-year study of the use made of churches and chapels in England by bats aimed to improve the conservation and management of bats in churches. Volunteer bat workers carried out the survey work and visits to 538 churches and chapels, of which 142 were occupied by bats. There are estimated to be 30,534 churches and chapels in England and the results of this survey indicated that, correcting for those no longer in use by parishioners, 6398 could be occupied by bats. The summary below shows the relative abundance of species occurring in churches and chapels as found in the National Bats in Churches Survey.

Species	Churches occupied by bats	Chapels occupied by bats	Proportion of roosts occupied by species (%)
Pipistrelle	63	16	50.6
Long-eared	44	12	35.9
Serotine	7	3	6.4
Natterer's	4	1	3.2
Lesser horseshoe	3	0	1.9
Greater horseshoe	1	0	0.6
Daubenton's	2	0	1.3
Unknown species	24	12	-

Source: *The Bats In Churches Project*, Sargent (1995).

3.4.2 Evening/dawn bat detector back-tracking

A technique of locating roosts using bat detectors has been developed in the Netherlands and a full description of the method can be found in Kapteyn (1993). The technique is based on four principles:

1 The earlier a bat is seen at sunset or the later it is seen at sunrise, then the closer it is likely to be to its roost (the exact time depends on the species under study).

2 Bats fly away from their roost at sunset and surveyors should move towards flying bats to locate the roost.

3 At sunrise bats fly towards their roost and surveyors should move in the same direction as the bats to locate the roost.

4 At sunrise some bat species 'swarm' at roost entrances before entering for between 10 and 90 minutes. Surveyors should look for swarming bats at sunrise.

Surveyors search for bats at emergence time, noting down the time bats were encountered and the direction and style of their flight, e.g. west, commuting. This information is pooled on a map to identify potential commuting routes and possible roost sites. Close to dawn surveyors search again, this time for returning bats. Potential routes identified earlier at emergence time are surveyed for bats swarming at roost entrances. Although the technique is biased towards early emerging species with loud echolocation calls and which form large roosts, it is possible to locate roosts of any species using this method.

3.4.3 Identifying and counting bats in roosts

Identification

Bats roost in a wide variety of sites within buildings, so the ease with which the bats can be seen is very variable. The horseshoe bats are probably the easiest to identify because they generally hang in accessible locations and are readily distinguished by size difference. Long-eared bats sometimes hang in obvious locations, often clinging on to timbers near the apex of the roof. However, many of the vespertilionid bats tend to roost in cracks and crevices, often using narrow spaces under soffits or between roofing felt and slates or weather boarding, and so can be much more difficult to see. Always try to keep disturbance of bats to a minimum and

spend as little time inside the roost as possible, especially when females are at the end of pregnancy.

Some species are very similar and need to be examined in the hand to be certain of the identification. Bats can be caught by hand during the day or by static nets placed outside the exit holes at sunset. When catching at sunset, it is important that a sample of bats is caught at different times because where mixed species are present they can emerge at different times. For example if noctules and Daubenton's bats roost together the noctules will emerge at least 30 mins before the Daubenton's.

Although identifying live bats is the most accurate way of determining the species present, it can be disturbing and for some species other methods may be satisfactory, particularly when the bats are absent or inaccessible. Bat detectors in combination with visual clues can be used to identify species leaving the roost, although confidence in identification is restricted to certain species. Where two or more species are present, species can often be distinguished by size, but there is room for confusion between whiskered and pipistrelle bats and between Daubenton's and Natterer's bats. A well-used roost may contain mummified corpses or skeletons in the guano pile and these can be identified from a key such as that of Yalden (1985). Other clues to the identity of the bats come from the size, shape and texture of the droppings and the presence of host-specific ectoparasites. Further information about the use of droppings for identification can be found in Stebbings (1993).

Counting

By far the most common and least disruptive way of estimating bat numbers in summer roosts is to count the bats leaving the roost at sunset. The most successful period over which to make counts so that yearly comparisons can be made is when the colony is at its most stable. Maternity colonies continue to grow into early June as pregnant females arrive from pre-maternity roosts. Later in the summer young bats begin flying and counts at this time will include both adults and young. Just prior to birth of the young, a peak in adult female numbers is reached and many or all of the adult females emerge every night. In general, young are born between mid- to late June in most species, although there is variation from year to year. Counts in late May to mid-June are likely to reflect the most stable numbers. This is the time that is recommended by the National Bat Monitoring Programme (see Walsh *et al.*, 2001; Appendix 4).

When attempting to count a colony for the first time, it is important to establish the number and location of access holes and this may require several people surrounding the roost. Once all access point have been discovered then fewer surveyors may be required for future counts. Assign observers to a specific exit or field of view because often two exits close together may be counted simultaneously. Be in position at the roost about 15 minutes before sunset (earlier on overcast evenings) and listen for the sound of bats moving at access holes or for squeaks as bats jostle for position. Poor weather conditions with overcast skies and rain may delay emergence and particularly bad conditions should be avoided in case bats choose to abandon foraging and remain inside the roost. Remain counting until at least 10 minutes after the 'last' bat has emerged.

As a general guide, bats may begin emerging from just before sunset onwards. The noctule is an early emerging species, whilst Natterer's and long-eared bats are late emerging (up to 40 minutes after sunset).

Do not shine white lights directly on the roost exit because this can often delay or prevent emergence. Excess noise, particularly ultrasound from keys, coins or nylon jackets, may disturb bats and inhibit or delay emergence. Emergence counts are most effective when departing bats are silhouetted against a light background (normally a clear sky or sometimes a light coloured wall). It is best to observe from the side of the emergence point(s), rather than from in front. Sometimes the structure of the roost and behaviour of the bats means this is not possible and the additional use of a bat detector is always recommended.

The behaviour of bats at emergence varies between species. Some, such as noctules, tend to fly off fast and direct to foraging grounds while others, such as the horseshoe and Natterer's bats, may exit and re-enter the roost several times before departing for foraging grounds (called 'light sampling' behaviour), which makes counting more difficult. In all cases, a running total of both exits and entries should be recorded so that a final net emergence figure can be calculated. This is essential when several exits are being counted simultaneously, so that bats that emerge from one and subsequently

re-enter at another may be properly accounted for. A small tally counter is useful for 'clicking up' bats as they emerge.

Automatic counting equipment or video equipment at roost exits can be a useful substitute for observers, although even the most sophisticated systems have their problems. Most automatic counting systems are based on one or more infrared light beams that are broken as a bat emerges from the roost. A single beam is unable to distinguish between emerging and returning bats but beam breaks should be proportional to the number of bats emerging/returning and so could be calibrated by combining beam counts with observer counts. More sophisticated systems use two sets of beams so that emerging and re-entering bats can be counted separately. Both types of system are unable to cope with bats that emerge without breaking the beams or when two bats break the beam simultaneously. Problems also arise when two or more species are using the same roost or if insects fly close to roost access points. When using automatic systems results must be cross-checked with simultaneous visual checks to identify errors or consistent biases.

Counts of bats within summer roosts are generally more difficult, cause more disturbance and are less accurate than emergence counts. One or two visits to a breeding roost in a season would probably be acceptable provided that every care was taken to keep the disturbance to the minimum. The exception to this is for counts of non-flying young, which may be counted on a weekly basis once all the adults have left to forage. This method is mainly applicable to horseshoe bats.

3.4.4 Finding hibernation sites

Bats use a very wide range of sites for hibernation, including trees, caves, mines, ice-houses, grottoes, lime-kilns and tunnels of every description. In some parts of the country such sites are plentiful but in others they are a scarce resource for bats and are therefore well worth preserving.

Hibernation sites can be located in a number of ways. Examination of maps can reveal the location of old quarry workings, disused tunnels (railway, canal etc) and, sometimes, old lime-kilns. Most large old country houses will have an ice-house, usually not too far from a lake, and many also have extensive cellars that may be accessible to bats. Old mining and local history books can be a valuable source of information about workings that may not appear on maps, because many small mines and trial workings are not recorded. Local sources of information may be important; for example, farmers may know of old workings on their land. Similarly cavers, mining research/history groups, industrial archaeology groups and others with interests in underground structures may be able to help.

If extensive underground sites, such as caves or mines, are to be explored for bats, safety must be a prime consideration. Simple rules for safety underground are given in Chapter 2 and a model risk assessment for entry into disused mines may be found in Appendix 8. Even relatively small structures such as ice-houses or lime-kilns can be dangerous places if they are in bad condition so always proceed with caution and be prepared to abandon the visit if the structure looks dangerous.

Always observe common courtesies when searching for new sites. Seek permission from landowners before going on their land and check that entering a site is not going to interfere with other people's interests. Some sites are used for storage, dumping of rubbish, mushroom-growing or water supplies and their owners are naturally sensitive about allowing others access.

3.4.5 Identifying and counting bats in hibernation sites

Ideally, hibernating bats should be counted when outside temperatures are both low and most stable. This is when the numbers of bats visible in underground sites will be highest and also most stable. In Britain, January and February are generally the months with the most stable cold temperatures. Because of the negative relationship between temperature and the number of visible bats, it is recommended that temperature be recorded when making a count and notes made about the previous night's weather conditions. As the size and complexity of the hibernation site increase, the probability that all bats will be observed and counted decreases, thus it is also good practice to record some details about the site.

Horseshoe bats hang in the open from ceilings or walls but vespertilionid species often tuck themselves away in cracks and crevices and may not be immediately obvious. Horseshoe bats can also hang

from rocks and boulders close to the floor and other species may hibernate in loose rubble on the floor so tread carefully. Careful searching with a light suited to the circumstance is essential. Bats select a variety of places to roost but most vespertilionid bats are found within a few 100 m of entrances, which are associated with the lowest temperatures. Lesser horseshoe bats can also be found in such places but are commonly found much deeper underground where temperatures are warmer and more stable.

In all survey work great care must be taken to avoid disturbing bats unnecessarily. Do not make excess noise or stay near bats longer than is necessary and do not shine bright lights on bats for longer than is required to identify them. Arousing hibernating bats can affect their ability to survive through to the spring, so the aim of surveyors should be to count and identify bats without handling them. If identification is difficult, as with whiskered and Brandt's bats for example, make a note of the uncertainty rather than arousing the bat. Identification of the Myotis species without handling them takes practice and experience and the best way of learning is to accompany an experienced bat surveyor. Further guidance is given by Greenaway & Hutson (1990). No licence is required to search sites where bats have not previously been found, but unlicensed surveyors must withdraw if bats are found so that bats are not intentionally disturbed.

Many bat hibernacula or potential hibernacula can be improved for bats by appropriate management such as grilling or altering the air flow (see Chapter 11). The scientific evaluation of the effects of such practices is an important part of these projects and as much information as possible should be collected both before and after any changes have been made. The value of such work is greatly increased if numbers of bats at the site can be monitored for one or two winters before any works take place or if a comparable 'control' site can be monitored at the same time. Examples of such studies are given by Stebbings (1965, 1992) and Voûte & Lina (1986).

3.4.6 Bats in flight

Field surveys of flying bats can incorporate one or more of four basic techniques. Direct observations of bats may be made in the early evening or later by using spotlights or infra-red night-vision scopes.

Captured bats may be fitted with chemiluminescent tags so that individuals can be observed readily in the dark (Racey & Swift, 1985). Mist-nets or harp traps for capturing bats in flight can be useful in certain circumstances for survey work, but they are not recommended for general purpose use (see Chapter 4). Mist-nets are particularly useful in intensive small-scale studies when verification of species difficult to identify in flight is necessary. If mist-netting is to be used, the survey project must be designed carefully to obtain the maximum benefit from the results obtained. Simply erecting nets on a casual or random basis rarely produces worthwhile results.

Recent advances in portable ultrasonic detectors have led to bat detectors becoming invaluable tools with which to study bats. Their use to identify bats in flight is now widespread, although it is important to realise that the technique has its limitations.

Bats and echolocation

Bats emit rapid, ultrasonic pulses and, by processing the information contained in the returned signals (echoes), are able both to orientate themselves and to detect prey in their environment. Bats have to use ultrasound because the wavelengths of lower frequencies are longer than most insects. However, the disadvantage of using high frequencies is that they are strongly attenuated in air, which limits the distance they can travel. The varied ultrasonic repertoires of bats are related both to the species of bat and type of environment in which they are flying.

There are two broad types of ultrasonic signals: constant frequency (CF) and frequency modulated (FM). Echolocation pulses are generally composed of various combinations of the two.

CF is a sound produced at one frequency. There are two distinct types of CF calls, of short and long duration, which are used in different situations and by different families of bats.

FM is a pulse that sweeps through a range of frequencies. These pulses are less suitable for long-range detection than CF pulses but can give other types of information such as distance to the target and texture discrimination.

The number of pulses a second emitted by a bat is related to:
- the wing-beat frequency;
- the environment in which the bat is found;
- the bat's behaviour at the time, e.g. searching for or approaching insects.

The pulse repetition rate of any species is not fixed. It is slowest and most characteristic in open environments but increases in cluttered situations when more information needs to be processed. This reaches a peak rate as a bat attempts to capture a prey item, when frequent updating of the distance to the target is required. The term 'feeding buzz' aptly describes a very fast pulse repetition rate.

Source: Extract from *The Bat Detector Manual* (Catto, 1994).

Species identification

Some species can be identified reliably from their echolocation calls using a bat detector; others can be identified only in favourable situations, with considerable experience or by computer analysis. Echolocation calls are made to perceive the environment and the nature of the environment dictates the type of calls that are produced. This is in contrast to bird song, which is a repetitive series of notes sung irrespective of the environment the bird is found in. For example, bats in open areas produce loud sounds, which travel far, whereas the same bat in cluttered areas produces quieter sounds so as not to be deafened by the echoes.

Horseshoe bats can be identified from their unique echolocation calls, and the frequency of the call identifies the species. Pipistrelle bats have a unique echolocation call, which distinguishes them from other bat genera in the UK and the species of pipistrelle can be distinguished, although only under certain conditions. Identification of other species in the UK requires a combination of visual observation and listening to the sounds heard through the detector. There is some overlap in the echolocation calls of noctules, serotines and Leisler's bat (although their calls are distinct from other UK species) but their size and wing shape can separate these species from each other. The identification of most *Myotis* species rests least with echolocation calls and comes mostly from the foraging style and environment in which the bat is found. The level of confidence of identification depends on the experience of the surveyor and the type of equipment used. The topic of identification of flying bats is complex and is covered in detail by Briggs & King, 1998. The use of time expansion techniques can help verify field identification of bats made with tuneable bat detectors. A detailed analysis of the echolocation calls of British bat species has been made by Vaughan *et al.* (1997).

Conducting bat detector surveys

Bats have distinct activity patterns both seasonally and nightly. Their activity is strongly influenced by time of night and prevailing weather conditions. Most species appear to follow bimodal nightly activity patterns with a large peak at dusk and a smaller peak at dawn. Thus conducting surveys for around 2 hours after dusk is likely to produce the maximum encounter rate. The most widely employed methods have been to use a detector to record the number of bat passes at particular spots or to walk a set route or transect and record the number of bats heard in each habitat type. An important aspect of such surveys is to ensure that the route taken visits cross-sections of available habitats and is not biased by visiting only the best habitats for bats. The NBMP carries out monitoring of free-flying bats with ultrasonic detectors and has standard protocols and recording sheets. To collect useful data, it is generally better to survey more shorter transects only a few times than to re-survey the same long transect many times. An example of such a study at a national scale is given by Walsh *et al.* (1993), Walsh & Harris (1996a, b). A general finding of such work has been that, not surprisingly, bats tend to forage most in the habitats with the greatest concentration of flying insects. For many species this is very often close to woodland or over open water.

Bat detectors

In recent years a wide range of bat detectors has become available both for the amateur bat worker and professional bat researcher. The transformation of ultrasound into audible sound can be made using one of three main techniques:
• Heterodyning
• Frequency division
• Time expansion

Heterodyning and frequency division are real-time methods so you will hear the sound from the detector at the same time as it is emitted by the bat. Heterodyning is sensitive and the detector can be tuned to specific frequencies. The resultant sound from the detector can have tonal qualities such as 'ticks' and 'smacks', which are important because they are related to the type of ultrasound the bat is producing and hence form the basis for identification. Frequency-division detectors can also be used for the laboratory analysis of sounds.

Recently, low cost frequency division/time expansion detectors have entered the market. Recordings made via these detectors can be played through a computer with suitable software to produce sonograms.

When purchasing a detector a number of points should be considered in addition to cost:
• accuracy – detectors with digital frequency displays can be read more accurately;
• bandwidth – this refers to the range of frequencies to which the detector is sensitive when set to a given frequency – the bandwidth will affect the number of species that can be heard when the detector is tuned to any frequency;
• frequency range – in the UK a detector should be sensitive to frequencies within the range 19 kHz to 118 kHz; some types of detector are more sensitive at certain frequencies, which is an important consideration when carrying out surveys because an element of bias can be introduced if a number of different types of detector are being used.

Source: Based on extracts from *The Bat Detector Manual* (Catto, 1994).

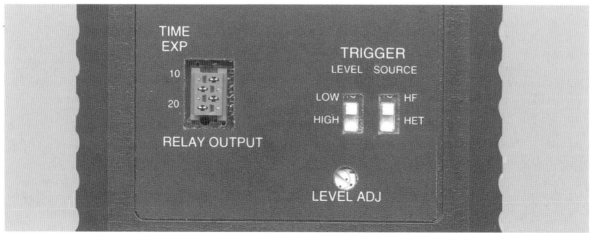

Pettersson D240x Bat Detector. © Alana Ecology.

Sonogram analysis

Producing sonograms of bat echolocation and social calls is a useful aid to identification. Sonogram analysis is most appropriate for identifying open/edge species with reasonable confidence such as *Pipistrellus, Eptesicus, Nyctalus* but *Rhinolophus* and *Barbastella* species can also be identified. However, separation of *Myotis* species remains problematic due to the large overlap in call structure of this group.

The process of making recordings and producing sonograms is complex and requires some specialised equipment and reasonable computer skills. Mastering the whole process requires a basic understanding of sound theory.

Basic equipment required:

Detector systems
Time expansion or frequency division detector – both these systems retain frequency information. Although time expansion detectors are more expensive, they produce better quality sonograms, but the advantage of frequency division is that it works in real time thus making it a better survey tool. Although sonograms derived from both systems are of sufficient quality to identify many bat species, analysis is generally easier with recordings derived from time expansion systems.

Recording devices
At the time of writing recording systems are undergoing a revolution, with tape cassette recorders being phased out and replaced with digital recorders such as mini discs, MP3 systems, .WAV recorders etc. Due to this fluid environment, recommendations for particular equipment can become outdated quickly so up-to-date specialist advice should be sought before purchasing expensive recorders. At present mini-disc recorders offer the cheapest recording system and resultant sonograms are suitable for analysis. There are many models available but for sonogram production it is important that they have both LINE IN and LINE OUT sockets. A date/time stamp is a useful addition for keeping track of recordings. Mini-disc recorders are not particularly robust so should be handled with care in the field.

Devices that record directly as .WAV files and can be attached to the computer via the USB port have started to appear and these are useful because sound files can be copied across directly to the hard disk of the computer. This approach saves considerable time because recordings will no longer require to be played into the computer via the sound card.

Computer sound card
No special card is required because standard cards sample at 44 kHz. However it is important that they offer a LINE IN port because there is a growing trend, especially with laptops, for the LINE IN port to be dropped. The user should be able to access the sound card settings to optimise its performance.

Appropriate software
Software is required to convert sounds into sonograms. As the ultrasound has been converted to audible sound via the detector, sonogram software developed for bird/cetacean sonogram analysis is suitable for bat sonogram analysis. There are many suitable software packages available and some can be downloaded for free from the internet – search for 'bird sound analysis' for suitable sites. Useful sonogram analysis tools include a Power spectra function (this identifies which frequency contains the most energy) – filters for 'cleaning' the sonogram and a measuring cursor. 'BatSound' is the only sonogram software designed specifically for bat analysis and has all the relevant tools (available from Alana Ecology).

Turning a laptop computer into a bat detector with appropriate software, hardware and an ultrasonic microphone it is possible to convert a laptop computer into a bat detector. Although an expensive option the advantage of this system is that high quality sonograms can be produced in the field.

Suggested reading: Russ (1999).

Source: C Catto, National Bat Monitoring Programme.

3.4.7 Bat boxes

The primary function of bat boxes is to provide artificial roost sites for bats, particularly in areas such as coniferous plantations where there is a shortage of natural sites. However, the provision of boxes also makes the bats easier to find, so that surveys of bats in woodland become possible. In continental Europe this has proved to be a particularly valuable technique for Bechstein's bats, for which other survey techniques are inappropriate. Guidance on the setting-up of bat box schemes, including construction, siting and inspection, is given by Stebbings & Walsh (1991).

The frequency with which the boxes are inspected will depend both on the need to check that the boxes are well sited and available to the bats, and the requirements of any research project.

There is still much scope for experimentation with new designs. However, such projects are only useful if they produce results that allow comparison between different types of boxes or different situations. It is essential, therefore, that careful thought is given to the experimental design before the boxes are erected and that the location, type and subsequent usage of each box are carefully recorded. Large projects involving more than 100 boxes are more likely to give statistically meaningful results than small projects with just 20 or 30 boxes and it may well be worthwhile for researchers to co-operate on projects.

3.5 Monitoring the status of sites and populations

Monitoring studies are designed to quantify change over some time period. Most monitoring is carried out by repeating counts of bats at maternity roost sites in the summer, counts of bats at hibernation sites in the winter and counts of bats along set transects at regular intervals (Walsh *et al.*, 2001). Additionally, distribution studies of species can be repeated at regular intervals to provide valuable monitoring data. Often, changes to populations may be more obvious from range changes shown on a distribution map than from counts made at the centre of the species' range.

Monitoring objectives vary and can include annual checks on the status of the site, long-term studies of changes in bat numbers, investigations of the effects of management practices, scientific studies of hibernation and arousal mechanisms or the breeding biology of bats. Each of these purposes may require a different intensity of monitoring, although in each case the aim should be to minimise any disturbance to the bats.

Visits to sites for long-term monitoring or for checking on the condition of the site generally need be no more frequent than one or two visits annually, but it is important to keep the times of these visits the same and to use exactly the same methods each year. Standardisation is a key element if results are to be reliably compared over time. Although the number of bats will vary with the weather conditions at the time of the annual count, underlying long-term trends will show up once a number of years' data have been collected.

Brown long-eared bat roost site. © Frank Greenaway

References and further reading

BRIGGS, B. & KING, D. 1998. *The Bat Detective – a field guide for bat detection*. Stag Electronics, Shoreham-by-Sea. 56 pp. ISBN0 9532426 0 9.

BRIGGS, P. 1995. Bats in barns. *Hertfordshire Natural History Society Transactions*, **32,** 237–244.

CATTO, C.M.C. 1994. *Bat Detector Manual*. The Bat Conservation Trust, London.

GREENAWAY, F. & HUTSON, A.M. 1990. *A Field Guide to British Bats*. Bruce Coleman Books, Middlesex.

HUTSON, A.M. 1987. *Bats in Houses*. FFPS/NCC/VWT, London. Reprinted BCT, London, 1993. 32 pp. ISBN 1 872745 10 5.

HUTSON, A.M. 1993. *Action Plan for ConservatioN of Bats in the United Kingdom*. The Bat Conservation Trust, London. 49 pp. ISBN 1 872745 16 4.

KAPTEYN, K. (ed.).1993. *Proceedings of the first European bat detector workshop*. Netherlands Bat Foundation, Amsterdam.

LIMPENS, H., MOSTART, K. & BONGERS, W. 1997. *Atlas van de Nederlandse vleermuizen*. KNNV Uitgeverij.

MITCHELL-JONES, A.J. 1995. The status and conservation of horseshoe bats in Britain. *Myotis*, **32–33,** 271–284.

RACEY, P.A. & SWIFT, S.M. 1985. Feeding ecology of *Pipistrellus pipistrellus* (Chiroptera: vespertilionidae) during pregnancy and lactation. I Foraging Behaviour. *Journal of Animal Ecology*, **54,** 202–215.

RUSS, J. 1999. *The Bats of Britain and Ireland; echolocation calls, sound analysis, and species identification*. Bishops Castle, Alana Ecology Ltd. 103 pp. ISBN 0 9536049 0 X.

SARGENT, G. 1995. *The Bats in Churches Project*. The Bat Conservation Trust, London.

SPEAKMAN, J.R., RACEY, P.A., CATTO, C.M.C, WEBB, P.I, SWIFT, S.M & BURNETT, A.M. 1991. Minimum summer populations and densities of bats in N.E. Scotland, near the northern borders of their distributions. *Journal of Zoology*, London, **225,** 327–345.

STEBBINGS, R.E. 1965. Observations during sixteen years on winter roosts of bats in West Suffolk. *Proceedings of the Zoological Society of London*, **144,** 137–143.

STEBBINGS, R.E. 1993. *Which Bat is it?* Mammal Society and Vincent Wildlife Trust, London.

STEBBINGS, R. & WALSH, S. 1991. *Bat Boxes*. The Bat Conservation Trust, London. 24 pp. ISBN 1 872745 02 4.

STEBBINGS, R.E. 1992. *The Greywell Tunnel*. English Nature. 32 pp. ISBN 1 85716 103 3.

TUPINIER, Y. 1997. *European Bats: Their World of Sound. Editions Sittelle*, Mens. (Book and double CD). 132 pp. ISBN2 809815 01 X.

VAUGHAN, N., JONES, G. & HARRIS, S. 1997. Identification of British bat species by multivariate analysis of echolocation call parameters. *Bioacoustics. International Journal of Animal Sound & Recording*, **7,** 189–207.

VOÛTE, A.M. & LINA, P.C.H. 1986. Management effects on bat hibernacula in the Netherlands. *Biological Conservation*, **38,** 163–177.

WALSH, A.L. & HARRIS, S. 1996a. Foraging habitat preferences of vespertilionid bats in Britain (I). *Journal of Applied Ecology*, **33,** 508–518.

WALSH, A.L. & HARRIS, S. 1996b. Factors determining the abundance of vespertilionid bats in Britain: geographical, land class and local habitat relationships (II). *Journal of Applied Ecology*, **33,** 519–529.

WALSH, A.L., HUTSON, A.M. & HARRIS, S. 1993. UK volunteer bat groups and the British bats and habitats survey. In: *Proceedings of the first European bat detector workshop* (ed. K. Kapteyn). Netherlands Bat Foundation, Amsterdam.

WALSH, A., CATTO, C., HUTSON, A., RACEY, P., RICHARDSON, P. & LANGTON, S. 2001. *The UK's National Bat Monitoring Programme, Final Report 2001*. Department of Environment, Food and Rural Affairs, London. 155 pp.

WILSON, D.E., COLE, F.R., NICHOLS, J.D., RUDRAN, R. & FOSTER, M.F. 1996. *Measuring and Monitoring Biological Diversity. Standard Methods for Mammals. Smithsonian Institution Press*, Washington & London.

YALDEN, D.W. 1985. *The Identification of British Bats*. Occasional Publication No. 5. Mammal Society, London.

Lesser horseshoe bats. © Frank Greenaway

Catching bats

M. Finnemore & P. W. Richardson

Before attempting to catch bats, think carefully about the justification for catching in view of the potential for damage or disturbance to the bats. Bats may be caught by a variety of techniques both at the roost site and in free flight. Once bats are trapped, great care is needed to ensure that they are dealt with quickly and harmlessly. The welfare of the bat is of paramount importance and if any method of catching bats causes, or seems to cause, distress or harm, it should be stopped immediately and further advice sought. Several of the methods described below can injure bats if used carelessly and should be employed only when fully justified. Take particular care when heavily pregnant bats may be caught because these may give birth or abort their foetus while captive.

The bat roost visitor licence normally licences capture by hand or static hand held net at the roost. All other capture methods will require a special licence from the relevant SNCO (see Chapter 1).

4.1 Hand-nets

4.1.1 Types

Round and kite-shaped frames and handles are available from entomological suppliers (Figure 4.1). Kite-shaped nets are often more useful, particularly when bats are in corners, but folding circular nets are convenient to carry. Fine meshed nets as used for butterfly or dragonfly nets should be used. Mist-netting material or other open mesh nets should not be used for hand-nets as the bats become entangled far too easily.

4.1.2 Methods

Static net

Outside roost sites, nets can be held just under the exit hole and will catch emerging bats at dusk (Figure 4.2). It is usually best to arrange ladders or any other equipment before dusk and wait until the first few bats have emerged. Then position the net around the hole as closely as possible. In some cases, it is advantageous to fix an extending handle on to the net because this avoids prolonged periods spent on a ladder outside a roost. Avoid noise of any kind because this delays emergence. Excessive delay will reduce the feeding time for bats, and too much disturbance can lead to the abandonment of roosts. Inside roost sites, such as attics, the hand-net

Barbastelle bat. © Frank Greenaway

should be carefully positioned around the bat before it flies. This may prevent it from flying so that it can be taken by hand, but if it flies it will be caught in the net. Angling the net at 45–90° from the pole can increase the catch rate. In high roofs a second thin stick may be used to touch the bat gently, causing it to fall into the net. Do not attempt to catch bats in flight. As soon as a bat is netted, the net frame should be rotated so that the bat is enclosed in loose netting and is unable to escape (Figure 4.3).

Moving net

Large kite-shaped hand-nets have been used for catching bats in flight. Unfortunately, bats are too easily killed or injured by this method for it to be recommended.

Extraction from hand-nets

When netting and extracting bats good lighting is essential. Head torches are recommended because these leave both hands free; the torch should not be switched on until the bat is netted.

If a suitably sized mesh is used, bats should not become entangled in the hand-net, so extraction can be achieved merely by sliding a gloved hand through the closed opening and getting a hold on the bat. Move one hand around the body of the bat, ensuring that the wings are folded carefully and that thumb and toe claws are unhooked and not pulled. Often it is best to place the bat and net on a flat surface to achieve better control; this applies particularly to larger bats, when it is necessary to avoid being bitten.

4.2 Cone trap

This trap is used mostly for research projects where large numbers of bats must be caught. Bats can be damaged (for example by biting each other) and these traps should not be used when females are in late pregnancy.

The trap is simply a large cone made of plastic, nylon sheet or other suitable material, sometimes with a collecting bag at the narrow end. The open end is held in position over an exit hole and emerging bats slide down (Figure 4.4). Various sizes and shapes can be employed to suit individual roost sites and the method works best where the bats are emerging from a small hole, so it is not generally suitable for capturing horseshoe bats. This method is ideal for catching a large number of bats at a roost as quickly as possible. Captured bats should be quickly transferred to holding bags.

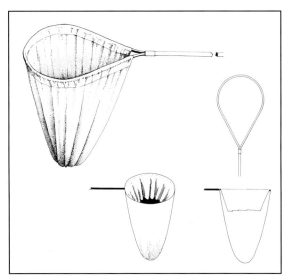

Figure 4.1
Hand-nets. Polythene around the lip prevents bats climbing out.

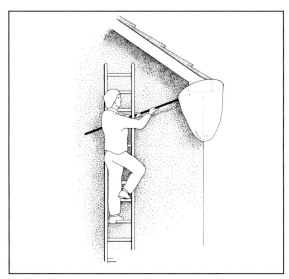

Figure 4.2
Use of hand-net to catch bats at the roost entrance. Always follow the safety code when using ladders.

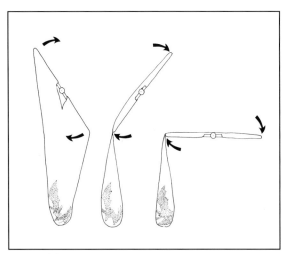

Figure 4.3
Rotate the hand-net frame to ensure the bat cannot climb out.

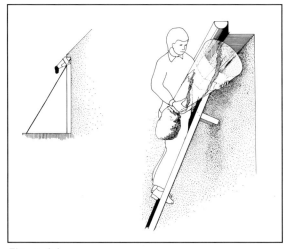

Figure 4.4
Cone trap. These can be constructed from a variety of smooth materials, such as acetate sheet. The collecting bag must be securely tied on.

4.3 Harp trap

This trapping method works best where bats are at a high density or are concentrated in narrow flyways. They have been used successfully in the UK outside cave and mine entrances, particularly in the autumn.

4.3.1 Design and operation

The trap consists of a frame supporting two banks of vertical strung nylon or wire lines (Figure 4.5). The trapping area is generally much smaller in size (2 m x 2 m) than a mist net. When set up in the flight path of bats this trap can be very successful. Bats fly into the lines, slide down them and land in the collecting bag underneath. The lines are carefully arranged and tensioned so that the risk of damage to the bat is minimised. The traps are especially suitable for catching bats that weigh less than 30 g. Detailed information on the use of harp traps may be found in Kunz (1988).

4.3.2 Extraction

The advantage of this system is the ease of extraction. The bats are not tangled and can be removed from the collecting bag when required.

4.4 Mist-nets

4.4.1 Description

These nets consist of fine nylon or terylene netting, which is usually held in tension between two poles (Figure 4.6). Mist-nets are supplied to responsible licence-holders through the British Trust for Ornithology (BTO), in standard lengths of 6 m (18'), 12 m (42') and 18 m (60'). Loose netting can also be purchased to make up nets of any length. The height of the nets is divided into 'shelves', each with a loose pocket of netting that holds the trapped animals. Nets can have between one and four shelves, but four are most usually used for catching bats. The nets have a mesh size of 13" or 12", the latter being preferable as it is apparently less easily detected by bats.

The main problems with mist-nets are entangling bats, risk of damaging them during extraction and potential predation. Mist-netting should be avoided between mid-June and mid-July because adult females may be heavily pregnant, lactating or carrying youngsters, which may become dislodged. They should not generally be used outside roost entrances, where large numbers of bats are likely to emerge/enter.

The use of mist-nets will be licensed only following adequate training in setting of nets and extraction of bats.

4.4.2 Static nets

Static nets are usually detected by bats and avoided. Some skill is required, therefore, to use them effectively. Bats have good memories and it is best only to attempt to catch them in one place on one occasion. Nets must be attended continuously. Cats and other predators can easily kill bats caught in mist-nets.

Setting a net, which must be well supported and firmly guyed, needs training and experience if the net is to be operated successfully. The length of net that can be safely operated will vary from site to site and the net must be set at an appropriate height for the target species. Set nets with the minimum amount of 'bag' required to enclose the size of bats likely to be caught. Over water, nets must always be set with the bottom pocket well clear to ensure that trapped bats do not become immersed. The operator should stand quietly beside the net with no light or bat detector, as both these can frighten away bats. The net must be closely supervised at all times and, if more animals are caught than can be safely dealt with, it should be taken down or temporarily furled as soon as all bats are removed.

There are a number of ways of increasing the probability of catching bats.

Concealment

If the net is set in front of a background (e.g. vegetation) it is less likely to be detected. It is most effective when placed in vegetation. Stand beside the net with a long-handled hand-net ready to place over any bat which lands on the mist-net. Great care needs to be exercised and if the bat flies before the hand-net arrives do not swipe at it.

Surprise

Bats often fly along the same flight paths and may fly into a net that is set up in this path, merely through lack of attention. This method works particularly well when the net is set up just round a corner where the bat always makes a sharp turn or where it is funnelled through encroaching vegetation.

Confusion

Setting nets in a funnel arrangement may guide the bat from its usual flight path into the net at the end. Such methods work best where the bat has a regular flight path, such as around the edge of water, or where the flying area is limited, as in narrow woodland rides. A well tried method of luring bats to the net is by flicking a small pebble upwards as the bat flies overhead: it will swoop down to investigate and, if the pebble is well directed, will be netted. Do not throw the stone so that it hits the bat or so that the bat catches it!

Nets should not normally be set until most birds have settled to roost, but occasionally they may be caught. Some guidance on removing birds from nets is given by Redfern & Clark (2001) but again there is no substitute for experience. Always be prepared to cut the net with scissors or a quickunpik, but avoid cutting where possible as it may result in increased entanglement of bats caught subsequently.

4.4.3 Moving nets

Single-pole flicking

This method, which requires two people in normal use, can be employed in any area with some success, including from bridges over canals and rivers (Figure 4.7). In this case, a 6-m or 9-m net is lowered over the bridge, being fixed to the parapet at one end by the top shelf string and having a weight tied to the bottom shelf string. The other end has a pole, to which the net is firmly fixed by elastic bands on both top and bottom shelf strings. This stops the net sliding off the pole. The pole is held vertically down by one operator, and approaching bats can be caught by moving the pole quickly upwards through an arc so as to encircle them. Once a bat is netted, the tension on the netting should not be altered, especially by stretching it, and the second person should retrieve any bats gently. Illuminating the catching area from the side with a strong spotlight makes catching easier. Bats may soon be frightened away, so periodically remove the net or move to another bridge.

Two-pole flicking

In this method, which requires three people, a net is supported on poles at each end and held horizontally and taut by two people (Figure 4.8). Approaching bats can be detected visually by careful positioning of the workers or audibly by setting a bat detector on the ground in front of the net. Often, bats can be attracted by throwing a small pebble in the air. Once a bat is in range, the net is flicked up, following the flight of the bat and ensnaring it. It is important not to increase the tension of the net, or the bat may be damaged by wings or legs being pulled apart. The third person can extract the bat. This method is very difficult, partly because of the synchronisation required between two people.

4.4.4 Extraction from mist-nets

This can be a difficult and time-consuming operation, which requires patience, skill and training. However, any bat which cannot be removed in about 2 minutes should be cut free with a quickunpik or scissors. When doing this, be most careful to ensure that no netting remains embedded in the fur or in the bat's mouth.

First, ascertain the direction from which the bat entered the net (see Figure 4.9 for general guidance) and start from that side. If the bat is above normal working height, lower the net to bring the bat within reach and open the pocket so as to expose it. The extraction of a bat must follow in reverse the stages by which it became entangled. Wearing suitable gloves, clear the netting away from the feet; this will require gentle teasing of the net from the toes by a stroking movement of one's fingers. Gently raise the bat by its legs, which should now be free, and slowly work the net down and away from the body of the bat. Wings need to be extracted one at a time and each wing may need to be partly opened to remove the netting. When one wing is clear, firmly hold the bat by the forearm, allowing its feet to grip the fingers of one's hand. Finally, check that the net is not caught in the teeth.

Occasionally, bats may be so badly entangled that they cannot be freed quickly. In these situations the net should be cut free, using scissors or a sharp quickunpik (available from BTO), before the bat begins to show signs of distress. Badly holed nets should be destroyed safely, as they entangle animals too easily. Always check nets carefully when they are being dismantled just in case a bat has been caught and not noticed.

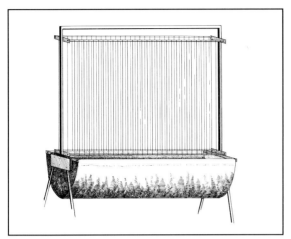

Figure 4.5
Harp trap. Bats fly into the rows of vertical lines and slide into the collecting bag below. Traps are usually collapsible.

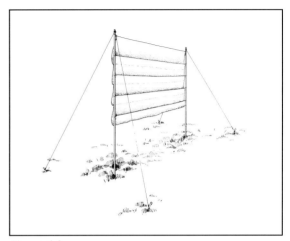

Figure 4.6
Mist-net correctly set and guyed.

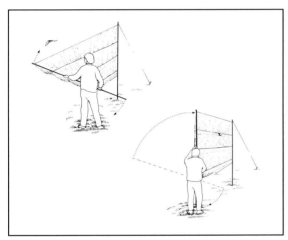

Figure 4.7a
Single-pole flicking. The pole should be held slightly above horizontal so the net can be accelerated fast enough to catch the bat.

Figure 4.7b
Single-pole flicking from a bridge. Great care must be taken not to pull on the net once the bat has been caught. An assistant at the water's edge is needed to remove the bat safely.

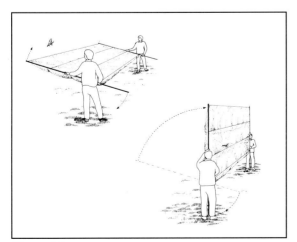

Figure 4.8
Two-pole flicking. Practice is required to ensure that the two poles move in synchrony.

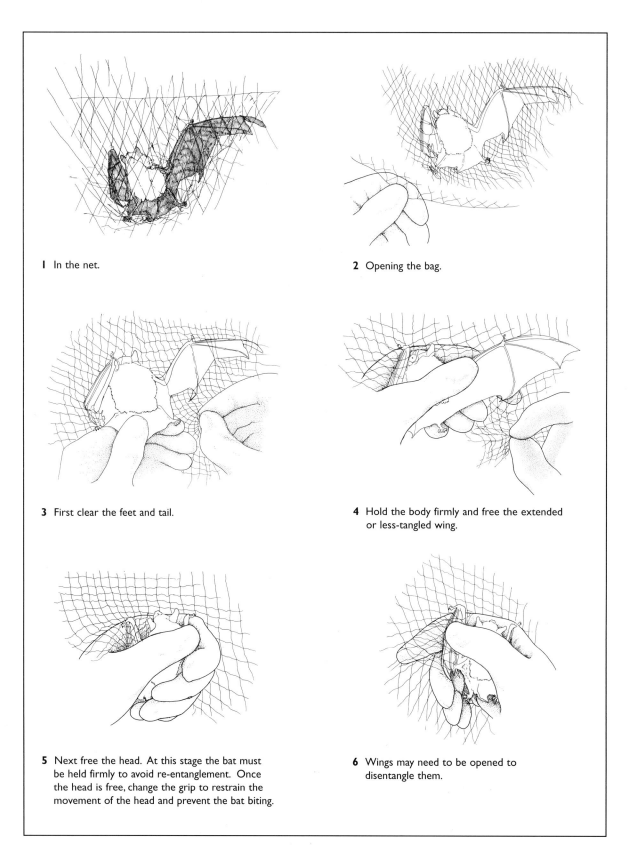

1 In the net.

2 Opening the bag.

3 First clear the feet and tail.

4 Hold the body firmly and free the extended or less-tangled wing.

5 Next free the head. At this stage the bat must be held firmly to avoid re-entanglement. Once the head is free, change the grip to restrain the movement of the head and prevent the bat biting.

6 Wings may need to be opened to disentangle them.

Figure 4.9
Removing a bat from a mist-net. Many variations on this method are possible and training and experience are essential.

4.5 Additional equipment

It is important to have suitable equipment to help with the swift removal of a bat from a trap and to hold it safely until released.

4.5.1 Head-torch

Ample illumination is essential when removing bats from traps and especially from mist-nets. A head-torch leaves both hands free for the extraction of bats. A floodlight is also useful to illuminate the whole area when dismantling equipment.

4.5.2 Scissors or quickunpiks

A pair of fine scissors can quickly cut a bat from a net in an emergency. Some bird-netters favour using a quickunpik, but this must be sharp or it will pull the net, causing damage to the bat.

4.5.3 Holding bags

Soft cloth bags with closure-strings and with seams on the outside are most suitable. They should be kept clean and dry. A clip (e.g. small carabiner) can be hung round the neck as a safe way of carrying bags at night. Suitable bags are available from the British Trust for Ornithology.

4.6 Captive bats

Bats should not be held for more than 2 hours and it is preferable to release them within a few minutes; they should be held in soft cloth bags until ready for processing. Bags should never be put on the ground but always hung up. Large bats, such as greater horseshoes, should be kept singly, especially if they are active, but small bats from the same roost may be kept in groups, which may help to calm them. Only keep one species in a bag, never mix species. Sometimes it is less stressful if bats are wrapped in a cloth (e.g. a holding bag) when they are being examined or worked on.

References

KUNZ, T.H. (ed.). 1988. *Ecological and Behavioral Methods for the Study of Bats*. Smithsonian Institution Press, Washington & London. 533 pp. ISBN 0 87474 411 3.

REDFERN, C.P.F. & CLARK, J.A. (comp./ed.). 2001. *Ringers' Manual*. 4th edition. British Trust for Ornithology, Thetford. 269 pp.

Bat workers erecting bat boxes. © Hugh Clark

Serotine bat. © Frank Greenaway

Examining bats

A. M. Hutson & P. A. Racey

5.1 Field identification

Bats are identified most easily in the hand, but practice allows identification by a variety of other means, such as bat detectors, droppings or flight pattern. Such methods have varying reliability and identifications may not be acceptable to recording authorities. A beginner will have to use an identification key (see Appendix 5) and, by looking at a number of characters, achieve a correct identification. It is essential, then, to be able to handle bats properly and confidently.

Bats are very vulnerable to disturbance, particularly in their nursery colonies, where excessive disturbance can cause them to desert their young, or during hibernation, where arousal uses up energy reserves. They should, therefore, be disturbed as little as possible. Similarly, if they are being handled, they should be confined for as short a time as possible; but a bat in the hand offers additional data that can be recorded for various personal or wider studies, e.g. sex, biometrics, physiology and parasites.

A museum specimen is no longer necessary to provide an acceptable record, and a preserved specimen often masks useful features. While a museum specimen is (or should be) available in perpetuity and will continue to provide research material, the live bat has many advantages. It allows both the opportunity to see pelage and skin in their natural colours and textures, and the monitoring of changes in certain physiological and morphological features.

Complete familiarity with the topography of a bat is essential for successful identification and further studies. Features used in the identification and other aspects of the study of British bats are described on the generalised bats illustrated (Figure 5.1) and there are a number of guides available that give further details (see Appendix 5).

Callipers will be needed for any essential measurements. Almost all essential dental characteristics can be seen with a x10 hand lens – and a co-operative bat.

5.2 Sexing and ageing

5.2.1 Sex and reproductive assessment

Reliable assessment of the reproductive status of bats is important to field and laboratory studies.

Handling a greater horseshoe bat. © Frank Greenaway

However, it is often difficult to assess age and reproductive status accurately (see Kunz, 1988; Crighton & Krutzsch, 2000).

5.2.2 Sexing and sexual dimorphism

Males of all species have a conspicuous penis. Females have a single anterior pair of mammary glands and nipples. Pubic 'false' nipples are found in rhinolophids and are used by young bats to hang on to their mothers.

Although sexual dimorphism is well documented in bats, with females larger than males, it is seldom marked enough to be of use as a field characteristic. Males make characteristic social calls during the mating season, which may allow identification of sex in the future.

5.2.3 Reproductive status of males

Testicular descent

The position of the testes varies among the families of bats. In many Microchiroptera they are descended at birth and lie close to and on either side of the base of the penis, where they form bulges beneath the skin. Several authors have referred to seasonal testicular descent corresponding with seasonal spermatogenesis, but this has not been recorded in British bats.

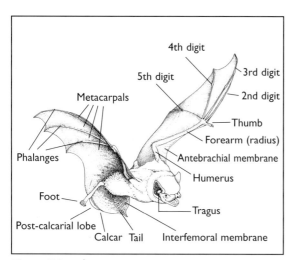

Figure 5.1
The features of a bat.

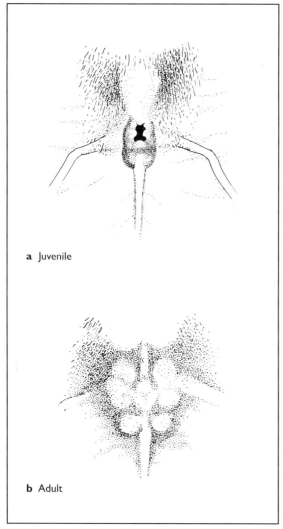

a Juvenile

b Adult

Figure 5.2
Sexual development in the male.

Puberty and spermatogenesis

Puberty is reached in most bats in the year following birth. However, in some vespertilionids some individuals achieve sexual maturity in their first autumn, while some horseshoe bats become sexually mature only after several years.

Both testes and epididymides are covered with a sheath of peritoneum - the tunica vaginalis. In juvenile and sexually immature male vespertilionids the tunica round the cauda epididymidis (= tail of the epididymis) can typically be seen through the skin as a densely pigmented sheath (figure 5.2a). Increase in the size of the testes, associated with growth of the seminiferous tubules and spermatogenesis, can be seen through the skin. After their release from the testes, spermatozoa pass through the epididymides to the caudae, which become distended between the layers of skin forming the interfemoral membrane. The rapid shrinkage of the testes at the end of spermatogenesis and the correspondingly rapid swelling of the caudae is very striking in captive bats. As a result of this swelling, the tunica vaginalis over the epididymis becomes stretched and the black pigment cells (melanocytes) separate so that the distended epididymal tubules appear white through the skin (figure 5.2b). After this initial separation has occurred, the melanocytes seldom return to their former density (in pipistrelles), so the apparent reduction in pigmentation, accompanied by varying degrees of distension of the epidydimis, can be used as a criterion of sexual maturity (although this is not proven in all genera). Where testicular swelling is apparent but the cauda is still heavily pigmented, the individual is probably undergoing its first spermatogenesis and is therefore described as pubertal.

Not only do immature bats have pigmented tunicae, but their testes are also smaller than those of individuals that have experienced spermatogenesis. This may be seen when the testes are examined through the skin.

The distinction between those males that have lost most of their epididymal spermatozoa and immature individuals is complicated when fat is deposited within the tunica vaginalis around the convoluted tubule of the epididymis and causes this membrane to appear stretched. In very fat hibernating bats, both testes and epididymis may be completely obscured from view.

The distinction between adult and immature individuals is further complicated by an autumnal moult when the dark pelage of immature individuals is replaced by the lighter one characteristic of adult animals, and a substantial error may occur in allocating males taken from hibernation into categories of sexually mature or immature.

These characteristics, which are the result of detailed study of pipistrelles and noctules, are not so clear in some other species such as long-eared bats.

5.2.4 Reproductive status of females

Oestrus

Oestrus is the time when females will allow males to mate with them, and the best criteria of its occurrence are behavioural, particularly in females soliciting copulation.

Copulation

A male mounts a female dorsally and often holds on by biting the neck of the female while curling its tail and penis underneath. Copulation is generally accompanied by much vocalisation, and some vespertilionids such as the serotine may remain in copula for several hours, without moving, giving the impression of one bat roosting on top of another.

Pregnancy

Early pregnancy is difficult to diagnose in bats. The nipples of nulliparous females (those that have never given birth or reached an advanced stage of pregnancy) remain tiny until around the time of first implantation of the egg in the wall of the uterus and so may be used as a criterion of nulliparity. Palpation can diagnose pregnancies that are between one-half and two-thirds progressed.

Parturition and lactation

The pubic ligament expands before parturition to allow the foetus to leave the birth canal. For a day or two after parturition, the vulva may appear blood-stained and swollen and the pubic symphysis is still separated. The mother encourages the baby to attach to a nipple immediately after birth and the mammary glands can be seen under her skin.

Milk may be extruded from the nipple by gentle finger pressure on the base of the nipple.

After lactation, the nipples retain (except in the case of Daubenton's bats) their enlarged, often darker, appearance and in most species of bat, as in other mammals, such nipples show that the bat has given birth. Bats that have had several young tend to have large nipples, but distinguishing between primiparous (having given birth once) and nulliparous females outside the breeding season often requires careful examination with the aid of a lens. The nipples of nulliparous females are rudimentary and often have tufts of hair on them. The nipples of parous animals show the expected characteristics of previous suckling: they are dark and cornified, either with no hair or with short, wavy hair.

5.2.5 Ageing

Juveniles

These are bats from the age of first flight until the loss of the characters described below. There is no widely accepted term other than 'baby' to describe the period from birth to first flight, although the use of the term 'pup' is becoming more widespread.

Ossification

At the time of first flight the bones are not completely ossified. This is most obvious in the joints of the digits (Figure 5.3). If held up to the light, the cartilaginous ends of the finger bones are apparent as pale bands either side of the joint. As cartilage is replaced by bone, the joint becomes more rounded or knuckle-like. The bones usually appear fully ossified by the autumn (60–75 days after birth).

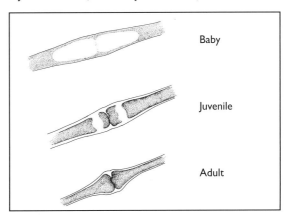

Figure 5.3
Development of the joints of the digits.

Size

Bats will fly before they are fully grown, so forearm lengths of early juveniles may be smaller than average for the species.

Fur colour and texture

Juvenile bats of all British species are darker and greyer than the adults. This is not always obvious, especially if the bats are born early in the year, when they may moult before hibernation. Fur of juveniles is often matt and frizzy rather than glossy or sleek.

Wing membrane colour/texture

Wing membranes of juvenile bats are often clean and unblemished and feel soft and tacky. The colour is generally darker than in adults. These juvenile characteristics may be detectable for up to a year.

Moult

Except for juveniles, bats have a single annual moult, usually in June and July. The moult usually starts from the back of the head and shoulders.

5.2.6 Abnormalities

It is worth noting unusual coloration, injuries or deformity to re-identify individual animals and monitor changes or healing processes. A number of bats are seen that have had serious tears to the wings, but which have healed. Bite marks are sometimes apparent.

5.3 Measurements

Measurements are generally only of value when taken as part of a larger project studying some aspect of bat morphology or for the field identification of certain species. Research projects may involve recording growth rates or assessing the normal and expected range of variation in size. If weight studies are being undertaken, it is useful to record at least forearm length to relate the weight to the size of each animal. All measurements should be in grams and millimetres.

Forearm measurements (by far the most useful), should ideally be taken with callipers, although a short steel ruler with a stop end can be used.

All other measurements should be taken with vernier or dial callipers. When measuring, rotate the callipers or animal slightly along the axis of the callipers to ensure that you have the maximum measurement. For right-handed people, it is best to control the bat in the left hand, leaving the right hand for the more delicate manoeuvring of the callipers.

Wing span, and head and body length

These are often quoted in books, but they are not useful field measurements because too much variation in measuring technique is possible. Their main use is in conveying the size of bats to the public.

Ear length

Take the longest measurement from the notch at the anterior base of the pinna to the tip. Ensure that the ears of Plecotus are fully extended.

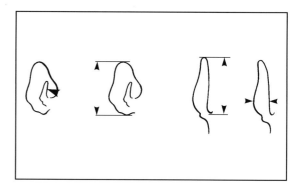

Tragus width

Take the greatest width. In *Plecotus* it may be necessary to eliminate curvature by slightly bending the tragus at its widest point.

Tragus length

Record the maximum length from base to tip, ignoring curved edges.

Forearm

With the wing folded, take the maximum measurement from elbow to wrist. With the elbow of the bat resting on the movable jaw of the callipers, the callipers are adjusted to the correct maximum length when you can see or feel slight movement of the skin of the wrist against the fixed jaw as the forearm is rotated within the jaws of the callipers.

Fifth digit

Measure from the inside (posterior) of the wrist to the tip of the finger. This is best done on a flat surface. This measurement is needed to distinguish Pipistrellus pipistrellus from P. nathusii. This is a difficult measurement to take accurately and some authors use a measurement from outside the wrist to the finger tip as an easier and more reliable measurement.

Calcar

The length of the calcar compared with the total length of the edge of the uropatagium is an aid to identification of some species (e.g. whiskered and Daubenton's). The calcar will not be perfectly straight, but spread the tail membrane and measure the chord from the base of the calcar at the ankle to the tip and similarly from the tip of the calcar to where the membrane joins the tail.

5.4 Weight

The weight of an individual bat can vary by as much as 50% seasonally and by a considerable, although lesser, percentage over a 24-hour period. These factors must be borne in mind when comparing weights of individuals or population samples. Weights are of greatest value in long-term studies of growth and body condition, and there is little point in amassing data in a casual way.

Two convenient types of spring balance are available. A 50-g Pesola (long scale) balance can be used for all British species and can be read to an accuracy of 0.1 g. Other Pesola balances (including the 30-g) and the much cheaper Salter balances should only be read to an accuracy of 0.5 g. The balance should swing free from the ring at the top either from a fixed hook or from a well supported hand. Ensure that the balance and bat are free from obstruction and that weighing is carried out in a draught-free environment.

Torpid bats can be hung by the feet onto the clasp of the balance. Active bats should be enclosed in a small cloth bag and the difference between the weight of the empty bag and the weight of the bag plus bat recorded. The bat must be confined sufficiently to discourage movement without injury. Small cones of cloth open at both ends with the bat's head inserted down into the narrow end of the cone can also be used. If very light cones or bags are used, the balance can be adjusted to give a reading of

zero when they are empty, but their weight should be regularly checked, as it will vary.

Remember that a bat's weight will vary greatly during the course of 24 hours when bats are active. This will put great limits on the use of weight data. Record the time of weighing, using the 24-hour system.

5.5 Rare bats

If a bat, which cannot be identified with a good key or which is clearly a rarity, is found seek expert advice immediately. Help can be obtained from an SNCO, The Bat Conservation Trust or through local bat group contacts. If it is not possible to arrange for a second opinion from a bat worker or an expert to see the bat within a reasonable time, take detailed notes before releasing the bat at the site of capture. Weigh the bat and measure the forearm and any other characters used in the identification of species of its genus. Note other non-measurable characters, such as colour, texture and extent of bare areas and of fur; the fur colour may change from the base of the hairs to the tip, and such colour banding should also be recorded. Take colour photographs and make sketches if possible. Make detailed notes of the circumstances in which the bat was found. These details will not only help your record to be accepted, but, by virtue of the fact that such bats are rare, the data will be useful to add to the limited amount of data available on the species.

5.6 Parasites

The word parasite is a loosely used term and here applies to any organism living in close association with a bat for at least part of its life cycle. Parasites fall into two groups – those that live within the bat's body or in the gut (endoparasites) and those that live on the surface or only very superficially below the skin (ectoparasites). The animal used by these organisms as a means of transport, for food or for shelter is called the host. Usually the bats live in harmony with these parasites, but occasionally (especially with the endoparasites) disease or debilitation may occur.

5.6.1 Endoparasites

Bats are hosts to a range of endoparasites but the only ones readily obtainable from a live bat are those that live in the blood. A drop of blood can be taken and spread as a thin (one cell thick) or thick (several cells thick) smear on a glass slide. In Britain, blood smears have demonstrated the presence of trypanosomes, malarias and babesias.

The taking of and examination of blood smears is a specialist occupation and should not be attempted without training and except for specific projects. It will also require a Home Office licence.

Other parasites may be found by examining saliva or droppings (e.g. *Coccidia*), but little work has been done in this country and, again, studies should be attempted only by those with a special interest and adequate training.

5.6.2 Ectoparasites

Many arthropods live on bats for at least part of their lives. In Britain these include a variety of mites (Acari), species of flea (Siphonaptera), bat-flies (Diptera, Nycteribiidae) and bat-bugs (Hemiptera, Cimicidae). These parasites are in a very vulnerable position and so have become very specialised in their morphology, physiology, life cycle and ecology. For this reason they are of interest in themselves, although relatively little is known of the composition of the fauna occurring on British bats, or, for individual species, of their distribution, host-specificity, ecology and, in the case of mites, even their food. We also know little of the relationships between many of the parasites and their hosts and about any role they may play in the transmission of disease organisms. The study of these parasites can also provide additional information about the bats.

Some mites are so small that a hand lens is required to see them on the host; most are reasonably visible at least to the practised eye. Parasites can be found by inspecting the flight membrane, feet, ears and face and by blowing through the fur. They can be carefully removed with fine forceps or a fine paintbrush and are best stored in 70-80% alcohol. Some of the insects are very agile, but they can be immobilised with a dab of ethyl acetate. Some mites may be very firmly attached and there is the possibility of leaving mouthparts embedded in the host. Not only does this create problems of identification of the parasite, but there is a risk of the embedded parts causing an infection.

Specimens should be stored in small tubes of alcohol with full data of host, position on host, locality, date and collector. Some specimens will need to be mounted on slides. Full details of preparation and storage are given in some of the identification guides, or the advice of an expert should be sought.

A general guide to ectoparasites can be found in Hutson (1971). A detailed catalogue of the parasites recorded from bat species occurring in Italy (which includes all UK species) can be found in Lanza (1999).

Mites, including ticks (Acari)

Larval mites have six legs; nymphs and adults generally have eight legs. They can be flattened or globular, rounded or elongate, long- or short-legged, and they are not obviously segmented. In some species it is only the larva that is parasitic, in others only later stages; mites may feed on blood, glandular secretions or skin debris. They can occur anywhere on the bat. The star-like spinturnicids are most obvious on the wing membrane; other mites may also be found here. A great range of mites are found in the fur, and specialist mites can be found on facial whiskers, in sacs on the wings or feet, or in cones of dried plasma on the lips or feet. Some species, such as the ticks, spend more time off the host than on, but they or their cast skins can often be found around the roost. A good introduction to mites can be found in Evans *et al.* (1961) and a recent review of species found on British bats in Baker & Craven (2003).

Bat-bugs (Hemiptera, Cimicidae)

Sandy brown and flattened dorso-ventrally, these bugs are very closely related to our own bedbug and can bite humans. Eggs are laid around the roost, and the nymphs and adults venture on to the bats to feed on blood. They are not well adapted to travel with the bats and it is more likely that they or their cast skins will be found around the roost site or in the guano. One species is quite common on a variety of bats; a second species is doubtfully recorded. A monograph of the family was published by Usinger (1966) and Péricart (1971).

Fleas (Siphonaptera, Ischnopsyllidae)

Adult fleas are brown to yellow, laterally flattened, blood-feeding insects; the white, actively wriggling, legless larvae are found in the guano below the roost. Some species are host-specific and, if bats are not visible at a roost, collecting fleas from the guano can help to identify the bat species involved. *Pipistrellus pipistrellus* and *P. nathusii* can be difficult species to separate, but they have quite different fleas. The larvae of some species are poorly known. Fleas can be identified from Smit (1957).

Bat-flies (Diptera, Nycteribiidae)

These blood-feeding flies are so highly modified that they are barely recognisable as true flies. Wings are absent and the thorax is so reduced and distorted that the head and long legs arise from its top. They do not lay eggs, but produce fully developed larvae, which are deposited near the bat roost site. A well-used traditional roost will be encrusted with the old puparia of these flies. Three species are recorded from Britain and all are virtually host-specific. They can be identified from Hutson (1984).

Guano dwellers

Apart from certain stages in the life cycle of some of the ectoparasites, the guano associated with a well established bat roost provides a habitat for a variety of mites and insects. In Britain the associated fauna is very limited, but it has been poorly documented. Some flies (Diptera) previously thought to be very rare have been found to be quite common in this habitat, and further investigation is worthwhile. If you collect guano samples, enclosure in an airtight container will kill any fauna through excess ammonia; it is better to keep the samples in a well-ventilated container, e.g. a cloth bag or an insect box with a fine-meshed gauze or muslin ventilation area. The guano should not be allowed to dry out completely. Different insects will require different methods of preparation and storage.

5.7 DNA analysis

A biopsy punch can be used to take 3-mm skin samples from the wing. This can be done only by scientists licensed to do so by the Home Office and SNCOs. The resulting hole heals within three weeks without impairment to flight or reproductive success.

5.8 Dead bats

Dead bats should never be discarded. Apart from being of value as voucher material for a species record, they may be of use for training, educational or more scientific purposes. Ensure that full details of locality, date and collector are attached to each specimen as soon after acquisition as possible. This information may also be required if you are

questioned, under the Wildlife and Countryside Act, as to the provenance of any dead bats you hold.

5.8.1 Preservation and storage

Bats can be skinned or stuffed, but in British bats the body is so small that it can be easily dried out and will retain some of the body shape in a desiccated condition – as long as it is kept dry and free from pest beetle. A better way is to store it in 70-80% alcohol (industrial methylated spirit) with the abdomen opened to allow preserving fluid into the body cavity. A piece of matchstick can be cut to prop open the mouth so that the teeth can be examined. Specimens should be kept in the dark and alcohol levels should be kept topped up. Bats are also suitable for freeze drying if such facilities are available. Long-dead bats may be useful for skeletal material, particularly skulls. Such 'museum' specimens will have a variety of purposes, but there may be other useful purposes for a dead bat that require different forms of preservation. Some uses for dead bats are outlined below.

5.8.2 Uses

Rabies surveillance

Specimens can be submitted to the Veterinary Laboratories Agency as part of the programme to monitor for European Bat Lyssavirus. (see Chapters 2 and 9). All dead bats should be sent there unless they are needed for any other specific purpose.

Museums

National, county or local museums and other institutes may be very grateful for well-documented specimens, and such institutions will be best equipped to preserve specimens for posterity.

Exhibitions

Good, well preserved specimens may be useful for exhibition. Generally even the best-preserved specimens maintain little of the character of live bats and photographs are better, but an actual specimen can demonstrate size, fur texture and other features.

Demonstration

For the more seriously interested audience, even badly preserved specimens can be useful as aids to identification and the understanding of bat structure.

Ageing/sexing criteria

Some of the criteria for assessing age are based largely on external examination. Fresh material is always useful for confirming the accuracy of such characters, especially in ringed bats whose age is known.

Pesticide analysis

At present it is too expensive to do routine chemical analysis of bat tissues to check for pesticide residues and few laboratories can undertake the work. If specimens are ever required for a specific project (and it is obviously a very important subject for enquiry), requests will be made. Specimens will need to be very fresh and sent rapidly to the analyst.

If the illegal use of pesticides to poison bats is suspected, the relevant agriculture department should be informed. All the Agriculture Departments have laboratories, which are equipped for pesticide analysis and can investigate such incidents. Incidents in the United Kingdom can be reported on a free telephone line: 0800 321 600. The relevant SNCO should also be informed.

Parasites

Bats are subject to a variety of endoparasites (particularly parasitic worms) and some of the mites associated with bats occur almost internally (e.g. inside nostrils or mouth) and hence can only be collected by dissection of freshly dead or well-preserved specimens; others can be missed in searching a live animal. These mites can be treated as for other mites (see Section 5.6), but the endoparasites may need special preservation (e.g. a mixture of glacial acetic acid and alcohol for some worms) and the advice of experts should be sought.

Sending dead bats by post

Nobody likes smelly parcels: they are a problem for the recipient as much as for the postman. If you are sending unpreserved specimens by post, wrap them in absorbent tissue, put them in a sealed crush-proof package and try to ensure that the addressee wants and is expecting them. Packaging must comply with GPO regulations for pathological material (see Chapter 2). Send them by first class mail and preferably not on a Friday or just before a Bank Holiday. Full data should be included with each specimen. Unless a fresh specimen is particularly requested, the dead bat can be kept in alcohol for some time or have alcohol injected into the abdomen. It can then be sent sealed in a plastic bag in a crush-proof container. If sending specimens for rabies surveillance refer to the instructions in Chapter 2.

References and further reading

BAKER, A.S. & CRAVEN, J.C. 2003. Checklist of the mites (Arachnida: Acari) associated with bats (Mammalia: Chiroptera) in the British Isles. *Systematic & Applied Acarology Special Publications*, 14, 1–20.

CRIGHTON, E.G. & KRUTZSCH, P.H. (eds). 2000. *Reproductive Biology of Bats*. Academic Press, London/San Diego. 510 pp. ISBN 0 12 195670 9.

ENTWHISTLE, A.C., RACEY, P.A. & SPEAKMAN, S.A. 1998. The reproductive cycle and determination of sexual maturity in male brown long-eared bats *Plecotus auritus*. *Journal of Zoology (London)*, **244**, 63–70.

EVANS, G.O., SHEALS, J.G., & MACFARLANE, D. 1961. *Terrestrial Acari of the British Isles. Vol. 1. Introduction and biology*. British Museum (Natural History), London. 219 pp.

HUTSON, A.M. 1971. Ectoparasites of British bats. *Mammal Review*, **1**, 143–150.

HUTSON, A.M. 1984. *Keds, flat flies and bat flies, Diptera, Hippoboscidae and Nycteribiidae*. Handbooks for the Identification of British Insects, 10(7). Royal Entomological Society of London.

KUNZ, T.H.(ed.). 1988. *Ecological and Behavioural Methods for the Study of Bats*. Smithsonian Institution Press, Washington/London. 533 pp.

LANZA, B. 1999. I Parassiti dei Pipistrelli (Mammalia, Chiroptera) della Fauna Italiana. Monografie 30. Museo Regionale di Scienze Naturali, Torino. 318 pp. ISSN 1121 7545, ISBNB 88 86041 25 X.

PERICART, J. 1972. Hémipteres Anthocoridae, Cimicidae, Microphysidae de l'Ouest-Paléarctique. *Faune de l'Europe et du Bassin Méditerranéen*. **7**. 402 pp. Masson et Cie. Paris.

RACEY, P.A. 1974. Ageing and assessment of reproductive status of pipistrelle bats *Pipistrellus pipistrellus*. *Journal of Zoology (London)*, **173**, 264–271.

SMIT, F.G.A.M. 1957. *Siphonaptera. Handbooks for the identification of British insects*, 1(16). Royal Entomological Society of London. 94 pp.

USINGER, R.L. 1966. *Monograph of Cimicidae*. (Vol 7). 585 pp. Thomas Say Foundation

WHITBY, J.E., JOHNSTONE, P., PARSONS, G., KING, A.A. AND HUTSON, A.M. 1996. Ten year survey of British bats for the existence of rabies. *Veterinary Record*, **139**, 491–493.

Greater horseshoe bat in cave. © Frank Greenaway

Ringing and marking

R. E. Stebbings

Recognition of individual animals plays an important part in much ecological research in many taxonomic groups. Marking can provide information about persistence and faithfulness to roosts, population dynamics, social behaviour, feeding ecology and almost every facet of bat ecology. Several techniques are available, few of them perfect, and the method used will depend on the species, duration and aims of the project. All methods of marking affect the subject to a greater or lesser extent, and research that requires individual recognition should not be undertaken without a careful appraisal of the risks involved and the potential harm to the bats. All marking methods require a specific SNCO licence. A Home Office licence is also required for activities involving invasion of the tissue of the bat. Further guidelines on marking are in preparation through the Agreement on the Conservation of Populations of European Bats (Eurobats).

6.1 Short-duration marks

For many projects it is sufficient to be able to recognise individuals or classes of individuals for periods of less than a year. Where circumstances permit, such temporary marks are generally preferable to permanent ones, because the potential for long-term damage is very slight.

6.1.1 Fur-clipping

Fur, usually dorsal, can be cut with scissors. Often up to four distinguishable patches can be cut. This is a useful and harmless technique for identifying an individual or group temporarily. No known inconvenience is caused to the bats, but the mark may grow out rapidly (in 2–3 weeks) when bats are moulting (see Chapter 5). Clipped fur is often visible without handling the bat.

6.1.2 Claw-clipping

The removal of toenails (not toe joints) has been used as a harmless and temporary method of marking juvenile bats while they are too small to accept a more permanent mark such as a ring. The method will also mark adults for a short period.

6.1.3 Colour-marking

Bats can be marked by gluing coloured tape to the fur in a variety of positions. These are mostly groomed off fairly quickly when the bat is active

Brown long-eared bat in a roof space. © Frank Greenaway

6

but may remain in position over long periods when the bat is hibernating. Reflective plastic tape, obtainable from cycle shops in white, yellow, orange, blue or red, can be stuck to the body using the sticky back or with additional non-toxic adhesive (e.g. tissue-bonding). The difference between white and yellow and red and orange is not always easy to distinguish and may depend on the type of lighting used. Blue reflective tape is the least easy to see. The fixing position depends on the species and situation: low-flying bats, such as Daubenton's, are best marked on the back, whereas high-fliers, such as the noctule, are better marked on the ventral surface. If the bat is marked with a forearm ring, it can be covered with a thin strip of tape. A thin coating of transparent glue helps prevent loss of the tape by grooming. The marked bats can be detected at distances up to 50 m and this technique has been used in studying the dispersal of bats from roosts and foraging behaviour.

Hibernating bats can be marked by gluing a small strip of tape or a plastic disk to the head of the bat. Plastic disks can carry a two-letter code, so that a few hundred individual markings are possible (Daan, 1969).

6.1.4 Lights

Two main types of light tag have been used. Betalights are small glass containers coated internally with phosphor and filled with tritium; the radioactive decay of tritium causes the phosphor to fluoresce. The apparent brightness depends on the colour, surface area and activity of the tritium. The most visible colour to the human eye is light green, which is the colour commonly supplied. The half-life of the devices is 15 years but they are groomed off by bats within a few days. Detectable range for lights small enough to be carried by bats (less than 5% of body weight) may be up to 100 metres when binoculars or an image intensifier are used. Betalights covered with an infra-red filter are also available and are detectable with an image intensifier.

Chemiluminescent tags can be produced by filling a capsule with the two liquids from a Cyalume tube (American Cyanamid Company: obtainable from camping shops or outdoor centres). The two liquids react when mixed, to produce a green chemiluminescence, the brightness and duration of which depend on the relative proportions of the chemicals. Equal proportions produce a very bright light for about 2 hours. The liquids can be sealed in glass spheres or tubes or, more conveniently, in short lengths of 6-mm diameter plastic tubing (as used for air hoses in fish tanks) with both ends sealed with disks of the same material cut out with a cork borer and superglued into place. The capsule is pierced with a syringe, squeezed to remove air then injected with the mixed fluids. The tag is stuck to the dorsal fur with non-toxic glue and the movements of the bat can be followed at distances of up to 200 m for several hours. The light will have failed by the time the bat returns to its roost and the tag will be groomed off in a day or two. The chemicals are reputed to be fairly harmless after mixing, but one contains a corrosive, so mixing should be carried out carefully, perhaps using syringes.

6.1.5 Radio-tracking

Radio-tracking is a successful way of locating bat roosts and tracking bats at night. As a rule, mammal researchers have tried to keep transmitter weights below 5% of the animal's weight. This means that a 0.35-g transmitter, the smallest that can reliably and repeatedly be produced and fitted, should be carried by no bat smaller than 7.0 g. However, bats have much greater natural variation in their body weights than other mammals and experience shows that species with low wing loadings can carry somewhere in the region of 10–12% of body weight without noticeable stress. Greater horseshoe

bats weighing as little as 16 g have been tracked successfully when carrying transmitters which weighed close to 2 g (when fitted), about 12% of body weight, though this is no longer recommended now that smaller and lighter transmitters are readily available. With the very smallest transmitters, it has proved possible to radiotrack the smallest species of bats (lesser horseshoes, whiskered and pipistrelle bats) without any apparent welfare problems. Whatever species is being tracked, catching and marking bats in late pregnancy and early lactation should be avoided because these are the times when energetic demands or wing loadings are highest.

Most biotelemetry and radio-tracking in the UK now operates on the 173.2 MHz and 173.7–174 MHz frequency allocations. The smallest are generally designed for a battery life of about 8–15 days and a line of sight range of 1–2 km. Range, pulse-rate and battery life are direct trade-offs. Tags are usually constructed with a short whip antenna and are glued to the bat's dorsal surface either by matting into the fur with a natural rubber adhesive (e.g. Skin-Bond by Smith & Nephew, available from most tag suppliers) or by gluing directly to the skin with Skin-Bond after trimming the fur. The weight of the tag should be close to the centre of gravity of the bat and the antenna should protrude towards the rear. Receiving systems usually consist of a purpose-built double-conversion superhet receiver with BFO and a directional antenna, most commonly a three-element Yagi.

6.2 Long-duration marks

6.2.1 Rings (bands)

Plastic or metal rings fixed over the forearm are the most widely used and successful long-duration marking method.

6.2.2 Metal rings

The only type of metal ring that is approved for use in the United Kingdom is a magnesium-aluminium flanged ring manufactured by Porzana Ltd and supplied by the Mammal Society. The design of this ring is the result of many years experimentation and is characterised by a lack of sharp edges or burrs. The ring carries a unique serial number and the inscription 'Lond Zoo'. (London Zoo has an arrangement with the Mammal Society to notify it of any ring or number sent in. This occurs only a small number of times each year.)

Bats are generally very much more sensitive to ringing than birds, for two reasons. First, the sensitivity of bats to disturbance and the fact that the majority are taken at the roost mean that desertion of roosts can be caused by excessive disturbance or careless holding or handling techniques. Secondly, the ring is in contact with soft tissues, whereas bird rings are fitted to a hard and scaly leg. In the past, great damage has been caused to bat populations in a number of countries for both these reasons, so much so that ringing has been abandoned or severely curtailed.

Two sizes of ring, 2.9 mm and 4.2 mm, are currently supplied and should be used as in Table 6.1. It is important that the ring is fitted as loosely as possible so that it is free to slide up and down the forearm. If this is done correctly, the possibility of ring damage is minimised. The gap should be closed sufficiently, however, to prevent finger bones becoming trapped when the ring is closed. If a worn ring or any degree of tissue damage is encountered, the ring must be removed carefully and a new ring fitted to the opposite wing. Training is required in fitting the ring so that it remains circular and is closed to the correct gap.

A full record of all rings applied to bats should be maintained, including details of ring number, species, sex, date, place of ringing and ringer.

6.2.3 Plastic rings

Split plastic (celluloid) rings are available in a variety of colours and sizes with or without numbers from A. C. Hughes, 1 High Street, Hampton Hill, Greater London TW12 1NA or from the caged-bird section of large pet stores. As purchased, these are unsuitable for bats and must be carefully modified by filing the gap wider and smoothing and rounding the edges. As with metal rings, the gap should be as wide as possible so that the ring is free to slide on the forearm. Up to three rings can be carried by each bat, allowing a large number of colour combinations. These rings may remain on bats for up to a year, although some discoloration of the plastic occurs. Some damage can be caused by this technique, so constant monitoring of marked animals is necessary so that any damage caused by rings can be rectified.

Table 6.1 Ring (band) sizes for British bats[1,2,3]	
2.9 mm	**4.2 mm**
Pipistrellus pipistrellus	*Nyctalus noctula*
Pipistrellus pygmaeus	*Nyctalus leisleri*
Pipistrellus nathusii	*Eptesicus serotinus*
Plecotus auritus	*Myotis myotis*
Plecotus austriacus	*Rhinolophus ferrumequinum*
Myotis bechsteinii	
Myotis brandtii	
Myotis daubentonii	
Myotis mystacinus	
Myotis nattereri	
Barbastella barbastellus	
Rhinolophus hipposideros[4]	

Notes
[1] A specific licence is required for all ringing.
[2] The ring sizes stated above refer to the approximate internal width when the gap is closed to 1mm. Other ring sizes are available for researchers working with non-British species
[3] Bat rings of the appropriate size may be obtained through the Mammal Society.
[4] *R. hipposideros* may be vulnerable to disturbance and ring damage.

6.2.4 Passive Integrated Transponder (PIT) tags

PIT tags, also known as microchips, consist of a small integrated circuit chip enclosed in a biologically inert glass capsule. When the microchip is interrogated by a reader placed close by, it responds by transmitting a unique serial number. The tag contains no power source of its own, but is powered by a signal emitted by the reader.

Tags are commonly 12 mm long and just under 2 mm in diameter. They are inserted under the skin using a 12 gauge needle. Alternatively, they can be glued to the dorsal fur of bats. If used in the latter way, no Home Office licence is required, because this is a recognised marking method, but a SNCO licence to mark protected species is essential.

Tagged animals can be detected at distances up to 150 mm and it is also possible to use a loop antenna, for example around a roost entrance or a bat box. Thus the system would appear to have potential for detailed studies of roost usage or emergence behaviour.

Tags have been used successfully on big brown bats *Eptesicus fuscus* in the USA (Barnard, 1989) and on pipistrelle bats in the UK. Tags and reading equipment are marketed by a number of companies in the UK, including Avid, Destron and Trovan. Avid and Destron equipment is cross-compatible, but Trovan is not.

References and further reading

AMLANER, C.J & MACDONALD, D.W. 1989. *A Handbook on Biotelemetry and Radio Tracking.* Pergamon Press. ISBN 0 08 024928 0 (out of print).

BARNARD, S.M. 1989. The use of microchip implants for identifying Big Brown bats. *Animal Keepers Forum*, **16**(2). 50-52.

DAAN, S. 1969. Frequency of displacements as a measure of activity of hibernating bats. *Lynx*, **10**, 13–18.

KENWARD, R.E. 2000. *A Manual for Wildlife Radio Tagging (2nd edn).* Academic Press. ISBN 0124042422.

KUNZ, T.H. (ed.). 1988. *Ecological and Behavioral Methods for the Study of Bats.* Smithsonian Institution Press, Washington & London. 533 pp. ISBN 0 87474 411 3.

MILLSPAUGH, J.J. & MARZLUFF, J.M. 2001. *Radio Tracking and Animal Populations.* Academic Press. ISBN 0124977812.

Handling, releasing and keeping bats

7.1 Handling

Bats, like all animals, suffer from a number of diseases and there is now a possibility that any bat may be infected with European Bat Lyssavirus (bat rabies), which can be fatal to humans (see Chapter 2). It is important to avoid being bitten and suitable gloves should be worn when handling bats. If you are bitten, you should wash the bite thoroughly with soap and water if possible, and seek immediate medical advice, even if you have had pre-exposure treatment. It is recommended that all bat handlers receive pre-exposure rabies vaccination. Guidance on suitable gloves for handling bats is available from the Bat Conservation Trust.

The recommended method of handling, which is suitable for all species, is to hold the bat loosely in the palm of a gloved hand with the fingers curled gently around the body. Depending on the part of the body to be examined, the bat may be held either with the head protruding between the thumb and forefinger, which can be used to keep the jaw shut (Figure 7.1a), or between the little finger and distal side of the palm (Figure 7.1b), in which case the pressure of the little finger will keep the jaw shut. This method of holding appears to minimise the stress caused to the bat and allows one wing to be opened by pulling the forearm between the palm and fingertips. The bat can be shifted to the other hand to examine the other wing. Wrapping the bat in a cloth can be a useful way of keeping it calm to allow the examination of individual limbs.

Other methods of handling such as that illustrated in Figures 7.1c, are also possible but tend to be more useful for the larger species or where the bat must be held still for detailed examination. For most purposes, the recommended method is to be preferred as bats are less likely to struggle.

Moribund or obviously sick bats need to be handled with particular caution, as there is a higher probability of disease being present, and the bat should not be given any opportunity to bite. See the sections on rabies in Chapters 2 and 9.

7.2 Releasing

Although bats have been known to home from considerable distances, it is always preferable to release them close to the point where they were found or captured. This ensures that the bat is in familiar territory and is able to locate suitable feeding areas and roost sites rapidly.

Members of Kent Bat Group showing bats to television crew.
© Neville Thompson

During the summer, bats which have been captured and held for a short time for identification or other purposes can be released simply by opening the bags in which they have been held and allowing the bats to fly. They should not be thrown into the air, but fast-flying bats such as noctules need to be held well clear of obstructions. If the bat is torpid and unwilling to fly, it should be warmed for a few minutes before release. In winter, bats should be replaced near where they were found, though most will arouse fully and probably fly.

The success with which bats can be returned to the wild may depend on the length of time for which they have been held captive and on other factors such as their flying ability. Bats are long-lived animals, so it seems reasonable to suppose that they have a good long-term memory for their home range. Bats that have been kept in captivity for months have subsequently been found in their original colonies after release. This means that keeping bats in captivity for a period may not disadvantage them significantly, though obviously the less time in captivity the better and bats should certainly not be taken captive without good reason.

Bats born or raised in captivity may not be suitable for release to the wild for a number of reasons. For example their lack of contact with conspecifics, lack of detailed knowledge of any area, inability to forage successfully, lack of experience of dealing with many insects and inexperience in selecting suitable roost sites. For these reasons it has generally been considered that the survival rate of these bats would be low. However, there are examples of bats raised in captivity habituating to the wild (e.g. Devrient & Wohlgemuth, 1997) and further study is required.

There is increasing evidence (but as yet unverified) that healthy wild bats held in captivity for long periods and then released can successfully return to their original roosts / foraging areas.

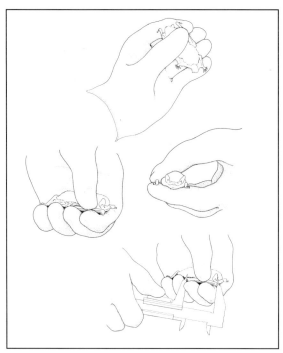

Figure 7.1a
Handling and measuring bats. The palm grip is suitable for all species and bats will often cease struggling when cradled securely in the palm. Right-handed workers find it most convenient to hold bats in the left hand.

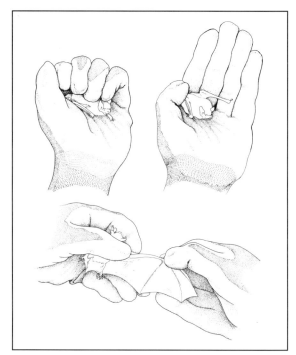

Figure 7.1b
Handling bats. Variations on the recommended method and extending a wing for examination.

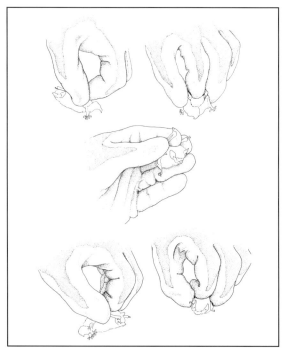

Figure 7.1c
Handling bats. This grip is useful when the bat needs to be examined closely, but appears to cause more distress than the palm grip. Great care must be taken not to strain the forearms or flight muscles.

7.3. Keeping

7.3.1. General environmental conditions

Bats of temperate latitudes are able to lower their body temperature at any time of the year in adverse environmental conditions. Torpid bats can, however, be awakened by handling and exposure to warmth, though they require several minutes to become fully active. They can be kept in a wide range of environmental temperatures from those found in a roof space during summer (15-50°C) to those that simulate hibernacula at 5-10°C, depending on circumstances. To be able to keep hibernating bats successfully it is essential that the natural environment be simulated as closely as possible. Any unheated, poorly lit room will serve, provided that the winter temperature is in the range 5-10°C depending on the species. If females are kept too warm during the second half of winter they may ovulate early and become pregnant. If deprived of food in a cold environment, bats will become torpid but will arouse when restored to more equable conditions. If the bats are healthy they should suffer no apparent ill effects from this. If a bat is sick or injured or is an abandoned juvenile a

Bat Conservation Trust - guidelines on bats in captivity

Members of the public bring to bat workers many bats with injuries or weaknesses, and those abandoned when young. These guidelines are designed to help bat workers to reach difficult decisions. Information on housing and feeding bats is dealt with elsewhere.

ADULTS

Temporary debility or injury likely to heal

Bats likely to recover fully should be isolated from other bats, kept in conditions that will encourage rapid recovery, handled just sufficiently so as to achieve this, but otherwise kept in a state as close to that of the wild as possible. They should not be tamed.

Before release they should be of good body weight (refer to *Handbook of British Mammals*, ed. Corbet and Harris), in good condition and be able to fly continuously for many minutes (test the latter on at least one occasion in a large, closed room or corridor).

They should be released at the site of origin. If this is not known then release should be in the general area of origin. Release should occur as soon as possible, preferably at dusk and not in extreme conditions of weather.

On the rare occasions where a bat fully recovers after a prolonged period in captivity, (eg two months or more), then it should be released next to an active roost in the area of origin.

In winter, release should not occur in extreme weather conditions and only when the bats have sufficient extra body weight for hibernation.

Permanent captives

Any bat with injuries that prevent grooming, feeding, reasonable mobility or roosting should be subjected to euthanasia. Bats with a single wing seem to cope well, provided the thumb is still present, but other amputations are not acceptable.

Bats of a species generally do best when caged together, but males should be segregated from females during the mating season (which may get out of phase in captivity) to prevent more captive bats being produced. Those wishing to undertake captive breeding programmes should do so under licence.

Bats should be given regular exercise. If the captives can fly then they should be given that opportunity each evening in a large, closed room. Bats can cope without hibernating, and seem to show no ill effects. If facilities for ensuring safe hibernation are not available, the captive should be kept warm and regularly fed. If a bat shows signs of wishing to hibernate, then reduce handling and feeding and keep at a lower temperature than normal. This will allow longer periods of torpor.

Educational use

The educational value of permanent captives is high, but it is important to tame the bat as much as possible. Recently

'grounded' bats should not be shown in public for at least two months in case of the onset of rabies. Bats should look acceptable so not be bald or have unsightly injuries.

Lack of a wing invokes sympathy and the inability to fly may be reassuring to those trying to overcome a fear.
Always explain how the bats come to be in captivity and the legal position concerning such bats.
Never allow a bat to fly at public showings.
It is unwise to advertise the fact that live bats will be on show, and the showing of bats should only be a minor or secondary part of the talk (see Zoo Licensing Act 1981).
The handling and showing of captive bats should vary with situations, and the good sense of the handler (who will know the foibles of each 'pet' bat) is paramount.
The public should not be allowed to touch or handle the bat.

YOUNG BATS

Abandoned baby bats should always be rescued - it is important for public relations and may lead to the discovery of new roosts. Great effort should be made to locate the roost and try to return the babies on two or three consecutive nights.

If babies are taken into captivity then the adult roost sites should be regularly checked and if the bats reappear, the babies should be returned immediately to the roost.

Babies abandoned completely, if reared in captivity should not be released into the wild.

Bats born in captivity should not be released into the wild unless accompanied by the mother when she has fully recovered or unless they are carefully habituated.

LEGAL ASPECTS

Legal implications regarding holding native bats in captivity have not been tested, but we should discourage untrained people from keeping sick, injured or abandoned bats. Sick bats should be tended by those expert in such matters.

A full record must be kept of each animal, detailing the origin and circumstances as to why it is in captivity (see The Veterinary Surgeons Act 1966, The Abandonment of Animals Act 1969, The Wildlife and Countryside Act 1981). The BCT can supply suitable recording forms.

MORAL CONSIDERATIONS

The natural distaste of seeing wild animals in cages can be offset by the beneficial educational effect to the public of seeing a captive bat, providing that these guidelines are adhered to.

GENERAL

Before taking any bat into captivity, carefully consider its likely fate. The welfare of the bat is paramount and this relates to the availability of sufficiently skilled keepers in an area. Like all guidelines, borderline cases will arise where difficult decisions will need to be taken. Do not let your heart rule your head.

Source: The Bat Conservation Trust

cold environment may be harmful and for this reason the keeping of live bats in a domestic refrigerator is not recommended.

Bats live naturally in a wide range of light intensities. The effect of natural day length in the timing of activity is now well known and is exemplified by the emergence of bats to forage at dusk. Many bats prefer to roost in darkness in caves and in the roof spaces of buildings. In captivity all bats should be given the opportunity of selecting a roost where light intensity is low. However, captive bats rapidly become conditioned to the time of feeding, and this, rather than changes in light intensity, becomes the most important factor governing activity patterns.

In winter, most bats seek hibernacula where the relative humidity is at or closely approaches saturation, so that water may condense on their fur. Failure to provide similar conditions in artificial hibernacula may lead to desiccation and death of some species, and relative humidity below about 80% is fatal to hibernating *Myotis* species and below about 90% to *Rhinolophus* species. *Pipistrellus* and *Eptesicus* are more tolerant of low humidity. Soaked cotton wool can be used to achieve high humidity. Horseshoe bats prefer a saturated atmosphere during hibernation, but most vespertilionids will live throughout the year in a humidity of about 80%. A drier atmosphere appears to be deleterious to the wing membranes and one which is too wet may lead to fungal and bacterial diseases affecting the wing membranes. Access to clean water is most important for all bats. Most British species have been kept in captivity for long periods, but lesser horseshoe bats are particularly difficult to keep and captivity is not recommended.

7.3.2. Caging

Two types of cage are widely used. Perhaps the most widely used type is a wooden cage divided into a roost box and feeding area, which can be separated (Figure 7.2). Although such division is not essential, this gives a choice of roosting conditions. Dishes containing food are placed in the feeding area, the floor of which is covered with absorbent paper for ease of cleaning. A thick polythene sheet on the floor can also help to make cleaning easier. More recently plastic pet carriers have been used successfully and have the advantage of being easy to clean, cheap and readily available in pet stores. Additional materials with a rough surface may need to be placed in the

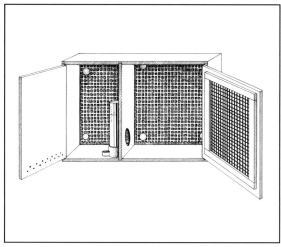

Figure 7.2
Keeping cage. The roost box is partially lined with semi-rigid plastic netting, which provides an ideal surface for the bats to grip. Bats almost invariably roost head down in the top corner of the box or behind plastic foam if this is provided.

box to provide a secure surface for the bats to roost on. Wicker baskets or walk-in net cages are increasingly used to house bats. Whatever sort of cage is used, it should provide a dark area for the bats during the day.

Several species of vespertilionid seek contact on both dorsal and ventral surfaces and will thus squeeze into narrow crevices. Cages can be modified slightly to provide for this crevice-seeking habit by pinning thin sheets of plastic foam to the walls. Grooved plywood or semi-rigid plastic netting will support the normal movements of bats, but during parturition, when the bats hang in more awkward positions, plastic foam also provides additional support. Some bats will also use secured, upright hollow log sections.

7.3.3 Exercise

Daily exercise is essential if bats are to be kept healthy. All species should be allowed free flight daily where possible and appropriate. Horseshoe bats deprived of exercise develop swollen wrist joints in a few days and make frantic attempts to escape from small cages, often causing themselves injury.

Bats have been kept successfully in a large outdoor flight cage (2.5m x 2.5m x 5m) containing a removable roosting box (30 cm x 30 cm x 12.5 cm). The cage was made from 5 x 10 cm timbers bolted together and covered with wire mesh large enough to allow ingress of insects but small enough to prevent the escape of bats (Figure 7.3). Two ultraviolet lights in standard fluorescent tube fittings were hung from the roof of the cage, separated by a reflecting cloth, and these attracted enough insects to satisfy the needs of small numbers of bats. When large numbers of bats (40-50) were maintained in this cage, however, it was necessary to provide mealworms. Water was provided in a large trough placed on the floor of the cage, and bats occasionally swam in this. If using a large trough it is important to provide a rough timber ramp at a shallow angle to permit bats to climb out of the water.

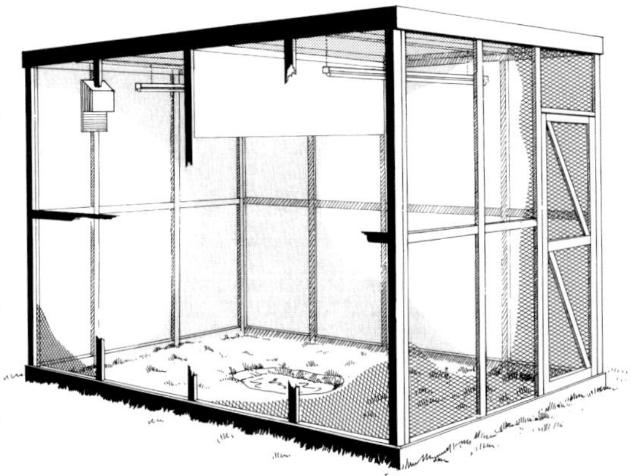

7.3.4 Feeding

Insects and substitutes

Insectivorous bats eat mostly insects within certain size ranges, but in captivity most species will accept a diet of mealworms (*Tenebrio molitor* larvae or other stages). These can either be purchased from local pet shops or cultured. Bats may also eat waxmoth larvae, blowfly larvae and pupae (from fishing shops), chopped liver or cat or dog food. These are a cheaper, but less preferred, source of food. The larger species will also take the early instars of many Orthoptera, the most commonly cultured of which are locusts and crickets. Cockroaches (Dictyoptera) may also be cultured and used as food.

In the wild, bats usually catch their insect prey in free flight, though some species such as long-eared bats and Natterer's glean a proportion of their food from foliage. In captivity, where food is provided in dishes, they require some training. A decapitated mealworm held in gloved fingers or forceps is offered to the hand-held bat and the viscera applied to its lips. After it has licked the viscera, the bat is encouraged to chew the chitinous exoskeleton, which is pushed into its mouth. While it is chewing, the bat's nose is brought into contact with a dish of mealworms and frequently it will start snapping and eating. Mealworms can then be left in dishes in the cage for the animals to eat as required. This procedure is the most crucial and time-consuming stage in adapting bats to captivity. The success of training depends largely on the skills and efforts of the trainer: some bats may require little training but others require several sessions. With time, all common species can be trained satisfactorily.

Figure 7.3
Flight cage. Standard bat boxes provide a choice of suitable roosts. Ultraviolet fluorescent lights, separated by reflective cloth, attract insects into the cage.

Although mealworms are the most convenient food for insectivorous bats, they are becoming increasingly expensive and several workers have used compound diets. These consist basically of cottage cheese, banana, hard-boiled egg and vitamins mixed in a blender to a firm, crumbly consistency. Canned cat or dog food can be incorporated into the mixture. Mealworms can be added to such diets, as chitin (roughage) appears to be necessary for alimentary health. This artificial diet, often known as 'bat glop' is very much a second choice, and every effort should be made to provide live food.

If available, insect traps may be used to provide some variety in the diet. Light traps, which are now relatively cheap, are a good way of providing food for long-eared bats.

In captivity, there is a tendency for bats to overeat, and this, if combined with a reduction in exercise, can result in obesity unless intake is controlled. Long-term captives should be checked weekly and their food regulated in order to follow the annual cycle of loss and gain. For example, noctules and serotines weighing 25-40g need about 40-58 (8g) mealworms per day during the summer but only the same number per week during the winter. A pipistrelle needs about 8-10 mealworms per day during the summer (depending on size). These quantities should be doubled for lactating animals.

The extent to which bats are fed during winter will depend on the facilities available for simulating a hibernaculum. Noctules have been kept for several months in a cold room at temperatures of 4-10°C without food, even though they were disturbed because the cold room door was repeatedly slammed. Without a cold room it proved impossible to keep the laboratory breeding colonies of noctules and pipistrelles at low enough temperatures during winter for hibernation to be maintained and they aroused frequently. However, such arousals use up fat reserves and so the bats were fed twice weekly.

Water

Water should be freely available. All bats will drink from a shallow dish and some will drink from the nozzles of inverted water bottles or plastic dispensers used for small cage birds. Vespertilionids will also lap water from saturated cotton wool, and this is a useful way of providing water when it is likely to spill, as during transport. However, be aware that loose wool fibres can be a problem to bats (particularly juveniles) if ingested or they get into the eyes. Water holding polymers are coming onto the market which may prove suitable as a means of dispensing water.

Vitamins and minerals

It is difficult to provide bats in captivity with all the foods they eat in the wild and attempts should be made to replace natural sources of vitamins and minerals with substitutes. The health of bats whose diets are supplemented is generally better than those which do not receive such supplements, but even so conditions such as alopecia, which may be the result of deficiencies in the diet, still occur. Veterinarians have generally recommended Nutrobal (produced by Vetarks) as an excellent general vitamin and mineral supplement. Bats are unable to synthesise ascorbic acid and it should be borne in mind that this vitamin is often omitted from dietary supplements. It is also particularly important to use supplements with your mealworms when feeding lactating bats.

Mealworms have traditionally been fed on wheat bran. If fed only on bran the worms end up nutritionally inadequate having calcium levels which are too low and phosphorus levels which are too high. A pinch of Nutrobal added to a tub of mealworms provides the necessary supplementation. The mealworm diet can also be supplemented with vegetables rich in ascorbic acid (such as cabbage),

with white flour or bread (which may contain added calcium) or even with vitamin powder to increase their nutrient value. Some bats have refused to take mealworms which have been fed on cabbage so it may be worth trying other fruits and vegetables. Alternatively, diets formulated for laboratory species can be added to the mealworm culture medium. One veterinarian feeds pelleted dog food (Pedigree Adult Formula) to his mealworms. The rationale is that this food is better quality than bran and that the dog food will be in the gastro-intestinal tract of the mealworm when being eaten, thereby elevating the nutritional value of the worm.

Bat workers keeping captive bats will find the quarterly newsletter 'Bat Care News' a useful source of information about feeding and caring for bats (see Appendix 5, Section D).

Weaning and rearing orphaned bats

Rearing orphaned bats is difficult, time-consuming and often disappointing. Cross-fostering is rarely successful, so the baby must be hand-fed on some form of milk or milk substitute. Small bats have been reared successfully either on fresh goats milk or on powdered skimmed milk (Lactol) with a 1-2% fat content, perhaps with added glucose. However, more recently other milk replacements have come on to the market, the most widely used of which is Esbilac. For the time being Esbilac is the recommended choice of substitute for insectivorous bat milk although some users have reported problems with bloat. The West Yorkshire Bat Hospital can provide Esbilac. They recommend that young bats are fed only on one type of milk (i.e. do not mix milks or change the type being used) and that bats should be kept warm after feeding (25-28°C) to encourage digestion. Feeding may be required up to eight times per day for naked pups although it could be as few as four if using Esbilac and the bat is furred.

Baby bats do not need cleaning or grooming unless large amounts of milk are spilt during feeding. Gently massaging the stomach may be of assistance if the bat develops digestion problems.

The small physical size of young babies presents its own problems and a very fine pipette or possibly a small catheter which can be attached to a syringe is needed. A local veterinary surgery may be able to provide something suitable. Frequent handling of baby bats or even carrying them about may help with success, perhaps by providing the warmth and physical contact that are normally provided by the colony. However, if the juvenile is a short term captive and the intention is to release it then handling should be reduced to the minimum.

Bats are not known to bring back food to their young, so the babies exist purely on a milk diet until they are able to fly and feed for themselves. Captive young grow more slowly than in the wild, so the time to begin weaning must be judged by the size of the bat and the fusion of its phalangeal epiphyses rather than by its age. Once the bat appears willing to fly, weaning can begin, either by presenting it with soft food such as the squeezed-out insides of mealworms or by adding fragments of mealworm to its milk. Both methods have been used successfully, but this is a critical time for the bat and so its progress and growth should be monitored carefully. Some orphans appear to be most unwilling to move on to a solid diet, and great persistence may be required.

7.3.5 Release of juveniles

Once the bat has been weaned successfully, the problem arises of what to do with it. Bats have a complex social life and are believed to rely on learned behaviour to a considerable extent, so it is generally considered that bats reared in captivity should not be released into the wild, as their chances of survival will be small. However, the subject has been little studied and it may be that rehabilitation is possible in some cases, particularly if they can first be released into a flight cage so they can learn to catch wild food whilst still having mealworms available.

7.3.6 Transportation

Recently-captured bats are best transported in cloth bags such as those sold by the British Trust for Ornithology for birds. Cotton bags are preferable to artificial fabrics, and seams should be on the outside. Bats which have been held in captivity may be transported in small cages fitted with a suitable substrate for the bat to cling to. A bag hanging in a car is also a safe method for transporting bats. Water should be provided on all journeys.

7.3.7 Euthanasia

Bats which are severely injured or ill and are not likely to recover may legally be killed. This is best done by a vet, who may use an injection of sodium pentobarbitone or apply an overdose of a conventional volatile anaesthetic in an anaesthetic induction chamber. If a vet is not available, alternative methods of euthanasia include dislocation of the neck and compression of the chest between thumb and forefinger to prevent breathing and possibly stopping the heart. Both these methods are quick and humane provided that they are carried out with determination. See the BCT's leaflet 'Information for Vets' for more details.

References

BARNARD, S. 1997. *Keeping bats in captivity.* 194pp. Wild Ones Animal Books, Springville, CA. ISBN 1 886013 02 0

DEVRIENT, I & WOHLGEMUTH R. 1997. The noctule's new home. *Bats* **15**(3): 16-17.

KLEIMAN, D.G. & RACEY, P.A. 1969. Observations on noctule bats (*Nyctalus noctula*) breeding in captivity. *Proceedings of 1st International Bat Research Conference. Lynx* **10**, 65-77.

LOLLAR, A. & SCHMIDT-FRENCH, B. 2002. *Captive Care and Medical Reference for the Rehabilitation of Insectivorous Bats.* Texas, Bat World Publications. 340pp. ISBN 0 9638248 3 X.

RACEY, P.A & KLEIMAN, D.G. 1970 Maintenance and breeding in captivity of some vespertilionid bats with special reference to the noctule *Nyctalus noctula. Int Zoo. Yb.* **10**, 65-70.

RACEY, P.A.. Bats. In: Poole, T. (Ed.) (1999) The *UFAW handbook on the care and management of laboratory animals,* Vol. 1 - Terrestrial vertebrates. 7th Edition, Blackwell

7

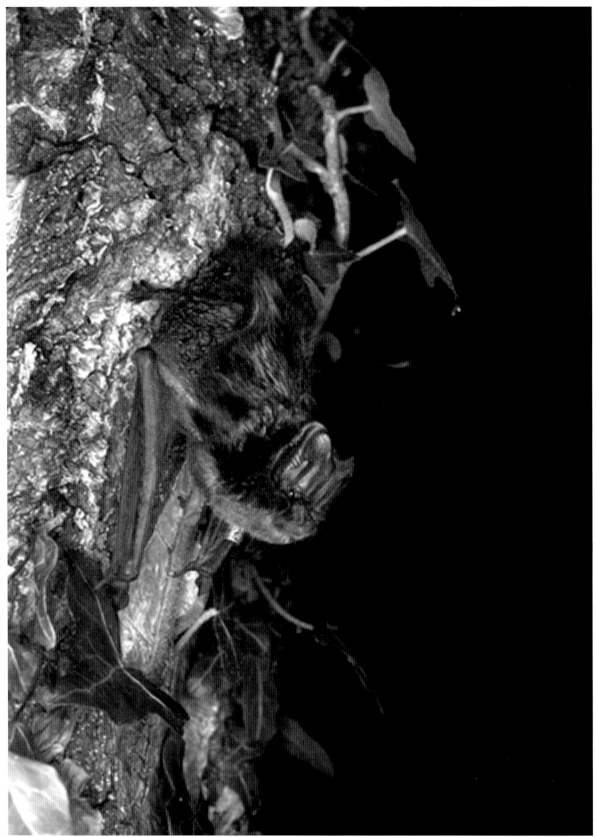

Barbastelle bat. © Frank Greenaway

The role of a Bat Group

G. Hinchcliffe

8.1 Introduction

Much of the grass-roots bat conservation work is carried out by voluntary bat workers operating from within the structure of local bat groups. Approximately 95 groups exist in the British Isles at present, many of which cover whole counties. Larger counties may be sub-divided, while other groups cover an individual town or city and its environs. Some groups are associated to The Bat Conservation Trust or local wildlife trust. Although the internal structure and the objectives of individual groups can vary enormously, the ultimate goal of conserving bats and their roosts involves most groups in:

- recording, reporting and monitoring roost sites and feeding areas;
- dealing with bat-related enquiries from members of the public;
- investigating and advising upon (via English Nature, SNH, CCW or EHS) enquiries relating to bats and their roosts;
- providing an informal information service to members of the public and a wide range of organisations;
- improving the public image and understanding of bats through planned educational and promotional events;
- raising funds for conservation projects.

Bat workers beginning hibernation visit to Dene Hole.
© Shirley Thompson

So, most bat groups combine the roles of a biological recording and monitoring unit with those of a public information and advisory service. This leads to a wealth of diverse activities (see Section 8.4) but, whichever a group pursues, if it is to function effectively it needs some form of internal organisation and a number of clearly defined aims, which its members understand and can contribute to, if they wish.

8

The Bat Conservation Trust

The Bat Conservation Trust is the national organisation dedicated to the conservation of bats and their habitats. It is a charity with a membership of about 4000. The Trust aims to stop further declines in bat populations and aid the recovery of threatened species. The BCT is the umbrella group for the local bat groups, providing support, information, resources, training and advice.

Each bat group elects a representative to attend regional meetings and to receive and disseminate information to the group. The BCT sends a regular information mailing to these bat group contacts which includes BCT's newsletters, Bat News and Young Batworker, and information of interest to bat groups, including new resources and details of training courses. Bat group members are invited to contribute to the volunteers' newsletter, which keeps people abreast of news and developments in bat conservation. An elected Regional Representative represents bat groups at the meetings of the Bat Groups Forum. The meetings are also attended by other organisations with an interest in bats and provide an opportunity for exchange of information.

The BCT holds an annual weekend conference of talks, workshops and exhibitions at the beginning of September. There are also regional meetings held for bat groups to attend. Their

Website (www.bats.org.uk) provides information on bats, legislation, bat groups, BCT and access to some of its leaflet resources.

Junior members of BCT belong to the Young Bat Workers Club and receive Young Bat Worker each quarter.

The BCT acts as a national voice for matters of concern and provides a link with similar organisations abroad (especially Europe). It lobbies at a national level for improved legislation affecting bats and to raise the profile among the public and professions of bats and their protected status. It organises national or county projects of conservation importance, including projects that allow local bat group participation, ranging from publicity campaigns, such as National Bat Week, to research projects, such as the Bats in Churches project and the National Bat Monitoring Programme. It runs the National Bat Helpline, which receives about 6000 inquiries per year. The Helpline gives advice and information to bat workers, members of the public, professionals and others about many aspects of bats.

The BCT maintains an insurance scheme, which provides public liability cover for its associated bat groups while they are carrying out bat group activities.

8.2 Starting up

The Bat Conservation Trust can provide specific help and advice to anyone considering starting up a bat group in a new area, or re-launching an existing one.

8.3 Running the group

8.3.1 Officers and organisation

Bat groups have developed into many different forms and the changing nature of both the membership and the demands placed upon it mean that most groups are continually evolving. However, certain jobs do need to be done, and most formalised groups have a number of officers such as Chairperson, Secretary, Treasurer, Enquiries Co-ordinator and Records Officer. Larger groups have found the need for named members to co-ordinate such areas as newsletters, press and publicity, sales goods, education, bat box schemes and church liaison. Specific projects or surveys may also need a co-ordinator. Subgroups may also form on a geographical basis, particularly in large counties, enabling enquiries to be dealt with more efficiently.

8.3.2 Meetings

Groups of any kind need to meet on a regular basis. The regularity of meetings is probably more important than the frequency – so that members know whether to expect some form of group activity once a month or once a year. It is probably best to seek members' views as to how often meetings should be held and what their main function should be. The section on bat group activities includes many ideas that could form the basis of meetings but the underlying reason for them – be it business, social, educational or a combination of these, needs to be clear, especially to those who are expected to organise them. While the group co-ordinator or secretary is often the one who plans and leads meetings, asking different people or small groups of members to take on non-business meetings may both share the load and lead to greater variety. Many formal groups have now developed a programme of indoor winter meetings and summer field outings, the details of which are circulated by newsletter or events list.

8.3.3 Recruiting/maintaining group members

This is probably the most difficult area on which to give advice with guaranteed results. What actually constitutes 'membership' varies enormously from group to group. It may be over a hundred annual subscribers, perhaps many bat supporters rather than active workers, or just a handful of keen, and probably licensed, enthusiasts. Whatever the size, the amount of potential bat work usually exceeds the time that a bat group's members have available and many groups are keen to attract new active workers.

In reality, one can rarely predict where the keen newcomer will be found. Membership of the 'subscriber' type can be promoted at walks, talks and countryside events but someone who is prepared to become seriously involved can just as easily turn up 'out of the blue'. Opportunities to watch out for include new intakes on environmental courses at local colleges and related adult education groups. Bat groups can even run their own course or contribute lectures within larger programmes. Displays and posters asking for volunteer help (in the usual places – natural history museums, libraries, visitor centres, local vets etc) may stimulate interest. Members of natural history organisations, wildlife trusts or bird clubs can also be approached. Another possibility is to cultivate the interests of positive roost owners. They may be able to do more than keep an eye on their own bats. Whatever the source of potential recruits, success depends on how welcome they feel within an existing group, how interesting and enjoyable the activities they participate in are, and, very importantly, whether their own skills and interests are utilised within the group.

The long-term maintenance of an established group involves similar considerations – with some new activities each year but also some old favourites, such as bat walks at regular venues. However, at this stage, the key to keeping active members is ensuring that the workload of individual bat workers remains within their capabilities while not letting the overall 'background' workload prevent the introduction of new ideas and stimulating projects. Whether the group is a new one or well established, those actively involved need to agree upon the group's priorities, be they roost monitoring, finding new sites, surveys and projects or education. It may be helpful to set objectives and deadlines. Certainly, areas of responsibility must be clearly defined, preferably for fixed periods of time, so that people know what they are expected to do and for how long. A formal group might wish to produce a development plan. An informal group should at least find the time to air ideas and discuss possibilities.

8.3.4 Training

The details of which bat worker activities require licensing and how training for these may be obtained are dealt with in Chapter 1, but several general points should be borne in mind. A great number of the possible activities (some of these being the most enjoyable) do not require formal licensing and hence require no formal training. However, many activities do require some prior experience, which will normally be gained through participating in group events or accompanying more experienced bat workers. A group tackling a new project or survey technique could learn from a more experienced group elsewhere, seek out a relevant course or a workshop at the annual conference or seek help from organisations outside bat work but carrying out studies with similar requirements. The Bat Conservation Trust organises training courses from time to time and there are usually a number of weekend training courses at Field Studies Council centres each year. The BCT also runs a number of courses for professional consultants. Participation in the BCT's National Bat Monitoring Programme and other national surveys can provide valuable experience and training. Bat detector workshops are held regularly, usually in collaboration with bat groups and bat workers.

In training bat workers for Statutory Nature Conservation Organisation (SNCO) licences, groups could consider keeping their trainer free from other official roles, thus reducing their workload. A log book could be maintained by trainees in which they record experience gained with other bat workers, which can then be taken into account as formal training progresses. As with all roles and responsibilities, it is important that both trainer and trainee have a clear understanding of mutual expectations in terms of time commitment, practical skills, baseline knowledge and long-term goals. Of course training does not finish with the acquisition of a licence. There are many opportunities to develop skills and knowledge further, at every level of experience. Dissemination of information from conferences and training courses is important for those who are unable to attend and could form the basis of an indoor group meeting.

8.3.5 Finance and equipment

Most groups operate a bank account with income originating from annual subscriptions, sales goods, fees or donations from bat talks and guided walks, occasional grants and specific fund-raising. Regular expenditure includes mailing, copying, printing and other membership- related maintenance costs. Excess funds or specific fund-raising may be used to purchase group equipment – typically more costly items such as ladders, rechargeable lamps, helmets and other safety equipment, catching and handling apparatus and bat detectors. Organisations such as BCT and the SNCOs may be approached for financial support towards the purchase of survey equipment or help with special projects, particularly those of a practical conservation nature. Bat groups in England and Wales should be aware that, because they have usually been set up for a purpose accepted by the law as charitable, there is a legal requirement to register as a charity if the group has a total income from all sources of more than £1000 per year. Individual bat groups are not covered by the Bat Conservation Trust registration because they are not subgroups of BCT. More information about this can be sought from either BCT or the Charities Commission. Groups operating as a specialist group of their county wildlife trust could be covered by the charitable status of the parent organisation. Groups would be well advised to determine their status and responsibilities, obtaining advice from the Charity Commissioners if needed. In Scotland and Northern Ireland the law is different, with charities registering with the Inland Revenue.

8.4 Bat group activities

The enthusiasm and inventiveness of the bat worker knows no limits. Thus, the activities outlined here are only an amalgamation of what many bat groups have already tried, not an exhaustive list. The activities are aimed at different audiences and each needs to be tailored to give those involved (both audience-member and bat worker) a positive experience. Group members should be encouraged to initiate or participate in activities whenever possible, while avoiding making others feel left out. Individual activities should be enjoyable rather than a chore, larger projects achievable rather than over-ambitious. The Bat Conservation Trust has a range of resources available to bat groups involved with organising events.

8.4.1 Roost recording and monitoring

Techniques for recording roost information and monitoring any subsequent change are discussed elsewhere (Chapter 3), but each group needs to decide upon methods that are manageable for themselves while allowing the transfer of information to other organisations, if required. In terms of group organisation it is important that the owner of each known roost has someone they can contact for further information or in an emergency. A useful way of doing this is to assign specific roosts to each bat group member who then reports to the Records Officer at the end of each season. A personal visit or a brief phone call or letter shows that the group is interested and organised enough to keep a check on significant sites. This is one of the keys to long-term conservation of roosts, particularly in people's homes. Positive roost owners should be encouraged to monitor colony size and arrival/departure dates themselves, perhaps using pre-stamped self-monitoring cards or by telephoning in dates and counts, or getting them involved with BCT's National Bat Monitoring Programme. One method of obtaining colony counts, which has been used successfully in recent years, is organising a co-ordinated count, where roost owners and volunteers all count their bats on a given evening. The idea of contributing to a mass effort has proved quite motivating and, in some areas, this has become an annual event.

The designated 'roost monitor' concept reduces the risk of duplication or confusion should different members of a group be arranging roost visits, training exercises or other activities. Liaison between neighbouring groups is also important for sites close to county or other geographical boundaries.

8.4.2 Other contact with roost owners

Maintaining contact with roost owners, particularly during winter months, can also be achieved through postal channels – sending Christmas cards, organising a competition or sending out a newsletter, or by social events, such as a roost owner's evening, with personal invitations and a programme of talks, activities and displays. A social event in the summer could also be promoted, such as a special roost owners bat walk or a barbecue and bat watch.

8.4.3 Gathering roost information

Information about existing or potential roosts may be acquired through a variety of means – posters, leaflet drops, questionnaires, press releases and so on. Much roost information reaches bat groups as a result of telephone enquiries. These may be of a general or problem nature, (sometimes via the SNCOs), or in response to walks and talks or other promotional activities. A system for logging incoming information and recording the initial action taken and by whom is essential. Distribution of roost enquiries or other information requiring urgent attention may be done on a geographical basis or a rota system.

8.4.4 Surveys

Bat groups and many individual bat workers together collect vast amounts of information on bat behaviour, roosts and feeding areas each year. Some groups specialise or concentrate their efforts into identifiable surveys or projects, others contribute data to regional or nation-wide schemes. Some of those aimed primarily at roost location have included systematic surveys of sites in churches, bridges, barns and other farm buildings, caves, mines, tunnels and various types of historic property. Attempts at 'whole-village' surveys have also been made. The recent developments in bat detector survey techniques have led to a more holistic approach where, combined with other methods, information about how bats use a given area includes feeding habitats and flight routes as well as roost sites. Subsequently many groups are now surveying specified areas of woodland, wetland, farmland and so on. Survey projects in conjunction with such organisations as the Bat Conservation Trust, National Trust, English Heritage, Forestry Authorities and the Ministry of Defence can also be very productive, yielding information which is useful to both parties. As with all survey work, it is vital that results, especially any roosts found, are notified to those responsible for them as quickly as possible. Some groups also carry out bat surveys that contribute to Environmental Assessments.

8.4.5 Research projects

Projects that look in more detail at certain aspects of bat behaviour or ecology may be seen as the realm of university departments or professional biologists, but many valuable contributions to our understanding of bats' requirements have been as the result of bat volunteers' work. A group, or an individual, needs to establish clear aims and time-scales for such a project and, where appropriate seek comment and discussion with other bat workers or relevant authorities at an early stage. The likelihood of special licensing, should additional disturbance to bats or roosts be created, must always be considered. Subjects that have been tackled by bat groups include studies of diet from feeding remains and faecal analysis, bat movements and roost fidelity by ringing, chemi-luminescent tagging and radio-tracking, and bat parasites, to name but a few.

8.4.6 Roost improvement and creation

There are many fine examples of groups' efforts to maintain, improve and create roosting opportunities for bats. Larger projects sometimes involve seeking grant aid, sponsorship (in the form of materials as well as money) and liaison with numerous authorities. At the other end of the scale, the offer of a little practical help from the bat group can lead to the maintenance of a roost site, which otherwise might be lost.

Many groups are involved in the creation and monitoring of artificial roosts through bat box schemes. They also improve known or potential sites, particularly hibernacula, by creating crevices and cavities with hanging boards or bat bricks, and grilling entrances to prevent disturbance. Members of groups regularly offer practical advice to builders, roofers and design engineers on maintaining and creating roosting opportunities within structures they are working on – houses, bridges, tunnels etc. Probably the most ambitious roost-creation projects are those where groups have built artificial hibernacula, either by modifying existing structures or designing and constructing entirely new ones.

8.4.7 Producing reports and publishing findings

Some groups produce reports on an annual basis, others occasionally. Summaries of a bat group's work can reach a wider audience through articles in the local press or wildlife trust magazines. However, interesting findings from completed research projects or analyses of specified survey results should be made available to other bat workers through publication in the BCT's Bat News or presentation at the annual bat workers' conference.

8.4.8 Dealing with enquiries from the public

Enquiries that result in survey of a potential roost site, dealing with stray or injured bats or necessitate advice on a bat problem are dealt with elsewhere. However, dealing with general enquiries about bats takes up a great deal of group members' time, especially in the summer months, and many bat workers are now experts in assessing exactly what the enquirer actually wants. 'Time-saving' ideas for dealing with general queries include lists of regularly used telephone numbers posted near the phone, information packs on popular subjects (school projects, building bat boxes etc.) made up ready in stamped envelopes and pre-prepared record sheets for incoming telephone information. The Bat Conservation Trust has a national help line, which all members of the public, professions and bat workers may call for general advice on bats (see Appendix 6).

8.4.9 Displays and countryside events

Static displays can be put up in libraries, museums, visitor centres and other high profile sites. The county or regional library service may be able to circulate a display around its branches, given a pre-arranged route and dates. This could make full use of a group's resources during the quieter winter months.

Groups receive many requests to attend countryside events during the spring and summer months – wildlife fairs, nature reserve open days, county shows and so on. Small groups may need to prioritise their commitments. Active participation in something will have more of an impact than just looking at the display. Brief guided walks (how bats could use the immediate area), bat box building or children's activities are worth considering.

The Bat Conservation Trust can loan display materials and resources to bat groups for events.

8.4.10 Bat talks and walks

The growth of public interest in bats and their conservation has led to a great demand for talks or slide shows and opportunities to watch bats in the wild. For an indoor talk the length of presentation, depth of information given and previous experience of the speaker needs to be carefully matched to the age and knowledge of the audience. While not all members of a group will be happy or competent to speak to an audience, it is well worth 'training up' and offering opportunities to those who are interested in order to build up a pool of presenters within the group. Thus requests should not have to be turned down due to lack of time or previous bookings. Make sure full details of venue, start time, expected size of audience and so on are confirmed in writing, also what equipment is available at the venue. For a children's talk or if the audience may include families with young children, consider a shorter talk followed by an activity for youngsters or have children's activities running alongside the adult's talk, if there are sufficient helpers and facilities.

Bat walks or watches can be one of the most effective and enjoyable ways of introducing bats to the public, given the right venue, timing and weather. Such events are often organised in conjunction with a local wildlife trust, council or other authority. In these cases they will usually advertise the event and send along someone to help with 'crowd control'. Consider a numbers restriction, through advance booking, if any of the sites you are visiting have limited space and ensure that appropriate safety precautions are taken (see Chapter 2) for all walks. Variations on the 'bat watch' theme include dawn, rather than dusk walks, and events designed for those with special needs. For example, a wheelchair route or a bat 'listen' for those with impaired sight. If the host authority is levying a charge, the bat group might expect payment for their services or a share of the income. The standard of bat talks and bat watches is now so high that a donation to group funds, if not a fee, seems reasonable in most circumstances. (For further ideas see BCT Guidelines for giving talks and lectures and for organising and leading a batwalk).

Bats on the internet

Bat groups and individual bat workers can now reach a world-wide audience through the internet. Some British bat groups have already established their own websites. Check out the local groups using search engines, or alternatively try some of the links and discussion forum on the BCT's website.

Both bat groups and batworkers will find the internet of use in a number of ways:
- searching for information on the web about bats worldwide;
- communicating with other bat workers by e-mail;
- posting and replying to messages in newsgroups;
- subscribing to automatic mailing lists;
- publishing their own information about bats on the internet;
- downloading useful programs, e.g. sound analysis software, photographs of bats;
- searching university libraries for books and published papers on bats.

The following list of internet addresses will get you 'surfing' some of the main bat sites around the world. More sites are listed in Appendix 6. You can also use a 'search engine' to locate other sites of interest by typing in keywords such as 'bats', 'bat box', 'Chiroptera' etc.

The Bat Conservation Trust http://www.bats.org.uk/
Bat Conservation International http://www.batcon.org/
Bat Ecology and
Bioacoustics Laboratory http://www.bio.bris.ac.uk/research/bats/

8.4.11 Running educational courses

Many opportunities for educating people about bats have been mentioned in earlier sections. Bat groups can organise their own seminars or short courses for other bat workers, for the general public (through environmental centres, local colleges or adult education groups) and for groups of professionals who might encounter bats during their work (for example 'Bats in Buildings' and 'Bats in Bridges' seminars). A lecture or field trip may be a welcome addition to a university or college course at any level.

8.4.12 Activities for children

The interest shown in bats by young people is remarkable and can only bode well for bats residing with these householders of the future. A wide range of imaginative and enjoyable children's activities has been developed, and are available from BCT and in published project books. Activities offered at public events or to accompany talks to children's groups should be short and simple, for example cut-out bats, masks, posters or quick quizzes. Never underestimate the number of helpers needed, or the amount of resources required, particularly for younger children. Older groups may be able to take on a more lengthy project or help with survey work such as roost counts or locating bat feeding areas.

Bats have been used as a school topic from primary to sixth-form level. They offer a fascinating context in which sections of the National Curriculum programmes of study can be delivered in England and Wales and the 5–14 Development Programme in Scotland. Seminars offered directly to groups of teachers enable them to pass on greater knowledge and enthusiasm to their classes and 'cascade' information efficiently. Individual workers should be aware of any Local Authority restrictions concerning taking captive wild animals into schools. (See also BCT Guidelines for activities with children and accompanying resource list).

A Scottish Education Pack on bats has been published by BCT which includes activities, slides, tape and games linked to the Scottish Curriculum and which has also been modified for use with the English National Curriculum (see Thompson 1997, 1998, Appendix 5).

8.5 Links with other bodies

It is essential that bat groups liaise with other organisations whose interests or responsibilities include bats. Groups should have a policy about which bodies receive information concerning bat roosts and other records and to which organisations data can be made available upon request.

8.5.1 English Nature, Scottish Natural Heritage, Countryside Council for Wales and Environment and Heritage Service (Northern Ireland)

Bat groups will be in regular contact with their area's Conservation/Area Officer who will be involved in any situation where bats are creating problems or disturbance is likely. Travelling expenses for registered volunteers will be paid by the SNCO for roost visits made at their request.

8.5.2 Local Wildlife Trusts

Many bat groups are affiliated to or are a subgroup of their local wildlife trust. Members of the public often seek advice from such trusts and bat enquiries will be passed on to local bat workers. Wildlife trusts may seek information about bat records when commenting on local development issues or monitoring planning applications.

8.5.3 Neighbouring Bat Groups

It is important for neighbouring groups to keep in contact, as they may be useful to each other in providing extra skills, equipment, people, advice and moral support.

8.5.4 Others

The RSPCA, SSPCA and local police should be provided with contact points for active bat workers. Making contact with Local Authority Environmental Health Officers, Local Authority Planning Officers and local pest control companies can also be useful. Developing and maintaining good relationships with any local caving group may bring benefits to bats.

Bechstein's bat. © Frank Greenaway

Public relations

A. J. Mitchell-Jones

9.1 Bat enquiries and visits to roosts

This section covers all those occasions when a request for advice about bats is received by any conservation organisation. Requests can arrive in many forms but can be split essentially into two types – those where bats have been discovered in a building, usually a house, and are causing concern and those where some action, such as development or repair work, is intended, which might affect bats or their roosts. In some cases a desire to get rid of the bats is expressed when advice is sought about some action that might affect them: these should be treated initially as of the second type.

Lesser horseshoe bats may be located in roofs of old buildings.
© Frank Greenaway

Emergencies

Although it is recommended that advice about bats is sought well before any proposed building work and it is normally possible to persuade the majority of householders to leave their bats to disperse naturally, there will, inevitably, be times when rapid action is required to save bats or their roosts. Serious problems are, fortunately, rare, but the following situations may be among the more frequently encountered:

- smell – householders can no longer tolerate it (see this Chapter);
- noise – householders can no longer tolerate it (see this Chapter);
- phobia – householder insists on immediate exclusion (see this Chapter);
- roof repairs – bats found after work has started (see Chapter 10);
- timber treatment – bats appear after spraying has begun (see Chapter 10).

Such situations may be divided into two broad classes. For the first three situations, any action may be covered by the defence in the Wildlife & Countryside Act or the Habitats Regulations that the action took place within a dwelling house. This covers the damage, destruction or obstruction of roosts and the disturbance of roosting bats, but not killing, injuring or taking. For the latter two, the potential damage to the bats or their roosts may also be covered by the 'incidental result of a lawful operation and could not reasonably have been avoided' clause in the legislation. This covers intentional/deliberate killing, injuring or taking as well as the damage, destruction or obstruction of roosts and the disturbance of bats. In addition, the availability of licences under the Habitats Regulations must also be taken into account. The legal position in these sorts of situations is complex and, as always, it is best to try and resolve the situation by persuasion and common sense rather than involving the law, which, in practice, is severely weakened by the defences referred to above as well as by the

difficulties of proving intent. This applies particularly to the first three situations, where, in a tiny number of cases per year, bat noise or smell may be quite intolerable. In such situations, a heavy-handed approach may well act against our long-term goal of improving the public's acceptance of bats in their houses.

The requirement to notify the appropriate statutory nature conservation organisations (English Nature, Scottish Natural Heritage, Countryside Council for Wales or Environment & Heritage Service) is, in essence, a consultation about the applicability of the defences in the Act/Regulations. Clearly, the SNCOs cannot advise on a course of action that would result in the law being broken, but they can advise about what they would consider 'reasonable' and they can also provide advice on how operations can be carried out with the minimum damage to the nature conservation interest.

Because of the complexity of many of these situations, it is impossible to give a simple set of rules that can be applied firmly and inflexibly in each case; each problem must be approached with an open mind and the various options assessed. The goals of any action that is taken should be, in order of importance:

- to ensure that bats are not killed or injured;
- to ensure that the roost is not damaged or destroyed;
- to ensure that the roost is left for the breeding season;
- to ensure that the roost is left for the future.

Sometimes, it may be advantageous to compromise one goal to achieve another. For example, it may be possible to persuade a colony of bats to use another entrance hole to a roost if this ensures that the roost will otherwise be left undisturbed. Or if a building is being re-roofed, it may be advantageous to accept a degree of disturbance in one season if this ensures, through maintaining the goodwill of the owner, that access will be left for the future.

9

9.1.1 Bats discovered and advice sought

The majority of callers in this category begin by stating that they have discovered bats roosting in their house and enquiring what should be done about them. Concealed within this introduction is a whole spectrum of attitudes ranging from those who know absolutely nothing about bats but have a vague feeling that they are not something one should have in one's house to those who are absolutely unshakeable in their conviction that they will not share their house with bats. Survey results show that about half these people can be persuaded to leave the bats undisturbed permanently and that almost all the others can be persuaded to leave the roost undisturbed until the bats disperse naturally. Even in this group, only about half will then take action, as advised, to prevent the bats returning.

Whatever the reason for the advice being sought, there is always a role in these cases for the Bat Group or bat enthusiast. This may range from the provision of advice on how to improve a roost for bats to persuasion about leaving the bats undisturbed. If persuasion is unsuccessful and action against the bats or their roost is intended, even in the future, the SNCO must become involved. Many enquiries in this category are received directly by the SNCO and, if the enquirer remains unconvinced about leaving the bats alone, it is likely that a local Bat Group volunteer will be asked to visit the site, assess the situation and send in a report.

Dealing with bat enquiries where an element of persuasion is required really requires a greater knowledge of people than of bats. Generally, it will be the conviction with which the case for bat conservation is made that will be the decisive factor rather than the ability to answer questions on the more obscure aspects of bat biology. Some people are naturally persuasive and, with a reasonable grounding in bat biology, will soon achieve a good success rate in persuading members of the public to tolerate or even to like their bats. Others find this role more difficult and may need extensive training to gain the confidence and experience to put the case for bats convincingly. A few may realise that they are temperamentally unsuited to such work and are better employed on some other aspect of bat conservation work; this is in no sense an admission of failure.

Enquirers who have discovered bats roosting in their house or other building but are quite happy to leave them undisturbed present no problems. Often the report of the roost will be accompanied by a request for factual information, which can be provided by leaflets or booklets. In other cases, a visit by the Bat Group might be welcomed to identify and count the bats, and many will be pleased to take part in the National Bat Monitoring Programme (see Appendix 4 for details) or join The Bat Conservation Trust.

Persuasion is a powerful weapon and must be used with care and respect for people's fears and beliefs, however strange these may be. The law appears to give bats considerable protection, but ultimately the existence of a roost in a private house depends both legally and practically on the continuing goodwill of the householder. Conservation should be based on understanding and co-operation rather than on a fear of the law or of public condemnation. In dealing with enquiries of this type, bat workers should rarely need to spell out the law, although they may perhaps make a passing reference to why bats are protected. There is no legal obligation on householders to have bats roosting in their house if they clearly do not want them.

Many enquirers will have had no previous direct contact with 'conservationists' and may well have no further contact in the future, so answering a bat enquiry gives an opportunity for the bat worker to present not only the case for bats but also, by inference, the case for conservation in general. If the conservationist viewpoint is presented carefully and with tact, then, even if the roost is lost, the enquirer may at least be left with a more enlightened attitude towards conservation generally.

Many people are unable to give a logical reason why they wish to get rid of their bats, but others will find some aspect of the bats' occupation objectionable. Table 9.1 presents an analysis of the reasons given; see also Moore et al. (2003). Despite all the publicity over the past few years, some people still think of bats as pests, which are infesting their house and which need controlling like mice. It is often a good starting point to explain that in most cases bats are only seasonal visitors to houses and use them for roosting in much the same way as swallows or house martins.

Table 9.1 Reasons given by a sample of 100 householders for wishing to be rid of bats roosting in their house (from Mitchell-Jones *et al.*, 1986)	
Reason	**Number of households**
Droppings outside the property	23
Droppings inside the property	20
Bats flying or crawling in the house	16
General fear of bats	15
Concern that bats are causing damage	11
Fear of numbers increasing greatly	5
Noise	4
Smell	3
Fear of transmission of disease to humans	3

Droppings

Droppings are the major cause of complaint, although in many cases they may form an obvious focal point for more general fears. Often the bats' roost entrance will be above a window, so that the glass becomes streaked with droppings and urine. This can be a cause of great concern to the house-proud, some of whom find any level of mess unacceptable. In other cases, droppings can fall on stored goods, patios, cars or doorsteps. In most circumstances some remedial action is possible, but this may not appear adequate or be acceptable to some people. On stored goods in lofts or other areas used for storage, plastic or cloth sheeting provides a cheap and easy method of protection. Plastic sheeting should be avoided where there is a risk of condensation. In many cases, especially where there are numerous entry points for the bats, the use of plastic sheeting is undoubtedly the most cost-effective solution to what is usually a seasonal problem. Where the enquirer remains unconvinced, an offer by the Bat Group to supply and fit plastic sheeting can often prove the decisive factor. In churches too, the use of dust-sheeting is often the most cost-effective solution to the perennial problem of droppings on the pews, altar or floor.

On the exterior of buildings, deflector boards fitted some way below the roost entrance can prove helpful in diverting droppings away from sensitive areas. Some examples and applications are shown in Figure 9.1. The boards, usually made of wood, can be fitted to masonry or wooden window frames with screws and brackets. Some roosts have a number of separate entrances or entry is possible anywhere along an opening, for example where a soffit adjoins a wall. If droppings beneath one particular area are a nuisance, it may be possible to close the offending access point and force the bats to use an alternative. This would require consultation with the SNCO. In a few cases, little can be done to alleviate the problem and so one will have to stress the seasonal nature of the bat colony and the harmlessness of the droppings. Success depends on the tolerance of the householder and the bat worker's persuasive ability.

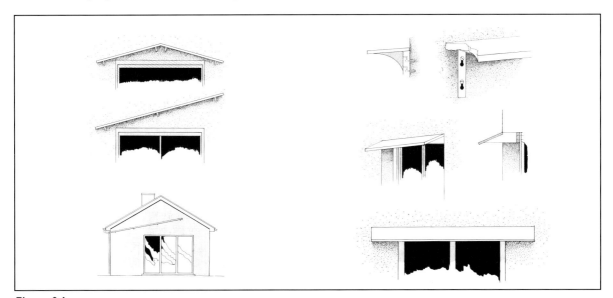

Figure 9.1
Deflector boards. These are most frequently screwed to masonry using plugs, or to the wooden window frame. Plastic guttering on standard brackets is also a possibility. If removable brackets, as illustrated, are used, the board need only be put up while the bats are in residence.

Bats in the living area

Bats flying or crawling in the living area of the house, the second most common cause of complaint, are generally soluble problems, though some detective work may be needed. Householders should be warned not to handle bats because of the risk of disease (see Chapter 2: Advice on bats and rabies).

The most common source of bats in the inhabited parts of a building is through some connection with an area habitually used by bats. In modern houses, such connections are common where pipes, such as sink waste pipes, pass through a cavity wall. The brickwork is rarely a perfect fit in such places and small gaps are often left. If bats are roosting at the gable apex, they can generally gain access to the wall cavity and may emerge many metres away, often in bathrooms or kitchens. If bats use the roof void, they may enter through gaps around pipes through the ceiling, especially in airing cupboards, or through badly-fitting loft hatches. In older houses particularly, there is a wide range of possible entry points such as between floor joists, around window frames where there is a gap between the wood and brick or stone, through gaps in corners of ceilings or skirting, through ventilators or through any other connecting hole or crack. Usually the householder will seek advice as soon as one or two bats have been found. As these may well have been found in different rooms, they may give little clue to the whereabouts of the connection, so it is probably best to begin by looking at pipes in the bathroom, kitchen and airing cupboard. In older buildings with solid walls the search may actually be easier, as the opportunity for the bats to travel away from their roosting area is more limited. Generally the difficulty of finding the access point is proportional to the size of the building.

Any gap wider than about 8 mm must be regarded as a potential bat entry point. Householders, who almost invariably overestimate the size of bats, generally overlook gaps of this size. Once discovered, the gaps should be carefully sealed, either temporarily with newspapers or rags or more permanently with plaster-based filler, expanded foam, wooden battens or other suitable material. Ventilators with bat-sized holes will need to be covered with a fine mesh less than 8 mm in diameter. Usually it is impossible to be absolutely certain that all potential entry points have been found on the first visit, so it is unwise to give absolute guarantees of immediate success; credibility suffers when the next bat is found.

Less commonly, bats will fly through open windows, particularly those that are hinged at the top. This may be an isolated incident, with no evidence that there is a roost, but usually the bats will have come from a nearby colony. The problem is most common when young bats are learning to fly or when the roost entrance is close to a window. The simplest advice is to keep the window shut during the sensitive time of the year, usually mid-July to mid-August. If the householder does not wish to keep the window closed during what is generally the hottest time of the year, a net curtain stretched across the window is an alternative. In some cases it may be possible to persuade the bats to use a more remote entrance, as was described in the previous section. Cats may also bring in live bats.

General fear of bats

General fear of bats is more common than its position in Table 9.1 would suggest, because many enquirers with a general fear try to present a more definite reason for wanting to be rid of the bats. The strength of such fears should not be underestimated; although the majority are based on ignorance and superstition (most people have never seen a bat at close quarters), a few are genuine phobias where the presence of the bats can cause real mental distress. Pressurising such people into leaving the bats undisturbed wins no friends for the conservation cause, and the public image of the conservation organisations is better served by the prompt provision of advice and even of practical help. The skill lies in assessing the extent of people's fears and knowing when to give in gracefully.

One of the most frequent expressions of a general fear of bats is the belief that bats in the roof are a permanent infestation, like mice. Many householders find it extremely comforting to be told that the bats are only resident seasonally and will move elsewhere once they have finished breeding. Although this may not always be strictly true, especially for species such as the long-eared bat, the bats will certainly not be obvious during the winter and will apparently have disappeared.

Other common fears are that bats are generally like mice, that they will become entangled in hair, that they will crawl into the house at night, that they will bring in lots of nesting material and that they are about the size of sparrows, starlings or possibly even pigeons. Such fears can often be calmed by the provision of factual information and showing them a real bat, but irrational fears are, by definition, not founded on fact. Children are more easily convinced than their parents, who, seeing their children's change in attitude may rapidly alter their views.

Damage to buildings

Concern that bats may be causing damage is common but almost entirely groundless. Many such fears stem from the belief that bats are similar to rodents in their ability to gnaw and construct their own entrances, runways and nests. Bats are often accused of dislodging hanging tiles, moving loft insulation or even bending lead flashing to gain access. Such accusations are completely groundless and can be countered with complete conviction by a description of the small size of bats and their lack of suitable teeth for gnawing. In very rare cases, bats can be implicated in minor damage to buildings through scrabbling claws or the accumulation of large quantities of droppings. The latter cases are generally associated with other building defects, which allow the droppings to become wet and thus act as a source of moisture, which can mark ceilings or walls or, in extreme cases, cause ceilings to collapse. However, it must be emphasised that such cases are very rare and that, provided that a building is structurally sound, the droppings present no danger at all.

In certain circumstances, particularly in churches, damage to valued items can occasionally be caused by bat urine or droppings. The droppings are most often noticed and constitute a nuisance in large numbers but it is likely that urine is more damaging because it contains ammonia, which is corrosive. Urine can leave a pale stain on surfaces such as polished wood, marble and brass. Droppings and urine may damage wall paintings. A project conducted by the Bat Conservation Trust (Bats in Churches) surveyed a random sample of 538 churches in England and reports were produced, which included some solutions to problems caused by bats and guidelines on the management of bats in churches. Revised guidance with respect to works of art can be found in Paine (undated).

The first approach to solving bat-related problems should be to attempt methods that do not disturb bats or their roosts and, hence, do not require consultation with the SNCOs. These include adjusting cleaning rotas so that the church is cleaned just before services and moving sensitive objects if they are kept under a roost. Covers of various types can be effective, elegant and easy to clean. They can take the form of hoods, drapes or canopies designed to cover a range of items such as candlesticks, textiles, statues or the pulpit. Covers can be removed before services and need only be used during the period when bats are present and active. Wax furniture polishes, applied regularly to wood, can provide some protection against damage caused by bat urine. Urine etches brass and bronze and, if the use of covers is not practical, both can be protected by a layer of strippable lacquer followed by a coating of micro-crystalline wax. A conservator should ideally apply these. Wall paintings in churches may be particularly susceptible to damage and protection methods described above may not be applicable. Attempts to dissuade bats from flying near wall paintings, such as the provision of time-switch operated lighting and side baffles should only be planned in collaboration with wall painting conservators. Some measures employed to alleviate problems may disturb bats or their roosting sites. In these situations the advice of the relevant SNCO must be sought. Positioning of devices such as canopies or deflector boards below roosts would require careful positioning to avoid disturbing access to the roost. The use of deterrents such as lighting, screening materials to protect specific areas of the church etc. should be discussed with the SNCO. There is no evidence to suggest that bats are affected in the long term by incense, ultrasonic devices or model predators such as owls. If a roost is in a particularly sensitive area, such as above the altar, it may be possible, after consultation with the SNCO, to relocate the roost within the church by blocking access to the original roost and, if necessary, providing an alternative roosting location within the building. In a minority of cases the presence of bats may be perceived as intolerable and the parochial church council may apply to the SNCO for exclusion. As exclusion involves blocking all holes that allow bats access to the interior these operations tend to be time-consuming and expensive. A crevice 1 cm wide will allow access to a pipistrelle so it is difficult to ensure that all potential access points are blocked. It should also be borne in mind that such an operation might restrict ventilation. Although there is

9

no guarantee that bats can successfully relocate to another roost, preventing re-entry is considered less disruptive than disturbing already roosting bats. Finally, it is important to be aware that the timing of bat occupation of churches is often at variance with the timing of maternity roosts in other types of building (e.g. Battersby, 1995).

Numbers increasing

Worries about the numbers of bats increasing greatly arise largely from the belief that bats are present all year and breed like mice, but are compounded by the way in which large numbers of bats can suddenly appear. Also, the numbers at a roost may build up as bats gather from other sites, such as in spring. Even in mid-summer the numbers can suddenly increase as bats move in from other sites, then just as rapidly decrease as the roost moves to other locations. Such fears can usually be allayed by an account of the seasonal and temporary nature of bat colonies, the fact that most colonies consist only of females, which have gathered to give birth and rear their single young, and the slow potential growth rate of the colony. Even if every bat survived, the colony could increase by only 50% a year (half the young being males), and in reality rates of increase are very much lower (<10%). The maximum size of colonies is very variable but the average is about 50 for common pipistrelles (larger for *P. pygmaeus*, especially in Scotland), 20–30 for long-eared bats and perhaps 20 for serotines.

Noise

Noise from bat colonies can be a temporary but annoying problem during the summer, particularly with pipistrelle colonies in modern houses, where walls are thin and sound-insulation is poor. Noise is usually most noticeable at dusk and on hot days. The problem can be particularly acute in houses with hanging tiles pinned directly onto blockwork walls. Serotines can also be noisy during the spring and autumn. Often, there is little to be done to reduce the problem, and one must stress the seasonal nature of the problem (only a few weeks a year except in cold wet summers when the breeding season is prolonged) and, if appropriate, suggest that other bedrooms are used temporarily. In a few cases it may be possible to install additional insulation or prevent the bats using the part of the roof that is the source of the problem. Cases of this

sort often need a careful and sympathetic approach, particularly where the noise is heard in bedrooms used by children or where the householder is suffering from lack of sleep. It may sometimes be necessary to try to persuade the bats to move elsewhere either by exposing their roost area or by restricting their access or by other suitable means. This would require consultation with the SNCO.

Smell

Genuine complaints about smell from droppings are relatively uncommon but can sometimes be well founded. Problems usually arise either where a building defect allows droppings to get wet or where large quantities of droppings are accumulating rapidly in a poorly ventilated area. When dealing with such cases, it is most important that these factors are investigated thoroughly so that the problem can be attributed to the correct cause. A satisfactory remedy may necessitate structural repairs or alterations to prevent a recurrence of the problem. Simply excluding the bats is unlikely to be satisfactory because the droppings and any moisture will still be present. In extreme cases, it may be necessary for the accumulated droppings to be exposed and removed before a satisfactory solution is reached. Building regulations now require roofs to be much better ventilated than formerly, and this should mean fewer complaints about smell. Some bats, for example soprano pipistrelles, have a particularly strong batty smell, and draughts through a house may draw in air over the roosting bats and downstairs, such as when a front door is opened. Keeping internal doors closed and sealed can alleviate this problem.

Transmission of disease

Fears are often expressed about the possibility of disease being spread by bat droppings or urine. Such fears are quite understandable in view of the number of diseases that can be spread by the excreta of other species, including domestic pets. In Britain, there is no evidence that bats can spread disease via their droppings or urine. However, one should not encourage close contact with either bats or their accumulated droppings.

In some parts of the world the fungal disease histoplasmosis (caused by *Histoplasma capsulatum*) has been associated with large accumulations of bat droppings. However, histoplasmosis is a very rare

Interior design for a huge roost of (smelly) bats

In a cottage on the National Trust's Attingham Park Estate in Shropshire, smells and stains from a huge bat roost had, by 1995, made an attic bedroom uninhabitable, and the ground floor dining room also suffered from the odour. Accumulated droppings and urine from the bats caused staining on the ceiling and an unacceptably strong smell of ammonia, which literally brought tears to the eyes. The problem was exacerbated by lack of access to the roof void, so that droppings could not be removed, and poor ventilation. Action had to be taken if the goodwill of the occupiers was to be maintained.

Some years ago, following a fire, a new roof was built on to one half of the house and an attic was converted into a bedroom. The bats may have been present before this work but the new roof clearly provided good roosting habitat because over the years an extremely large maternity roost (sometimes in excess of 1600 adult females) of soprano pipistrelles (*P. pygmaeus*) developed.

We needed to contain the smell, stop the staining and retain the roost. In discussions between the National Trust and English Nature it was agreed that the priority was removal of the accumulated droppings. A loft access was cut into the ceiling, through which several bin liners of droppings and soiled insulation were removed. In winter 1996/97 we agreed that the existing ceiling would be stripped out and replaced with a vapour barrier between the bats and the ceiling. New insulation, additional ventilation on ridge and eaves, hinged soffits to allow droppings to be removed and wooden rakes between the rafters with which droppings could be removed were also installed.

The usual advice would be to carry out such works outside the May to September breeding season when the bats are not present. However in January bats were found hibernating in remnants of insulation in the bays between the rafters. These had to be excluded for works to proceed and be completed before May when the maternity roost would, it was hoped, return.

During a warm period in March, lights were installed in the roof void and the insulation removed. No bats were found at a this time and it is likely that those present earlier in the year had already moved on. On subsequent nights the householder blocked the access points after dark and opened them the following morning, thereby progressively excluding any bats still using the roof void. He reported seeing no bats leaving and so after a week of blocking in this way the holes were left blocked to stop bats returning and to allow work to proceed.

In early April the ceiling was stripped, with bat workers on hand to deal with any bats (there were none). Removing the ceiling boards revealed that, in the bay used as the main entrance to the roost, the bats had reduced the scrim (cloth) lining of the felt to tatters. The soffit boards, also removed at this time, were so solidly packed with droppings that thick cakings of them stayed in place when they were removed. The soffits were probably the original roost site but as droppings accumulated the bats were progressively excluded and forced to use the main roof void, often roosting several metres from the access hole.

By the end of April the works had been completed. It could only be hoped that the bats would return. By mid-May the occupier reported counting 500+ bats leaving the roost and a count on 4 June revealed 769+ and by the end of June c. 1000. Importantly, 6 months after the works the bedroom had neither 'bat' smells nor 'bat' stains and was habitable! In subsequent years, the number of bats in this roost has declined steadily, but there is no apparent reason for this.

Close co-operation at every stage between the National Trust, English Nature and the householder was essential. The total capital cost of the works, including a grant for the hinged soffits from English Nature, was c. £6,000 (which at c. £6 per adult female bat seemed good value).

Source: The National Trust/English Nature, pers. com.

disease in Britain (all occurrences are of foreign origin) and there is no evidence that the fungus occurs naturally in this country. The climate is also generally unsuitable for this fungus, which requires a temperature of 20–35°C and a high relative humidity to flourish.

Concerns may be expressed about a form of rabies that may now be present in bats in the UK. In the past decade, rabies-like viruses, now characterised as European Bat Lyssavirus (EBL), have been found in bats in north-western continental Europe. One type (EBL1) appears to be endemic in serotines, and another type (EBL2) has been recorded, though rarely, from the pond bat *Myotis dasycneme* and Daubenton's bat *Myotis daubentonii*.

These viruses are serologically distinct from the 'classical' or sylvatic rabies virus (serotype 1), which is typically spread by terrestrial carnivores, and all the evidence suggests that there is no significant interchange of the bat virus with other wild mammals, although the virus can be transferred to other mammals under laboratory conditions. In 1996, a Daubenton's bat picked up close to the south coast of England, was found to be infected with EBL2 (Whitby *et al.*, 1996) and a further individual was recorded in Lancashire in 2002 (Johnson *et al.*, 2003). Later that year, a batworker in Scotland died from EBL2 infection (Fooks *et al.*, in press a). It is known that he had been bitten by bats and the assumption is that he acquired the disease by that route.

Smell, noise and phobias – emergencies

Legal position (simplified)

If action is taken against bats because of smell or noise problems or because they are not liked, the intentional killing, injuring or taking of bats is illegal. Disturbing bats or damaging or destroying roosts within dwelling-houses is covered by a defence in the Wildlife & Countryside Act/Habitats Regulations, but this cannot be relied on unless the SNCO had been consulted. Thus, if people take action against bats and deliberately kill or injure them, this would be illegal. However, if they disturb them or damage or destroy their roosts without first consulting the SNCO, this would probably be illegal, but only a court could decide.

Advice

Problems involving smell or noise are amongst the most acute that batworkers are likely to encounter. In a few cases per year, householders are faced with a situation, which they find intolerable and which they insist must be resolved at once. Unfortunately, such problems tend to become acute during the short period (about 4 weeks) when the bats have dependent young and when a straightforward solution is most difficult.

At this point, the law is of limited relevance, particularly as public sympathy (and often that of the bat worker) lies with the householder. In such instances, which amount to probably no more than five cases a year, bat conservation is probably best served by the provision of prompt advice on how to solve the problem with the least damage to the bats. This would normally mean the exclusion of the colony, followed, in some cases by subsequent remedial works. Wherever possible, the SNCO should be involved as early as possible, so that they can make the decision as to whether advice about immediate exclusion is appropriate.

Outside the breeding season (mid-August – mid-May)

Bats can be excluded by fitting a one-way bat excluder or blocking their access holes over three nights once they have left in the evening (see section on exclusion techniques in this chapter). Alternatively, the roost area could be exposed (preferably towards dusk), so persuading the bats to move on.

During the breeding season

No dependent young

If the bats have no dependent young, they can be excluded as described above, even if they are pregnant. Hopefully, the bats will know of alternative roosts nearby.

Dependent young

Attempting to move bats with dependent young carries a high probability of bats being killed, mainly through the abandonment of young, and must be advised against by the SNCO. However, if there are overriding reasons for attempting to move the bats, for example under a licence issued on public health grounds, action should be taken in such a way that casualties are kept to a minimum. The aim here should be to persuade the bats to move to a different roost during the night. Provided they are not panicked, they should carry their young with them. Persuasion can be achieved by partially exposing the roosting area, for example by removing a soffit board or an area of hanging tiles. This should be done during the early evening if possible. Part of the roost area can be exposed the first night, followed by more on subsequent nights until the colony moves. If dependent young are abandoned, these would have to be raised by hand or euthanasia could be considered. Note that adults may return to collect young up to two or more days after abandonment.

If action by the householder results in bats (adults and young) having to be rescued from a roof, these should be kept together if possible and placed in a bat-box located not too far from the original roost. The entrance to the box should be sealed up until all the bats have been rescued (provided this is not more than a day) and then opened at dusk to allow the bats to move on.

Illegal action

Occasionally householders will feel unable to wait while attempts are made to move the colony and will start to open up the roosting area. Such action, which would probably involve killing or injuring bats, would be illegal and the SNCO and the police should be informed immediately.

Although the outcome of being bitten by a bat carrying EBL2 may be a fatal disease, this is not considered to be a significant public health risk in the UK. This is because:
- The level of infection in bats seems to be very low. More than 3200 bats have been tested in the UK since 1986, with only two Daubenton's bats being found to be positive (see Table 9.2). Recent limited testing of live Daubenton's bats suggests exposure to EBL2 may be more widespread.
- Pipistrelles and long-eared bats, the species most commonly found in houses, have never been found to have the type of virus (EBL2) found in Daubenton's bats.
- Daubenton's bats are not strongly associated with houses. Out of 23,896 enquiries recorded by NCC/English Nature between 1982 and 1992 only 58 (0.24%) involved Daubenton's bat in domestic properties (see Table 9.3).
- EBLs can be passed on only through a bite or by contact between bat saliva and mucous

membranes, so the risk can be eliminated by not handling bats.

- Contacts between bats and the public, even those with bats living in their house roof, are relatively rare. Bat-workers are the only group at higher risk because they may handle bats more frequently.
- Post-exposure vaccine is available and appears to be effective. Nobody who has been bitten by a bat and received this vaccine has died.

Foreigners, particularly Americans, and people who have lived abroad are often horrified at the thought of bats with rabies. This very strong reaction is because 'classical' rabies is endemic in the New World. Although the main vectors are terrestrial carnivores (skunks, racoons and foxes), it is known to occur at a low incidence in bats throughout the USA. There have been about 22 human cases in the USA in the last 22 years resulting from contact with bats. Such fears can be calmed very considerably by the knowledge that the situation in the UK is very different and that rabies is not present in terrestrial carnivores. There have been one or two cases in the USA where people are believed to have contracted rabies after visiting caves inhabited by huge numbers (millions) of active bats. Conditions in the UK are very different and visiting bats roosts of any sort in the UK is not considered to present any rabies health risk to humans.

Concerns may be raised that cats that catch bats may become infected with EBL. There are no recorded instances of this happening, although one wild animal, a stone marten in Germany has been recorded with EBL1. Given the apparently low incidence of EBL and the lack of any recorded transmission to domestic pets, owners can be reassured that the risk to their pets is very low. If they remain concerned, suggest that they have their pet vaccinated against rabies.

Further advice about the health implications of EBLs can be found in Chapter 2. Updated information is available from the SNCOs, the BCT or the Health Protection Agency/Scottish Centre for Infection and Environmental Health and a leaflet 'Bats and human health' is available from the SNCOs. A review of EBLs can be found in Fooks et al. (in press b) and a review of the incidence and distribution of rabies and rabies-related viruses in bats (by A. M. Hutson) and their epidemiology (by S. M. Brookes) is included in a report compiled for Scottish Natural Heritage.

Table 9.2 UK bat rabies surveillance 1986-2002. Bats found dead were tested at the Veterinary Laboratories Agency (the positive Daubenton's bats were both found alive).

Species	Number tested	% of sample	Number with EBL
Rhinolophus ferrumequinum	3	0.09	0
Rhinolophus hipposideros	11	0.34	0
Myotis daubentonii	51	1.57	2
Myotis brandtii	27	0.83	0
Myotis mystacinus	83	2.56	0
Myotis mystacinus/brandtii	5	0.15	0
Myotis nattereri	83	2.56	0
Myotis bechsteinii	2	0.06	0
Myotis myotis	1	0.03	0
Eptesicus serotinus	69	2.13	0
Pipistrellus pipistrellus/pygmaeus	2202	67.90	0
Pipistrellus nathusii	38	1.17	0
Nyctalus leisleri	4	0.12	0
Nyctalus noctula	39	1.20	0
Plecotus auritus	532	16.40	0
Plecotus austriacus	8	0.25	0
Barbastella barbastellus	4	0.12	0
Other[1]	47	1.45	0
Unidentified[2]	34	1.05	0
Total	**3243**		**2**

[1] includes European species not normally found in UK (e.g. E. nilssonii, P. kuhlii, P. savii, V. murinus) and imports from elsewhere (e.g. M. lucifugus, L. noctivagans, E. fuscus, T. brasiliensis, some fruit bats and other exotics).

[2] includes specimens not present in sample examined for verification of identification, or insufficient material for identification (e.g. brain only).

Table 9.3 The occurrence of bat species in buildings. The frequency with which each species of bat was recorded in buildings from a sample of 1807 roosts where the species was identified.

Species	Number of roosts	%
Pipistrelle *Pipistrellus spp.*	992	54.9
Long-eared bat *Plecotus spp.*	548	30.3
Serotine *Eptesicus serotinus*	85	4.7
Whiskered/Brandts' bat *Myotis mystacinus/ brandtii*	61	3.4
Lesser horseshoe *Rhinolophus hipposideros*	39	2.1
Natterer's bat *Myotis nattereri*	32	1.7
Noctule *Nyctalus noctula*	21	1.2
Daubenton's bat *Myotis daubentonii*	18	0.9
Greater horseshoe *Rhinolophus ferrumequinum*	8	0.4
Leisler's bat *Nyctalus leisleri*	2	0.1
Bechstein's bat *Myotis bechsteinii*	1	0.05
Total	**1807**	

Note. These data were collected from a sample of bat enquiries in the 1980s where the bats were identified. Long-eared bats are probably over-represented because they are most frequently seen in roofs and are easy to identify.

Insects in droppings

Very occasionally large accumulations of droppings may contain small insects, either as adults or as larvae. The most common are the larvae of small moths such as the common clothes moth *Tineola bisselliella*. Numbers of these larvae are generally low and never warrant the application of any control measures. A few cases have been recorded of spider beetles, most often the Australian spider beetle *Ptinus tectus*, being associated with accumulations of droppings. The adult beetles are 2.4–4 mm long and are covered in brown or golden-brown hairs. They are nocturnal, spending the day in cracks and crevices and emerging at night to feed, when they will feign death if disturbed. The beetles are widely distributed throughout the UK and are often found in old birds' nests. In the roofs of domestic premises, the beetles are of no economic significance, though they may be a nuisance. They may be controlled by removing the bat droppings and any other organic debris and treating the area with a pyrethroid-based spray at a time when no bats are present. Another group of small insects that are occasionally associated with bat droppings are beetles of the family Dermestidae, such as the carpet beetle *Anthrenus verbasci* or the hide beetle *Dermestes maculatus*. Like the spider beetles, these are general detritus-feeders and, in roofs, are most often associated with old birds' nests or dried animal remains. The larvae, known as woolly bears, are more commonly encountered than the adults. In the unlikely event of control measures being required, they may be treated in the same way as spider beetles. The largest insect that is ever found in bat droppings in the UK is the mealworm (*Tenebrio molitor* larva). This is indicative of long-established bat roosts (see also Chapter 5 – Guano dwellers).

As the visit draws to a close it is often wise to introduce a cautionary note by explaining that there are many aspects of bat behaviour that are still not well understood and that any suggestions or interpretations made are based on the most likely behaviour of the bats. Ask the householders to contact you again if the advice proves unsatisfactory or the bats do not behave as expected so that further investigations can be made. This helps with your credibility and ensures that the householder is not left feeling dissatisfied with the advice he or she has been given.

9.1.2 Exclusion of bat colonies

If it becomes apparent that the householder is not going to be persuaded to leave the bats undisturbed and does not want them in the roost, it will be necessary to provide advice on how to rid the building of bats. This advice would be given under Section 10(5) of the Wildlife & Countryside Act or Regulation 40(4) of the Conservation (Natural Habitats &c.) Regulations and should be given or confirmed by the SNCO.

There are only two successful and approved ways of dealing with an unwanted colony, neither of

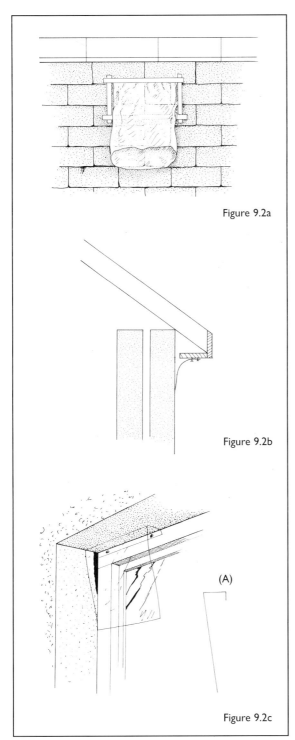

Figure 9.2a

Figure 9.2b

(A)

Figure 9.2c

Figure 9.2
a Plastic bag with bottom cut off fixed over roost entrance. The bag can be taped over the entrance.
b A sheet of acetate or similar stiff plastic pinned under the soffit. The plastic should be flexible enough to allow the bats to push past it, but be stiff enough to spring back into place.
c An A4 sheet of acetate bent to profile (A) then taped or pinned along its short edge to the top of the window frame adjacent to the roost entrance.

which should be used while there is the possibility of non-flying young being present.

The first is to install a one way door or valve (sometimes known after its inventor as a Constantine device) which allows bats to exit the roost but not re-enter. This method is now widely used in the USA. Because of its simplicity, exclusions in the UK should be carried out with this method where possible as any bats remaining inside the roost still have the opportunity to leave following installation of the device. The valve-like device is essentially a collapsible plastic tube, sometimes attached to a solid section of tube, fitted over the roost entrance (Figure 9.2a). The collapsible section allows bats to push past it but ensures they cannot re-enter once they have left the roost. Where the roost entrance is between a soffit and wall, a length of acetate sheet or heavy duty polythene attached to the soffit can perform the same function (Figure 9.2b) and this method can be adapted to other situations (Figure 9.2c). To install these devices, all secondary entrances to the roost should be sealed. The device can then be installed over the main exit, permitting bats to leave at dusk but not re-enter. Once in place, the device can be left for an extended period to ensure that no bats are left inside the roost. For late autumn or winter exclusions, it may be best to leave the device until the following spring to eliminate any possibility of hibernating bats being trapped.

The second method is to exclude the bats from their roost sites by blocking the entrances once the bats have left the roost, either for the night or for the season. This method carries the danger that not all the bats may leave. During the winter, bats may remain torpid for long periods, so this method should not be used after the weather turns cool in September.

In the great majority of cases the householder can be persuaded to leave the bats to disperse naturally before installing the device or blocking the access holes, but occasionally it will be necessary to provide advice on how to exclude bats that are still using the building on a daily basis. No action to exclude bats should be taken between mid-May and mid-August because dependent young may be present at that time.

The first step in any exclusion operation is to locate the access holes used by the bats. In many cases

9

they will be obvious, but in others it may be necessary to watch the building at dusk on one or two nights. Bats may emerge from more than one hole or may emerge from one hole but know of others that can be used if their main exit is obstructed, so the locating of exit holes must be done carefully and thoroughly if the exclusion operation is to be successful. There is also the possibility that bats excluded from a roost in one part of a building will simply move to another part of the same building, so it is always prudent to provide advice on bat-proofing the whole building even if the householder declines to carry out the recommended works.

If the householder can be persuaded to leave the bats to disperse naturally, advice should be provided on how to check whether bats are still present. This will include such techniques as looking for fresh droppings beneath the access hole (having swept up the old ones), listening for bats on a warm day or evening and watching for emerging bats at dusk. In winter bats hibernate so, unless it is known that bats are absent, blocking operations should be done in spring or autumn.

If, for any reason the one-way valve method cannot be employed to exclude bats while they are using a roost, the secondary exclusion technique can be applied, although it is a little more time-consuming and requires action over a 2–3-day period. During the first day any little-used access holes should be sealed permanently, leaving only the main hole open. The same evening the bats should be watched as they emerge to forage and, when no bats have emerged for more than 10 minutes, rags should be pushed into the hole to prevent their return. Early the

following evening, well before dusk, the rags should be removed and any further bats allowed to escape before the hole is once again sealed temporarily. If there seems any possibility of bats still being present, the process should be repeated for a third night; otherwise the temporary blockage can be replaced with a permanent one. A careful watch must be kept on the building while the bats emerge to ensure that the temporary blockage is in place before bats begin to return. These blocking operations are best done in warm weather, when a high proportion of the colony will emerge to feed each night; in cool, wet or windy weather few bats may emerge.

There are many methods and materials suitable for blocking bat access holes and the choice of method may often be left to the householder. For access points between soffits and walls, wooden battens fixed either to the soffit or to the wall are a common choice. Holes in brick or stonework or around window frames may need repointing with mortar or filling with mastic; larger holes can be filled with crumpled wire netting or expanding polyurethane foam (from DIY shops). Gaps in lead flashing can often be closed simply by bending the lead, though in some cases extra flashing may be required. Some roosts have a very large number of entrances, often under loose tiles (both roof and hanging) or between weatherboarding. Blocking individual holes may not be practicable and covering the whole area with 1 cm galvanised wire mesh may be required.

Whatever method of excluding bats is chosen, it is important to emphasise that all roofs require adequate ventilation to prevent the build-up of moisture and that provision should be made for this in whatever works are proposed.

Summary – visit to householders who have discovered bats

- Make an appointment for the visit. Don't turn up with a crowd of people.
- Listen carefully. Try to discover what is really worrying the householder and how he or she perceives the problem.
- Present the case for bats by showing knowledge, understanding and enthusiasm. Counter arguments logically. Respect true phobias.
- Advise on any measures that may be taken to abate any perceived problems.
- Take along leaflets and other information relevant to the visit/problem
- If exclusion will be required, explain carefully what is involved and the logic behind the process. Try to persuade the householder to wait until the bats have left. Liaise with the SNCO.

- Fill in a Bat Roost Visit Report Form and return it to the SNCO representative who requested the visit. If the request originated elsewhere, return the form to your SNCO contact with a clear indication if action is required.

Summary – exclusion of bats

- Ensure that advice is provided or confirmed by the SNCO.
- If bats may be present, adopt the appropriate exclusion technique (usually a one-way valve).
- If bats are known to be absent, block holes when convenient but before the following spring.
- Advise on ways of blocking holes but emphasise the requirement for ventilation.
- Advise on bat-proofing the whole building so that bats do not return to a different part of it.

Security alarm systems in buildings

Bats have been known or suspected to trigger burglar alarms in buildings. If it is confirmed that bats are the cause there are two courses of action.

First, the relevant SNCO can be contacted with a view to excluding bats from the space in question. This may be neither successful nor reliable.

Second, the alarm systems can be altered to make them less susceptible to bat-generated false alarms. The installers of the alarm should be consulted and the local Bat Group may be able to help.

Types of alarm

Light beam detectors – a transmitter sends out an active infra-red beam that is received by a receiver (e.g. across a window). The alarm is set off when the beam is broken. Such systems can be modified to prevent false alarms by installing two parallel beams, one 50 cm vertically above the other, wired so as both must be broken before the alarm is signalled.

Ultrasonic movement detectors – they emit ultrasound and receive an echo of the room that they get accustomed to. When the echo is altered by a person or animal entering the room, the alarm is set off.

Microwave movement detectors – are similar to ultrasonic detectors but emit much higher frequency waves.

Passive infra-red detectors – detect changes in radiant heat.

These last three types of detector can be re-located so that there is little chance of a bat flying close to them, i.e. as low as possible and away from corners. However, the detectors should not be mounted lower than 2.0 m to 2.5 m, in accordance with manufacturers instructions. Also, two detectors of the same technology, i.e. passive infra-red, can be mounted at opposite ends of the room, each covering the whole room, and connected in a series configuration. Both would be triggered by a large object in their common field of view, but a bat should not be large enough to trigger both at the same time.

Source: The National Trust, pers. com.

9.1.3 Activities that might incidentally affect bats or their roosts

Many enquirers request advice about the possible effects of repairs, alterations or remedial work on bats and their roosts. Such operations may be covered by the 'incidental result' or 'dwelling-house' defences in the Act/Regulations (see Chapter 1) and so will require advice from the SNCO. In such situations, the role of the batworker is more investigative than persuasive, and the SNCO will provide advice based on information supplied by the batworker. In making such investigations the batworker is acting, to some extent, as the SNCO's agent, but he or she is not empowered to give advice on behalf of the SNCO. This is because the nature conservation agencies are mentioned by name in the legislation as the organisations whose advice must be sought. This can easily lead to confusion, but it is essential that the correct procedure is followed if the enquirer is to be given the protection provided in the Act. Less experienced batworkers should make it clear that they are visiting only to collect information and that nothing should be done until advice has been received from the SNCO; more experienced batworkers may wish to predict what advice will be given but point out that action should not be taken until official confirmation is received.

A frequent type of enquiry in this group concerns remedial timber treatment. This is covered in detail in Chapter 10 but the most common situations are summarised below.

Infestations of 'woodworm' or common furniture beetle Anobium punctatum may be dealt with by a spray application of a suitable treatment fluid at a time of year when no bats are present. Solvent or emulsion formulations may be used, because both are effective, but emulsions have the advantage of lower solvent toxicity.

Death-watch beetle Xestobium rufovillosum infestations may be treated with a spray application of a suitable fluid supplemented by pressure injection or paste application to particularly heavily infested areas. Permethrin-based products for the latter purposes are widely available. If pastes are used, they should be kept as far as possible from bat roosting areas and, if the treatment of roosting areas is essential, attempts should be made to prevent bats coming into contact with treated surfaces.

Dry rot is relatively uncommon in roofs. It needs to be treated by cutting out and replacing damaged timbers. Cut ends of beams may be treated by pressure injection or paste application as for death-watch beetle, and the same remarks apply.

Other common problems, also dealt with in Chapter 10, include re-roofing, loft conversions, demolition of buildings, removal of dead trees, capping of

9

mineshafts and destruction of caves. Some of these situations may fall within the scope of the licensing arrangements under the Habitats Regulations, but in others the SNCO may have to provide advice. Here, the role of the batworker is largely one of collecting information and, perhaps, suggesting possible solutions to the problem.

9.2 The media

Over the past few years there has been a considerable interest in bats from the press, radio and television. On the whole, bats have received fairly sympathetic treatment, perhaps because the 'conservationists' are the main source of information, although most reporters seem unable to resist the old clichés of vampires, Dracula etc. For the amateur bat-worker, most dealings with the media can be through the local bat groups (see Chapter 8), but some guidance bears repetition here.

The most easily handled form of contact with the media is positive publicity where the conservation organisation or individual makes an approach with what is believed to be a good story. For such an approach to succeed, the story must be well thought out beforehand and 'newsworthy'. Generally, the local press and radio are much more receptive than the nationals, especially if you catch them on a slack day, and will often run quite small stories if these have a local angle and, for newspapers, are accompanied by a photograph or two. If you do agree to be interviewed for television or radio, try to get the reporter to take a positive line about how nice bats are rather than the more typical, 'Bats are horrid, aren't they?'; this gets the interview off on a much better footing.

Reactive publicity, where the media already have the bones of a story, is much more common and can be more difficult to handle, because the reporter will generally be working to a deadline and may already have spoken to the 'opposition'. In such cases, one may feel on the defensive from the start. When one is approached, the first decisions, which must be made rapidly, are whether one is competent to answer the enquiry and whether one is being consulted personally or as the representative of an organisation. In some cases it may seem most sensible to hand the enquiry on to someone who is more in touch with the story, but beware of giving the reporter the run-around; this does not help to gain a sympathetic hearing. The Bat Conservation

Trust can give advice or recommend bat experts in your area who have experience of dealing with the media. Television companies are showing a growing interest in covering bats and bat group activities and BCT can provide advice and, if required, help negotiate fees for the bat group.

- Answering enquiries from the press is largely a matter of common sense and experience, but it is worth bearing in mind a few basic rules.

- Ensure your facts are correct. If you don't know, say so or offer to find out later.

- Always respond in a friendly and helpful manner. This will help to ensure a fair hearing.

- Respond as quickly as possible. The media are inevitably ruled by deadlines and, if necessary, may run a story without your comments.

- Remember the press are not experts on bats. Keep it as simple as possible.

- Make it clear if you do not wish to be quoted, although making 'off the record' remarks can be a dangerous practice.

- Don't tell lies. It will severely damage your credibility if you're found out.

- Think carefully before replying. Don't be rushed into making unconsidered statements and remember that long pauses will be edited out of television and radio recordings.

- Don't be rude or sarcastic or make jokes. These often come across rather differently from how you intended.

- Avoid jargon and acronyms.

- Don't say 'no comment'. This can be interpreted in a number of unflattering ways.

Guidelines on writing a press release are available from The Bat Conservation Trust.

References and further reading

ANON (2003). *Bats and human health*. Scottish Natural Heritage & Scottish Centre for Infection and Environmental Health, Edinburgh or English Nature, Peterborough.

BATTERSBY, J. 1995. Bats, droppings and wall paintings at Clayton Church, West Sussex. *Bat News*, No. 36, 2–3.

FOOKS, A.R., McELHINNEY, L.M., POUNDER, D.J., FINNEGAN, C.J., MANSFIELD, K., JOHNSON, N., BROOKES, S.M., PARSONS, G., WHITE, K., McINTYRE, P.G. & NATH WANI, D. (in press a). Case report: Isolation of a European Bat Lyssavirus Type 2a from a fatal human case of rabies encephalitis. *Journal of Medical Virology*.

FOOKS, A.R., BROOKES, S.M., McELHINNEY, L.M., JOHNSON, N. & HUTSON, A.M. (in press b). European Bat Lyssaviruses: an emerging zoonosis. *Epidemiology & Infection*.

JOHNSON, N., SELDEN, D, PARSONS, G., HEALEY, D., BROOKES, S.M., McELHINNEY, L.M., HUTSON, A.M. & FOOKS, A.R. 2003. Isolation of a European Lyssavirus type 2 from a Daubenton's bat in the United Kingdom. *Veterinary Record*, **152**, 383–387.

MITCHELL-JONES, A.J., JEFFERIES, D.J., STEBBINGS, R.E. & ARNOLD, H.R. 1986. Public concern about bats (Chiroptera) in Britain: An analysis of enquiries in 1982–83. *Biological Conservation*, **36**, 315–328.

MOORE, N.P., JONES, S. HUTSON, A.M. & GARTHWAITE, D. 2003. Assessing the out come of English Nature advice on bat colony management and mitigation works. *English Nature Research Report No. 517*. English Nature, Peterborough. 59 pp.

PAINE, S. UNDATED. *Bats in churches*. English Heritage, London.

WHITBY, J.E., JOHNSTONE, P., PARSONS, G., KING, A.A. & HUTSON, A.M. 1996. Ten-year survey of British bats for the existence of rabies. *Veterinary Record*, **139**, 491–493.

9

Brown long-eared bat hovering. © Frank Greenaway

Timber treatment, pest control and building work A. J. Mitchell-Jones

10.1 Introduction

Apart from commensals, such as the house mouse, bats are the only group of mammals that rely heavily on buildings for shelter. This reliance on man-made structures, together with their colonial habits, make bats very vulnerable to a wide range of human activities, either directly, by being killed or injured, or indirectly by roost loss. This chapter provides guidance on dealing with activities that are likely to affect bats incidentally.

Legally (see Chapter 1 for full details), the protection afforded to bats against killing or injuring and the damaging or destruction of their roosts is limited by two defences in the Wildlife and Countryside Act and the Habitats Regulations. These provide a defence against prosecution where the alleged offence took place in a dwelling house (applies to disturbance of bats or damage or destruction of roosts) or was the incidental result of a lawful operation and could not reasonably have been avoided (applies to all offences). However, these defences cannot be relied on unless the Statutory Nature Conservation Agency (SNCO) had been notified and allowed a reasonable time to advise as to whether the proposed operation should be carried out and, if so, the method to be used.

In practical terms, this complex section may be interpreted as giving the SNCOs a statutory role in advising how damage to bats and their roosts can reasonably be avoided or minimised, but it does not give them the power to prevent lawful and necessary works. It is not, in itself, an offence to fail to consult the SNCO or even to ignore the advice, but to do so could lay an individual or company open to prosecution. In this circumstance, the onus of proof would be on the defendant to show that the alleged offence, whether killing or injuring bats or damaging or destroying roosts, was either the incidental result of a lawful operation and could not reasonably have been avoided or took place in a dwelling house. Although no true case law has yet been established, cases in Magistrates' Courts have shown that Magistrates take a serious view of offences where the defendant failed to consult and took action that the SNCO would have advised against. Note that in England and Wales it is sufficient to show that someone acted recklessly to disturb bats or damage or destroy roosts whereas in Scotland (until 2004) and Northern Ireland it is necessary to demonstrate intent.

Bat worker using fiberscope to inspect mortice joints in barn.
© Shirley Thompson

The word 'reasonable' in the 'incidental result' defence gives considerable scope for negotiation and interpretation in any particular case. In law, only a court could decide what is reasonable in any particular circumstance, so in practice, and in the absence of case law, common-sense decisions must be made.

The situation is further complicated by the existence of a licensing system under the Habitats Regulations which is administered separately by Departments in the four countries of the UK (see Chapter 1 and Appendix 6). This is available where work that might affect bats is required for preserving public health or public safety or other imperative reasons of over-riding public interest. Guidance is available from each of the Departments or SNCOs about how the system operates in their territory, but it is likely to apply mainly to operations on structures other than dwelling-houses or to major alterations to dwelling-houses.

In situ remedial timber treatment with organochlorine insecticides and some fungicides has been considered an important, although largely invisible, source of bat mortality in Europe. Evidence for its importance comes from a number of sources. Experiments have shown that bats kept in wooden cages treated with lindane, formerly a common insecticide in treatment fluids, die within a

10

few days, even if the cage had been treated 2 weeks previously. Although this was a severe test, the speed with which the bats died was both surprising and alarming. Similar results were obtained with the fungicide, pentachlorophenol (PCP), and bats still died when placed in a cage that had been treated 14 months previously with a mixture of lindane and PCP (Racey & Swift, 1986; Boyd *et al.*, 1988). As well as the acute poisoning that was observed in these experiments, bats can suffer from chronic poisoning by accumulating doses of a range of pesticides, particularly the organochlorines. In such cases it is unlikely that corpses will be found within the roosts and the only sign would be the disappearance of bats from a traditional roosting site. Such disappearances have been recorded many times after remedial timber treatment.

Pest control – for wasp or bee nests, cluster-fly swarms or possibly for rodent infestations – is much less of a problem than remedial timber treatment but can be treated similarly from a legal point of view. Many of the remarks about chemicals in the timber treatment section apply equally to pest control, although a wider range of chemicals is available for the latter use because there is not the same requirement for persistence.

Roof repairs and any other building work likely to affect bat roosts are covered by the same legal requirements as remedial timber treatments, although fewer consultations are received from roofing contractors. In many respects, the problems associated with such works are more readily definable, because the main dangers are either direct physical disturbance of bats, killing of bats (especially when torpid) or loss of the roost site. Experience has shown that bats will generally tolerate quite considerable changes to their roosts provided that they are not subjected to excessive disturbance during the course of the work.

10.2 Remedial timber treatment

10.2.1 Types of infestation

There are three species of wood-boring insect of economic significance.

Common furniture beetle or 'woodworm' *Anobium punctatum* is the most widespread species, occurring throughout the British Isles. Adults are

about 2–3 mm long and can be identified by the extended thorax, which almost obscures the head (Figure 10.1). This species attacks the sapwood of hardwoods and softwoods, particularly when these are damp, so timbers consisting largely of heartwood are resistant to attack. Some hardwoods are virtually immune.

Eggs are laid on irregularities in the surface of timbers by the adults, which emerge throughout the summer, and the larvae tunnel into the wood, where they remain for up to 3 years. Prior to pupation, the larva makes its way to just beneath the surface of the wood, and the emerging adult later bores a small circular 'flight-hole' 0.8–1 mm in diameter and emerges to mate and complete the life cycle. Relatively few eggs are laid by each female, so infestations of this species are slow to build up.

Death-watch beetle *Xestobium rufovillosum* (Figure 10.2) is most common in southern Britain and absent from Scotland. Adults are 6–8 mm long and dark brown with a golden mottled appearance caused by hairs on the wing-cases. They do not fly readily, except under extremely warm conditions, so that infestations are not readily spread between buildings. The larvae are up to 10 mm long and 2–3 mm in diameter. Death-watch beetle generally attacks only hardwoods, preferring areas that are damp and already subject to fungal decay. The larval stage of the life cycle can last up to 10 years, depending on the state of the wood. Wood with a high moisture content and active fungal attack will cause rapid maturation of the larva, while dry wood, if attacked at all, will result in slow maturation. Temperature is also an important factor. Adults emerge from March to June after boring a circular 'flight-hole' 2–3 mm in diameter. In churches or similar buildings, the adults can often be found crawling on the floor or window ledges after falling from the beams. As with *Anobium*, only small numbers of eggs are laid, so infestations are slow to build up. In severely attacked wood, adults can emerge into cavities within the wood and thus complete their life cycle without ever appearing on the surface.

The house longhorn beetle *Hylotrupes bajulus* (Figure 10.3) is the largest of the wood-borers. Adults are about 16 mm long with, as might be expected from the name, strikingly long antennae. (Note that there are a number of superficially similar species which do not cause damage in houses.)

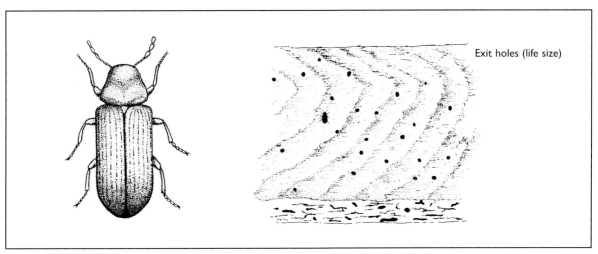

Figure 10.1
Common furniture beetle *Anobium punctatum*

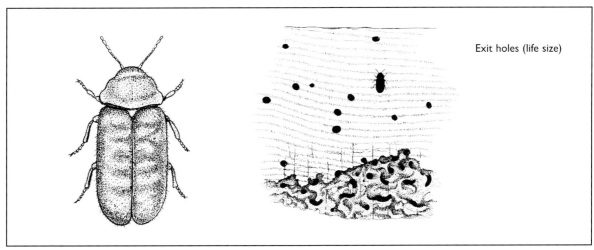

Figure 10.2
Death-watch beetle *Xestobium rufovillosum*

10

Figure 10.3
House longhorn beetle *Hylotrupes bajulus*

The larvae grow to a length of up to 25 mm and bore tunnels up to 4 mm in diameter. The 'flight-hole' is oval, about 7 x 3 mm. This species attacks the sapwood of softwoods and can be extremely damaging as the larvae can bore up to 25 mm of tunnel per day. Often there is no sign of damage to roof timbers until the adults begin to appear and reveal that the structural timber is just a shell. Fortunately, the species is confined largely to Surrey and parts of Hampshire, although it is widespread in continental Europe. In the local authority areas in Britain in which it is established, pretreatment of timbers is mandatory.

There are two fungi of significance:
Dry rot *Serpula lacrymans* attacks wood with an initial moisture content above 20% and can be extremely damaging. Once established in a damp area, fungal hyphae can travel considerable distances over masonry to reach other wood, because nutrients can be transported through the hyphae. Sound wood can be attacked provided that there is a damp area adjacent and humidity is high. When mature, the fungus forms a rust-coloured fruiting body, which releases millions of spores. Attacked timber develops cuboidal splitting and becomes dry and powdery. The fungus can survive for considerable periods within masonry, providing there is a source of nutrients, so treatment must be thorough and can be difficult.

Wet rot is a generic term covering a number of species such as pore fungus *Poria vaporaria* and cellar fungus *Coniophora cerebella*. These require moister conditions than those required to start dry rot. In practice, this means that in buildings they are always associated with defects that allow water to soak into timbers under sheltered conditions or through lack of ventilation or damp courses. Although considerable structural damage can be caused, wet rots do not have the same invasive capabilities as dry rot, so damage is usually more localised.

10.2.2 Treating beetle infestations

Although there are differences in the types of timber attacked, the three wood-borers have a broadly similar life history. The majority of the life cycle is spent in the larval form, feeding on cellulose or breakdown products of cellulose, and the adult does not feed but lives only long enough to mate and lay eggs. Thus the insect could spend almost its entire life deep inside timber, appearing on the surface for only a short period, first as an egg and later as an adult. This is of vital significance when attempting to halt the infestation.

When newly felled, timber is susceptible to attack by a wide variety of wood-boring insects including powder post beetles (*Lyctus* species) and wood-boring weevils (*Euophryum* species). However, these species all require fresh wood with a moisture content above 20% and, once the timber has been seasoned or kiln-dried, only the three species under discussion can survive. Even these need some moisture, and this fact provides the basis for an effective treatment, though one that is not always practicable. For example, furniture beetle infestations are uncommon in timbers in centrally-heated buildings as the wood is too dry. In some European countries, a well-established disinfestation treatment is to blow hot air into the roof void, thus heating the timbers. Once a critical temperature has been reached deep in the wood, all the larvae are killed and instant disinfestation is achieved. Of course there is no protection against reinfestation, but this is normally very slow.

In the UK, chemical treatment is almost universal, and this seems likely to continue in the foreseeable future. There are a number of factors that have to be taken into account when designing an effective treatment, but perhaps the most important are the relative impermeability of wood and the long life cycle of the beetles. With spray or brush treatment it is virtually impossible to achieve a significant loading of insecticide more than a few millimetres below the surface of the wood. Beneath this toxic 'envelope' the larvae can survive and continue to burrow. The only time the insects must approach this treated layer is during metamorphosis and as eggs. This means that, to be effective, the insecticide must persist at a toxic concentration for longer than the maximum lifespan of the beetle; longer persistence carries a bonus of protection against further attack.

For common furniture beetle, the continuing activity of the larvae beneath the treated layer is of little significance, because they are small, and structural weakening of timber will only occur after many years of uncontrolled infestation. A single brush, spray or fogging treatment with a persistent insecticide will therefore end an infestation over a 3-year period, both by killing the emerging adults and by preventing the establishment of new larvae. New flight-holes may appear during this time as some beetles may survive to complete their emergence.

For death-watch beetle, and even more so for house longhorn, the longer life cycle of the larvae means that their continuing activities after a surface treatment can cause an unacceptable increase in damage. In addition, the adults are much larger than furniture beetles and need a larger dose of insecticide, which can sometimes be difficult to achieve in practice. The death-watch beetle's habit of emerging into inaccessible areas or cavities in the wood can also lead to problems, so this species is considered difficult to eradicate. Attempts to increase the effectiveness of treatments include pressure injection (in which solvent-based treatment fluid is forced into the wood under pressure through injector nozzles), and the use of paste formulations, (in which a thick gel of insecticide is painted on to the timber to increase the time during which the insecticide is able to penetrate the wood). Both methods are widely used. Pressure injection is usually used for limited areas of heavy infestation such as the ends of joists or wall plates. Paste application is quicker and probably more widely used.

10.2.3 Choice of chemicals and fluids

The primary requirement for persistence greatly reduces the number of possible chemicals to use, because most insecticides are either broken down too rapidly or are too volatile or are unacceptably

---

Emergencies – bats discovered during remedial timber treatment

Legal position (simplified)

The killing, injuring, taking or disturbance of bats and the damage or destruction of roosts may be covered by the legal defences that 'the action took place in a dwelling-house' (disturbance or damage/destruction of roosts only) or that this was 'the incidental result of a lawful operation and could not reasonably have been avoided' (all offences). However, these defences may only be relied on if the SNCO had been consulted and allowed a reasonable time to advise as to whether the proposed operation should be carried out and, if so, the method to be used.

If the SNCO had been consulted, the defence could be relied on; if not, illegal activity may be taking place, so the police could be involved, but only a court can ultimately determine the legality of the situation. If the 'incidental result' defence is used, the decision of the court may depend on the interpretation of the word 'reasonably'.

Advice

The remedial timber treatment industry has had a considerable amount of publicity about bats and companies should have no excuse for not knowing what they are supposed to do. Nevertheless, some difficult situations can arise, particularly outside the maternity season where it is difficult to know what advice to give.

Outside the breeding season (where a small number of bats are present, suggest <5)

If bats are torpid

Catch carefully (do not handle bats, use box, gloves or cloth), keep safely and release nearby at dusk the same day. Proceed carefully with the work.

If bats are active

If a significant numbers of bats are present (suggest >5), abandon work and try again at a time of year when bat numbers may be lower (autumn to spring). You should consult with the appropriate SNCO as well. If small numbers are seen, wait a while or continue brushing down the roof to see if the bats disperse. If the bats are unwilling to leave, it may be possible to divide the roof with plastic sheeting and treat one section at a time. If appropriate fluids are used (see advice elsewhere in this Chapter), these are unlikely to harm bats unless sprayed directly on to them.

During breeding season

Breeding unlikely

(Only a very small number of bats present. No pregnant females or young and no significant quantity of droppings).
Treat as for the non-maternity season.

Breeding possible

Stop treatment until after the maternity season. In large roofs, it may be possible to continue treatment in part of the roof, particularly if a water-based treatment is used. Dividing up the roof with plastic sheeting may also be a possibility here.

Illegal action

It is well established that the synthetic pyrethroid insecticides and a range of fungicides including boron esters, IPBC, propiconazole and zinc compounds are 'reasonable' replacements for lindane or TBTO–based products. These latter two compounds are now either no longer Approved or not available commercially. However, if you have reasonable grounds for suspecting that a non-Approved product is being used, insist that work is halted immediately while the SNCO is informed. Call the police if it is not. All timber-treatment product containers, whatever their contents, should now carry a warning about bats.

10

toxic to humans. Until the early 1980s dieldrin, an organochlorine, was a common choice, but concern about its safety led to its withdrawal in 1984. Lindane, also known as gamma-BHC (benzene hexachloride) or gamma-HCH (hexachlorocyclohexane), another organochlorine but with lower mammalian toxicity and less environmental persistence, has also been widely used since the 1950s, but is now rarely used, though some products still hold statutory Approvals. There is a statutory requirement to label remedial timber treatment products containing lindane as 'Dangerous to bats'.

Currently, the most commonly used chemicals are the synthetic pyrethroids, a class of chemically synthesised compounds related to naturally occurring pyrethrum. Like pyrethrum, they have considerable insecticidal activity but are not generally very toxic to mammals (although they are very toxic to fish). They are fairly stable in air and light but are easily metabolised by mammals and broken down by bacteria in soil and other media. Two compounds, permethrin and cypermethrin, are now widely used. Tests on bats have shown that these both appear safe for use in bat roosts. In no case has there been any greater mortality than in bats kept in untreated cages.

Boron compounds, such as disodium octoborate and boric acid have an increasing use in the treatment of furniture beetle infestations. They are now considered as effective as the chemicals previously discussed but are relatively non-toxic to mammals and have been recommended for sensitive situations such as bakeries or other food preparation areas.

A new type of product for remedial timber treatment is Flufenoxuron, also known as Flurox®. This acts specifically as an insect chitin synthesis inhibitor and has a very low mammalian toxicity.

All products containing pesticides must be approved under the Control of Pesticides Regulations 1986 (COPR), which governs the advertising, supply, storage and use of pesticides. The Health and Safety Executive is responsible for administering these regulations for timber treatment products and all approved fluids will be labelled with an HSE number as well as statutory hazard warnings and directions for use. It is a criminal offence to misuse these products.

The properties of some insecticides are summarised in Table 10.1a.

There are two main types of fluid:

Solvent-based fluids consisting of the active ingredients (pesticide) dissolved in a hydrocarbon solvent such as odourless kerosene or white spirit. Water-based emulsions consisting of pesticides, emulsifiers, organic solvent and water. They are often supplied as concentrates to be diluted with water on site. Microemulsions are emulsions with particularly low solvent levels, which appear to give better penetration of the wood.

The main advantages of solvent formulations are the greater penetration into wood and the toxic effects of the solvent itself. In some instances, a solvent-based fluid may also be chosen because of possible damage to furnishings or decor. Penetration and solvent toxicity are probably most important in treating death-watch and house longhorn infestations, where a rapid kill of the larvae is advantageous, but are of less consequence when treating furniture beetle. The flammability of the solvents is a very real hazard. If fibreglass insulation is fitted, this usually has to be removed, as solvent-soaked fibreglass is a considerable fire risk.

The great advantages of emulsions are their lower cost and their lower flammability. When applied in emulsions, the pesticides probably do not penetrate as deeply as with solvent fluids because of swelling of the wood fibres. This could be a disadvantage when treating death-watch beetle, but could be a positive advantage when treating furniture beetle. Here, the lower penetration means that the pesticide is concentrated in a tight band within the top 2–3 mm of the wood rather than being diffused and diluted through perhaps 4–6 mm.

Emulsions have become increasingly popular over the past few years and this trend seems likely to continue. However, there may be a continuing requirement for solvent-based fluids for the spray treatment of death-watch and house longhorn beetles and for pressure injection, because even high-oil emulsions are unlikely to be successful when used in this way. In bat roosts, emulsions obviously have an advantage of low toxicity, although in practice any toxic effect of organic solvents is likely to be temporary, because evaporation is quite rapid, especially in a warm, well ventilated roof, and there is no residual effect. The SNCOs welcome the wider use of emulsions for the treatment of furniture beetle infestations, although there is no evidence that

Table 10.1 Common active ingredients in remedial timber treatment products.

a.   Insecticides

Common name	Usual solution strength	Toxicity to mammals	Acceptable uses within bat roosts/ comments
Permethrin	0.2%	Low	Any remedial use
Cypermethrin	0.1%	Low	Any remedial use
Deltamethrin	0.1%?	Low	Any remedial use
Boric acid, Disodium octoborate, Tri(hexylene glycol) biborate	5-20%	Low	Any remedial use
Flufenoxuron (Flurox®)	0.025%	Low	Any remedial use
Cyfluthrin	0.1–0.5%	Low	'May cause harm to bats' (HSE labelling requirement)

b.   Fungicides

Common name	Usual solution strength	Toxicity to mammals	Acceptable uses within bat roosts/comments
3-iodo-2propynyl-N-butyl carbamate (Polyphase/IPBC)	0.5%	Low	Any suitable application
Benzalkonium chloride		Low	Any suitable use
Boric acid, Disodium octoborate or tetraborate, Tri(hexylene glycol) biborate	3.5%	Low	Any suitable application
Dichlofluanid		Low	Decorative stains and finishes
Dodecylamine salicylate or laurate		Low	Any suitable application
Phenylphenol (+sodium salts)	2-5%	Low?	Wall sterilant for dry rot
Propiconazole	1.5%	Low	Any suitable application
Quartenary ammonium compounds	3.0%	Low	Any suitable application
Tebuconazole	0.1 – 1.5%	Low	'May cause harm to bats' (HSE labelling requirement)
Zinc naphthenate, Zinc octoate, Acypetacs zinc, Zinc versatate	1-3% Zn	Low	Any suitable application

10

solvent-based fluids, when applied at the recommended time, cause deaths of bats.

Fogging systems have recently been adopted by some companies which enable operators to treat buildings using a remote controlled fogging machine, which disperses the insecticide throughout the treatable area. The fog droplets are deposited on all exposed timber surfaces and provide a protective layer of insecticide. This considerably reduces the volume of fluid required to treat a given area and also greatly reduces the operator's exposure to pesticide and / or organic solvent. However, the effects of such treatments on any bats that may be present are unknown. Permethrin is now being replaced in many cases by boric acid in a glycol base.

Remedial fluids sometimes contain a fungicide (see Table 10.1b) as well as an insecticide. The fungicide is included to give some protection against moulds or surface fungi, but is unlikely to be effective against wet rot or dry rot, for which specialist treatment is necessary.

10.2.4 Treating fungal attack

Serious fungal attack always leads to structural damage of the affected timbers, so successful treatment must include remedial building works to prevent the further ingress of moisture and the removal and replacement of severely affected timbers. Simply treating affected areas with fungicide is not an effective treatment, because the structural damage remains and the fungus may continue to grow deep in the wood beyond the penetration of the fungicide. In addition, all fungicides break down with time and some can be leached out of damp wood. It is wise to view fungicidal treatment of wood, certainly for wet rot, as a temporary measure to slow down the fungus while remedial works allow the timber to dry to a moisture level at which the fungus cannot survive. However, there is considered to be a need for fungicidal treatment of areas surrounding any area of dry rot because of this fungus's ability to survive in masonry.

Fungal problems in roofs are uncommon, generally develop slowly and are associated with poorly maintained roofs or guttering.

A wide range of fungicides is in common use, many of which have not been tested specifically on bats, though some are known to have a low toxicity to rats or mice.

Pentachlorophenol (PCP) was, until recently, widely used, but is now carefully controlled and only available in exceptional circumstances. It is very toxic to bats.

Zinc- and copper-based fungicides generally have a low mammalian toxicity and all are likely to be suitable for use in bat roosts. Only zinc octoate, copper naphthenate and acypetacs zinc have been tested on bats and these proved to be safe. Similarly, boron compounds such as tri-hexylene glycol biborate or Polybor (disodium octoborate) have a low mammalian toxicity because they hydrolyse to form boric acid. They are not such potent fungicides as some of the others discussed and in some circumstances they can be leached out of the wood. However, they are perfectly adequate for preventative treatment in areas not subject to excessive damp.

10.2.5 Time of treatment

The replacement of lindane by the synthetic pyrethroids, which are known to be relatively harmless to bats, has largely removed any problems over the choice of chemical, so that the only variable factor is the time of year at which treatment takes place. Because the synthetic pyrethroids do have some toxicity and organic solvents may be used, the guiding principle is that treatment should take place at a time when no bats appear to be present.

In house roofs, the timing of treatment for species such as the pipistrelle, which is usually only present seasonally, is relatively simple. Treatment should take place after the bats have left in late summer or autumn or before they return in the spring. In some cases, treatment could safely be carried out between 1 October and 15 April, but this season could be extended into May or September, or possibly even further, if an inspection shows that bats are not present.

Long-eared bats and other species, such as the whiskered bat and serotine, which may be present throughout the year, present a much more acute problem for which there is no ideal solution. With these species, bats may be most obvious during the summer, when they are breeding, but at other times bats may still be present but concealed in crevices, under ridge tiles or behind roofing felt and even the most careful inspection may fail to reveal them. Many roosts of these species may be occupied throughout the year, whereas others may be used for short periods, perhaps during the spring or autumn.

If a roost is known to be used through the summer, it would be safest to assume that it is a maternity roost, regardless of the amount of evidence of droppings, so that, unless there are compelling reasons, no timber treatment should be carried out between approximately the beginning of May and the end of September. Outside this period bats may still be present, and a number of factors will have to be taken into account when deciding on the optimum time for treatment. If an inspection during the possible treatment period (October to April) reveals no bats and no fresh droppings, there would be no advantage in delaying treatment (although the area to be treated should be carefully inspected and any concealed bats persuaded to leave, perhaps by leaving lights on or by beginning to brush down the roof). In some cases it will still be wise to avoid key hibernation periods, e.g. January and February, and instead aim to carry out treatment towards the end of winter.

If one or two bats appear during the treatment, these should be caught and released outside, preferably at dusk, because it is vital that bats are not sprayed directly. This is 'common-sense' advice and so the catching can be justified when the treatment is in accordance with the SNCOs advice. In the autumn, if significant numbers of bats are still present, a delay of a few weeks before treatment may allow many to move elsewhere. In most cases, signs of bat activity will decrease as the weather cools, although it is generally not possible to determine whether this is because the bats have moved on or because they are still present but less active. If bats are still present in November even after a hard frost, it is likely that some at least will overwinter in the roost, so there seems little advantage in delaying treatment further. In spring, bats may be visible and active in roof voids as early as March or April, sometimes in quite large numbers. At this time of year bats are active enough to move elsewhere if disturbed but they are not yet breeding, so that timber treatment may be possible provided that the bats are persuaded to leave first. Usually, the disturbance caused by cleaning operations before spraying will cause the bats to disappear temporarily, but placing lights in the roof void may also be helpful.

10.3 Pretreatment of timber

There is no legal requirement to pretreat structural timbers in Britain with either insecticide or fungicide except in a designated area of Surrey and Hampshire where house longhorn beetle occurs and in other areas with local byelaws. Apart from timbers below the damp-proof course, which are routinely treated, it appears that the only treatment the majority of timber receives is a low dose of water-soluble fungicide to prevent sapstain fungi, which affect the colour of the wood. Pretreatment of timber does not, therefore, appear to be a major hazard to bat populations generally, although there is a continuing interest in the industry in extending the proportion of structural timber that is pretreated.

On some occasions, it may be necessary to replace damaged timbers in a bat roost with pretreated timbers to give protection against further attack by insects or fungi. In such cases, care must be taken to specify a treatment that is non-toxic to bats. The two main types are described below.

10.3.1 Solvent or emulsion processes

In this type of process, a fungicide or insecticide in organic solvent or as an emulsion is forced into the wood by a combination of vacuum and pressure treatment. Such processes generally end with a vacuum cycle to remove the solvents from the wood. The most common active ingredients include

boron compounds, zinc compounds, pyrethroids, triazoles (propiconazole and tebuconazole) and TBTO, though the latter is being replaced by the less toxic alternatives.

Timber pretreated with TBTO is best avoided for use in bat roosts, although it is probably less dangerous than wood that has received only a superficial treatment because the pesticide is distributed deeper into the wood rather than being concentrated at the surface. Timber pretreated with other active ingredients is perfectly acceptable.

10.3.2 Copper chrome arsenic (CCA)

Treatment with an aqueous solution of copper, chromium and arsenic salts, often known as Tanalisation, a trade mark of Hicksons Ltd, provides protection against fungal and insect attack. The chemicals are applied using a vacuum and pressure cycle and the treated wood is then stacked to dry. During the process, the mixture of salts reacts to form insoluble compounds, so that very little is lost by subsequent weathering and leaching. If the process is carried out correctly, very little preservative is left on the surface of the wood and there appears to be no safety hazard. Occasionally a white powdery deposit may be seen on the surface; this is either hydrated sodium sulphate (Glaubers salts), a harmless by-product of the CCA salts, or some resin that has exuded from the wood during treatment. Both these deposits are easily removed by scrubbing or brushing, and such treatment will also reduce the minimal amounts of arsenic, which may be present on the surface of the wood.

Provided that the treatment is carried out to the appropriate British Standard and the wood is allowed to dry before use, CCA treatment appears to present no hazard to bats. In fact, the use of such timber should be encouraged because its use obviates the need for any subsequent in situ treatment with more hazardous chemicals.

10.4 Pest control

10.4.1 Wasp, bee and hornet nests

Wasp nests are the most common problem and are usually dealt with by Environmental Health Departments, although some local Councils have now contracted out pest control activities to commercial businesses. The usual control method is by spray application of an insecticide into the nest, if accessible, or by local application of powder around the nest entrances. A wide range of insecticides is used. If the nest is accessible and not close to an area used by bats, strictly localised treatment with a pyrethroid is unlikely to harm or disturb the bats so that in these circumstances consultation with the SNCO would not be necessary.

If the bats and wasps share a common access point or the nest is very close to the area used by the bats, greater care is needed and advice should be sought from the SNCO. If the wasps are not causing any particular problems, it is usually possible to arrange for treatment to be deferred until after the bats have left, usually by late August, but in a few more difficult cases treatment with pyrethroids may be possible provided that the pesticide application is confined to the nest and the minimum amount of pesticide is used.

Hornets appear to be more common than formerly but still account for relatively few treatments every year. Most nests are quite small, so localised treatment, if required, can be carried out.

Bee nests are rarely found in houses and may be of interest to local beekeepers. A local contact can often be found by enquiring at the police station and in some cases it may be possible to have the bees removed rather than killed.

10.4.2 Cluster-flies

Cluster-flies and other swarming flies enter houses during the autumn for hibernation and remain until spring the following year. The term 'cluster-fly' generally includes the true cluster-fly *Pollenia rudis*, which is parasitic on earthworms, the autumn-fly or face-fly *Musca autumnalis* and the green cluster-fly *Dasyphora cyanella*, both of which breed in cow dung.

In the autumn, flies congregate on the outside of buildings and later move inside to hibernate in the roof void or other suitable areas. The criteria used by the flies to select hibernation sites are not known, but one building apparently indistinguishable from its neighbours may attract hibernating flies for many years in succession. It may be that the aspect of the building, the particular surface finish or perhaps even pheromones deposited by previous flies are important in attracting the flies, as obviously there is no

'tradition', as with bats. If the area that the flies have chosen remains cold throughout the winter, there are unlikely to be complaints during this time, although intermittent heating can cause the flies to become active and perhaps descend to inhabited parts of the building. Similar problems can arise during the spring, when warm weather rouses the flies and they attempt to disperse from their hibernation sites.

Because they do not breed or feed on meat or domestic waste, cluster-flies do not cause any hazard to human health, although large numbers can be a considerable nuisance. In any conflict between bat conservation and cluster-fly control, therefore, the requirements of bat conservation must take priority, although this does not mean that nothing can be done.

The majority of enquiries about cluster-flies in bat roosts are in late autumn or early winter when the flies are moving in to hibernate. Fortunately, few bats are present in roofs during this time, reducing the possibility of conflict over treatment, and it is usually possible to advise on control measures. If bats are present, obviously no chemical treatment should be permitted, but it may be possible to alleviate some of the nuisance by blocking the routes by which flies enter the living area of the house. If no bats are present, as is commonly the case, treatment with a synthetic pyrethroid, either as a spray or as a smoke treatment, would normally be permissible, though the recommended method is to use a vacuum cleaner to collect the flies. More persistent or toxic insecticides such as lindane (γ-HCH), fenitrothion or dichlorvos should not be recommended in view of the ready availability of less toxic alternatives. Vacuum cleaners have been used successfully to remove flies. In dealing with such cases, it is worth emphasising that the influx of flies is likely to be an annual problem and that insecticidal treatment is in no sense a 'cure'. Possible long-term solutions include changing the colour or reflectance of the building or blocking any gaps under the soffits that allow the flies to land on the wall and crawl up into the roof, but care should be taken that such measures do not obstruct any access points for bats.

10.4.3 Rodents

A need to control rodents in the roof voids of domestic properties is uncommon, but many larger institutions such as hospitals or hotels routinely practice rodent control, often as part of a pest control contract.

The most common methods of control are baiting with anticoagulants, such as warfarin, brodifacoum or difenacoum, snap-trapping or the use of tracking dusts (contact rodenticides).

Bats are not, of course, attracted to rodent baits, so these present no hazard from this point of view. However, there is a possibility that bats, particularly babies, could fall into open trays of bait or poorly-sited trays of contact rodenticide and accumulate poison on their fur. They could then be poisoned when this is groomed off. If the bait or tracking dust has been placed in position by professional pest control operatives, the possibility of such occurrences are remote, but cases have been recorded where bat droppings have been misidentified as rodent droppings and open trays of poison have been placed directly under the bats' roost site. Such practices are both undesirable and ineffective and should not be allowed to continue. Often this is simply a matter of pointing out the error that has been made and suggesting that, if rodent control is required, the baits are placed in more appropriate places. It is, of course, illegal deliberately to attempt to poison bats.

The only other possible interaction between rodent control and bats is the disturbance to roosting bats caused by the routine visits of the rodent control operative. As such visits are generally made at intervals of several weeks, this seems most unlikely to be a problem unless the operative deliberately interferes with the bats. In general, the SNCO would not wish to limit such visits unless particularly large numbers of bats or particularly sensitive species (e.g. horseshoe bats) were involved.

10.5 Building work

Building work, in its most general sense, can result in the total loss of bat roosts and disturbance to or death of the bats. Much of this damage can be avoided if operations are correctly timed and planned; although the loss of the roost is sometimes unavoidable. The earlier advice is sought, the easier it is to accommodate the needs of bats in building work.

Experience has shown that bats will accept considerable changes to the structure of a building without abandoning it as a traditional roost site.

For example, several greater horseshoe bat breeding roosts have recently been modified and re-roofed but all are still used by the bats. Bats' strong adherence to traditional sites and apparent willingness to accept change to them mean that roost loss is by no means an inevitable result of alterations, and efforts should always be made to allow the bats continuing access.

10.5.1 Timing of operations

Bats are at their most vulnerable in buildings during the summer, when large numbers may be gathered together and young bats, unable to fly, may be present. Operations to known breeding sites should therefore be timed to avoid the months of June, July and August if possible. Very large rebuilding or renovation projects may take many months to complete and may need to continue through the summer, which is naturally the favoured season for re-roofing. The aim in such cases should be to have the work sufficiently advanced by May or June for returning bats to be dissuaded from breeding in that site for that year. The bats will know of other less favoured sites, which can be used temporarily, but will return, if possible, to their primary site in the following summer. Another possible solution is to divide the roof with a temporary barrier and work on half at a time. This procedure has been used successfully on a number of occasions.

In most cases it is not known if a building is used for hibernation, except occasionally in the case of lesser horseshoe and long-eared bats in cellars. In such cases, excessive disturbance during the winter must be avoided and work should be delayed until after hibernation if possible.

The best times for building or re-roofing operations are spring and autumn. At these times of the year the bats will be able to feed on most nights and may be active or torpid during the day, depending on weather conditions, but will not have begun breeding. Active bats will usually keep out of the way of any operations, but torpid bats can be moved gently to a safe place (see Chapter 7), preferably without causing them to fly in daylight. Repeated disturbance to bats during the winter can seriously deplete their food reserves, but, unless significant numbers of bats are known to be hibernating in a building, there is no advantage in requesting a deferment of scheduled works.

10

Emergencies – bats discovered during re-roofing

Legal position (simplified)

The killing, injuring, taking or disturbance of bats and the damage or destruction of roosts may be covered by the legal defences that 'the action took place in a dwelling-house' (disturbance or damage/destruction of roosts only) or that this was 'the incidental result of a lawful operation and could not reasonably have been avoided' (all offences). However, these defences may only be relied on if the SNCO had been consulted and allowed a reasonable time to advise as to whether the proposed operation should be carried out and, if so, the method to be used.

If the SNCO had been consulted, the defence could be relied on; if not, illegal activity may be taking place, so the police could be involved, but only a court can ultimately determine the legality of the situation. If the 'incidental result' defence is used, the decision of the court may depend on the interpretation of the word 'reasonably'.

Advice

The advice to be given here would depend primarily on a number of factors, including:
Season;
number and species of bats involved;
type of roost;
state of progress of the work;
cost of delay (financial and human).

Outside breeding season (NB small numbers of bats only)

If bats are torpid

Catch (don't handle bats; use a box, gloves or cloth), keep safely and release nearby at dusk the same day. Proceed carefully with work. Leave access for bats to return in future.

If bats are active

If bats are uncatchable, leave roost partially exposed to encourage bats to disperse naturally overnight. Then proceed carefully with work. Leave access for bats to return in the future.

During breeding season

Breeding unlikely (for example, small numbers of bats)

Leave roost partially exposed overnight for bats to disperse naturally, then proceed carefully with the work. Leave access for bats to return in the future.

Probable nursery roost

Stop work and seek advice from the appropriate SNCO. If work has just started, consider reinstating it and postponing work until the bats have dispersed. If work is well advanced, consider sheeting roof and waiting until bats have dispersed. In many cases, the disturbance or exposure that has already taken place will persuade the bats to move elsewhere, taking any young with then, so the delay may not be long. On a large building, it may be possible to divide the roof into sections so that the work can proceed a section at a time. This technique has already been used successfully.

Illegal action

Generally, if roofers are concerned enough about the bats to seek advice from the SNCO or a bat group, they will be prepared to make at least some concessions and, it is hoped, enable the situation to be resolved without the threat of legal action. If roofers have found bats in a roof during the breeding season and refuse to stop to allow time for a consultation with the SNCO, there would be reasonable grounds for calling in the police on the basis that a roost was being destroyed and bats disturbed and possibly injured and killed.

10.5.2 Direct effects on bats

Bats are occasionally encountered during the course of building works. Usually, small numbers are discovered hibernating singly during roof repairs or repairs to exterior cladding, but a few reports are received each year of large hibernation colonies. These colonies, almost invariably of pipistrelles, are found in a variety of situations such as in wall cavities or under flat roofs and generally there are no obvious external signs of their presence.

Although bats may be inadvertently or deliberately killed by workmen, the main problems are disturbance and the permanent or temporary loss of a hibernation site. As the bats will already have been disturbed, the most appropriate solution is to collect any torpid bats into a box and either release them nearby at dusk or move them to a part of the building, which provides suitable conditions but is not going to be affected. Active bats can be left to make their own escape. Only bats that are apparently unhealthy or injured need to be taken temporarily into care, and these should be released at the site of capture as soon as practicable, preferably within 2 weeks. Healthy bats can be released safely in any weather except gales, when they should be kept temporarily.

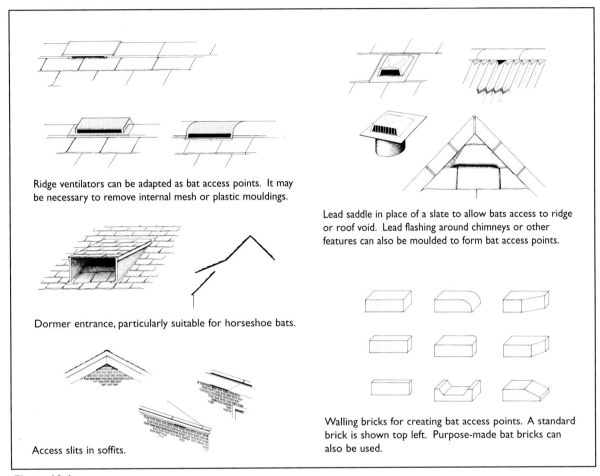

Ridge ventilators can be adapted as bat access points. It may be necessary to remove internal mesh or plastic mouldings.

Lead saddle in place of a slate to allow bats access to ridge or roof void. Lead flashing around chimneys or other features can also be moulded to form bat access points.

Dormer entrance, particularly suitable for horseshoe bats.

Walling bricks for creating bat access points. A standard brick is shown top left. Purpose-made bat bricks can also be used.

Access slits in soffits.

Figure 10.4
Bat access holes. Horseshoe bats prefer to fly into their roosts, but only small holes or slots are needed for other species and this also helps to deter colonisation by birds.

Fire doors in roof voids used by bats

Large roof voids, for example in historic houses, sometimes need to be partitioned in order to prevent fire spreading through the void. Access through these fire partitions is generally provided for maintenance purposes through 'fire doors'. Where bats that routinely fly through the roof void (such as long-eared or horseshoe) are present, access to and from their roost sites needs to be safeguarded and fire doors need to be kept open and close only in the event of fire. There are two types of fire door that can provide this:

Fusible link shutters operate when the temperature rises above 72°C. This system would not provide adequate fire protection in lofts, where heat or flame might travel between compartments prior to the fusible link operating. It is, however, routinely used in metal duct work with smaller aperture in boiler rooms, where it is designed to disconnect the oil or air supply in case of a boiler overheating or catching fire.

Electromagnetic doorstops are connected to the fire alarm system and close automatically when a smoke detector is activated. The National Trust in a Fire Guidance Policy Note recommends the use of electromagnetic door stops with the following system specifications in roof voids used by bats:

- the doors close on activation of smoke detectors only in the part of the roof occupied by bats;
- doors are connected to a backup battery that will keep them open for at least 72 hours if the power is cut;
- doors are connected to a security alarm that would go off if the doors are closed due to fire, accident or failure;
- the system is excluded from regular fire alarm tests and will only be tested annually outside the season when bats are present.

The SNCOs must be consulted in cases where fire doors are to be installed in roofs occupied by bats.

Source: The National Trust, pers. com.

10

10.5.3 Alterations to roosts

In some cases, such as demolition, the loss of the roost site is inevitable, but during repairs it is often possible to arrange for appropriate access holes and roost sites to be left so that the bats can reoccupy their roost at a later date. The size, shape and location of the access points and roosting areas will depend on the type of work being carried out and will need to be determined for every case, but some general guidance can be given (Figure 10.4). Ensure that the roost site is not made unsuitable for bats, for example by the use of inappropriate timber treatment chemicals or by the installation of large amounts of loft insulation near the access points (e.g. at the eaves of buildings).

Try to locate the new access points as close to the old ones as possible. This will ensure that they are found easily by the bats. If the main access point has to be moved, it is helpful if the old and new access points can both be available for a time so that the bats can become used to the new one.

If the roosting area is to be reduced in size or otherwise limited, ensure that the temperature regime is not altered too drastically. Breeding colonies of bats will generally choose the warmest parts of a roost but need to have some choice of temperatures. Hibernating bats need cool and stable temperatures, so heat 'leakage' from occupied parts of a building should be avoided. The installation of central heating boilers or uninsulated hot pipes in cellars used for hibernation is inadvisable, but, if it is unavoidable, try to isolate the heated parts from the rest by walls or doors.

If part of a roof is to be converted for human occupation, a good layer of sound insulation should be installed between the two areas. This will benefit both bats and humans. If ceilings are to be replaced or altered, a layer of boarding covered with polythene on top of the insulation will facilitate the removal of accumulated droppings.

Access holes should be kept small or birds may move in. For most bat species a slit 15 mm wide by at least 20 mm long is adequate and the ideal position appears to be between soffit and wall. The bats can then land on the vertical wall and climb up through the gap; most birds cannot manage this. Building regulations specify that roofs must have adequate ventilation around the soffit, so access for bats can easily be incorporated into this. Other suitable access points for bats are at gable ends, around lead flashing or through gaps between slates or tiles.

Horseshoe bats need special consideration because they may require an access hole large enough to fly through. This should, wherever possible, be modelled on the size and shape of the previous access hole, but new holes should ideally be at least 400 x 300 mm for greater horseshoes and 300 x 200 mm for lesser horseshoes. The hole can be either in a vertical wall or in a horizontal surface such as a soffit or ceiling. Use of the latter position may help to discourage birds.

All alterations to roost sites have the potential to damage the site, so the SNCO must always be consulted before any work begins.

Bat access and bat roost bricks are an innovation that, where sited appropriately, can provide access to roost sites (e.g the Marshall's bat access brick) or provide new roosting/hibernation opportunities. Bricks suitable for roosting (such as the Norfolk bat group 'bat-zzz-brick', see Appendix 6), consist of a series of slots or holes of exactly the correct size for species such as Daubenton's, Natterer's, brown long-eared, Brandt's, whiskered and barbastelle bats to hide in. These bricks would typically be used by replacing an existing, perhaps crumbling brick in a brick-lined tunnel or in a bridge. Roost units, suitable for incorporating into new structures have also been made; these are much larger and have the potential to be used as nursery roosts.

Case study - window and lintel replacement

English Nature in Kent was contacted by a property owner who knew that bats were roosting in a cavity brick wall above a bedroom window. The bats were gaining access through a hole in the mortar. The owner needed to replace a brick lintel beneath the window, which was disintegrating. The window frame was also to be renewed. If the work had been carried out immediately the roost would have been damaged and, possibly, the bats using it would have been injured or killed. A member of the Kent Bat Group visited the property and the

owner was advised to delay carrying out the work until the autumn, after checking that the bats had departed. It was also suggested that bricks with circular holes in them, or bat bricks were used. An access slit being left close to the original access point was also considered to be an option. The work was carried out during the autumn and the operation was a success, with bats continuing to use the roost thereafter.

Source: English Nature/Kent Bat Group, pers. com.

Case study - roof refurbishment

Early consultation between owners of properties where work is to take place, which may affect bats or their roosts, is essential. SNCOs and bat workers can increase the probability that the outcome will be successful. The maintenance of good liaison between the parties involved avoids misunderstandings and lessens the risk of damage being caused to bats or their roosts.

In Somerset an architect approached English Nature in February, requesting advice regarding some bats found in the roof of a large property, which, although in use, had been neglected for many years. Now under new ownership, major refurbishment of the roof of the building was planned. This was a project costing £250,000 (at 1991 prices) and work was due to start in May. The work included complete re-roofing, including the replacement of defective timbers, localised timber treatment, removal of a number of chimney stacks and the rebuilding of others, rebuilding parapet walls, installation of smoke detectors and lights in the roof void and the laying of glass fibre insulation.

A site visit revealed copious amounts of bat droppings, with concentrations throughout the roof. The roof was probably being used by three or four species of bats. Particularly large concentrations of lesser horseshoe droppings, one at least 0.6 m in depth and covering an area of about 1 square metre, were found in one part of the roof, indicating a sizeable summer roost. Six lesser horseshoes and two brown long-eared bats were seen on this initial visit.

The early consultation and subsequent good liaison with the architect, main and subcontractors resulted in an agreed plan to carry out the necessary works in phases. The lesser horseshoes' main nursery roost was worked on first. This was completed in good time to allow the re-establishment of the summer nursery of 60–70 bats. Brown long-eared bats were forced to move through the roof voids as work progressed. Both species remained in the roof during the whole summer and, as far as it was possible to determine, both species bred successfully.

The Somerset Bat Group has monitored the roost since the completion of re-roofing and has confirmed the successful outcome of this exercise by continuing to record similar numbers of bats using the roosting site each year.

Source: English Nature/Somerset Bat Group, pers. com.

Case study – timber treatment and roof renovation

In May, the Kent Bat Group visited a farmhouse, which required timber treatment. Building work on the property had already begun. A cluster of 10 brown long-eared bats was discovered in the oldest part of the roof void. The owners of the property were advised to delay the application of timber treatments until the autumn and they agreed to do this. However, it was not possible to delay the building works and so provisions enabling bats to continue using the roost were required. The alterations to the property included dismantling a free standing chimney in the roof space. While work on the exterior of the property continued, access points were left for bats when soffit boards were replaced. Prior to the dismantling of the chimney the bats' side of the attic was separated using a hardboard screen, which was stapled, rather than nailed into place to reduce noise. A dust cloth was also hung between the two areas to minimize dust and to keep the bats' side of the attic dark. Good relations were established with the builders, who were given an explanation of the need for the actions taken, and they carried out their work with the minimum of noise and disturbance. The outcome was successful, with the bat population continuing to use the roost.

Source: English Nature/Kent Bat Group, pers. com.

References

BOYD, I.L., MYHILL, D.G. & MITCHELL-JONES, A.J. 1988. Uptake of Gamma-HCH (Lindane) by pipistrelle bats and its effect on survival. *Environmental Pollution*, **51**, 95–111.

RACEY, P.A. & SWIFT, S.M. 1986. The residual effects of remedial timber treatments on bats. *Biological Conservation*, **35**, 205–214.

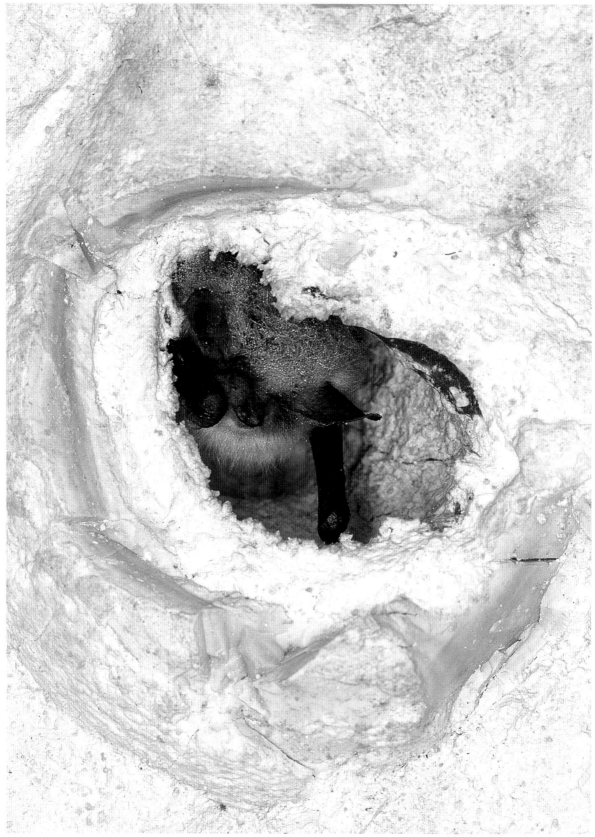

A Natterer's bat in hibernation. © Frank Greenaway

Conserving and creating bat roosts

A. J. Mitchell-Jones

11.1 Conservation measures in underground sites

Caves, mines and structures such as ice-houses, tunnels, lime-kilns and cellars provide the protected and stable conditions that many bats seek during hibernation. Within such sites, there is relatively little variation in temperature and humidity throughout the year, although each site will provide a range of conditions. Bats use such sites both as mating and gathering areas in early and late summer, as night roosts and as hibernation sites. A few species will form maternity roosts near the entrance of caves or mines if conditions are suitable. Table 11.1 summarises the usefulness of subterranean sites to the various species, although it is difficult to give hard and fast rules. In late summer a wider variety of species uses these sites at night than can be expected to hibernate in them.

11.1.1 Threats

Excessive disturbance

Although bats can tolerate a degree of disturbance during hibernation and can apparently become conditioned to a low level of human activity, excessive disturbance will cause bats to abandon a site. In one extensive cave system, bats seem to co-exist with cavers, who are aware of their vulnerability and take reasonable care not to disturb them, but bats in other sites have been adversely affected.

An artificial bat roost. © Frank Greenaway

The increasing use of a growing number of sites by outdoor pursuits centres, adventure holiday groups, tourism and the like is also a cause for concern, because members of such parties generally have less understanding of the impact of humans on these sites and their fauna than members of specialist clubs. Frequency of visits is also a problem: outdoor centres generally operate throughout the week, so that visits to sites by relatively large parties of inexperienced people can be frequent.

Some sites are readily accessible without any special equipment or preparation. Here, casual disturbance by the curious can be a problem, as can vandalism, the lighting of fires, the dumping of

Table 11.1 Occurrence of bat species in caves, mines and other similar situations

	Light zone	True cave	Notes
Greater horseshoe	HBO	HO(B)	Use caves almost throughout the year.
Lesser horseshoe	HBO	HO(B)	Use caves almost throughout the year.
Daubenton's	HBO	HBO	
Whiskered/Brandt's	HO	HO	
Natterer's	HO(B)	HO	
Bechstein's	HO	HO	Very rare
Common pipistrelle	H	Very rarely	Hibernates in caves in eastern Europe.
Soprano pipistrelle	H	Very rarely	Hibernates in caves in eastern Europe.
Nathusius's pipistrelle	H	Rarely	
Serotine	(H)O	Very rarely	
Noctule	-	-	
Leisler's	-	-	
Barbastelle	(H)O	-	Cave entrances in very cold weather.
Brown long-eared	HO	HO	Uses caves during cold weather.
Grey long-eared	HO	HO	Uses caves during cold weather.

H - hibernating   B – breeding   O - other

11

toxic waste or even the deliberate killing of bats. The Bat Conservation Trust's leaflet 'Bats Underground' gives guidance on conservation issues and site assessment.

Destruction, maintenance or change of use

Subterranean sites can suffer from a variety of operations, which can affect their use by bats. Safety considerations and concern over legal liability have persuaded many local Councils or land-owning organisations to seal disused shafts and, in some cases, block caves or adits. In some areas the loss of potential hibernation sites is continuing at an alarming rate. Tunnels have been repaired, converted to storage areas or rifle ranges, or reopened for their original use; caves have been opened for public access as show caves, and caves and mines have been quarried away as part of commercial quarrying operations. Even if a cave or mine is to remain open, gating or grilling in an inappropriate way can also affect the bats, so the SNCO should always be consulted.

Even quite subtle changes to the topography of a site, both inside and outside, can have far-reaching effects on its suitability for bats, mainly by altering the air-flow through the system and hence the temperature and humidity. Some changes, if carefully planned, can benefit the bats, but others can certainly degrade the usefulness of the site.

Bats tend to prefer dynamic cave systems, where there is a flow of air through the system and hence some variation in temperature. Horseshoe bats tend to prefer warmer sites than other species, though there is much overlap. In simple dynamic systems, such as blind tunnels or adits, which rely on convection currents, the size, configuration and aspect can affect the temperature within the site to a considerable degree. Convection will pull in warm air in summer and cold air in winter. Domes and recesses in the roof can trap warm air and cold air can be trapped in areas lower than the entrance. In the UK, the coldest sites are usually the best midwinter hibernacula for vespertilionid bats. The surrounding vegetation and topography are also very important because bats require cover around the site access. Figure 11.1 gives some examples. Non-dynamic systems with no air movement tend to be too warm for hibernation, although they may be used as temporary summer roosts.

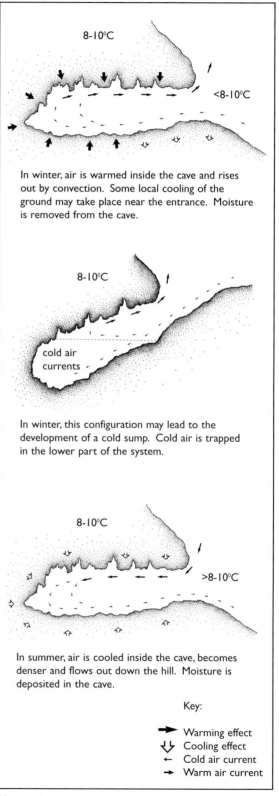

In winter, air is warmed inside the cave and rises out by convection. Some local cooling of the ground may take place near the entrance. Moisture is removed from the cave.

In winter, this configuration may lead to the development of a cold sump. Cold air is trapped in the lower part of the system.

In summer, air is cooled inside the cave, becomes denser and flows out down the hill. Moisture is deposited in the cave.

Key:

➡ Warming effect
⬇ Cooling effect
← Cold air current
➡ Warm air current

Figure 11.1
Convention currents in caves and mines. The extent and direction of the currents depends on the temperature differential between inside and out as well as the size and configuration of the site.

Bat conservation: site grading and protection

Site grading

Caves, mines and other underground sites can be graded according to their importance to bats. This grading takes into account not only the number and species of bats involved but also the physical nature of the site and the pattern of usage by the bats. Compared with other European countries, numbers of bats recorded in British sites are small; there are fewer than 30 known sites with more than 100 bats.

Grading gives an indication of where limits on human access would help bat conservation. Many sites also have access control for other reasons and these may take precedence over control for bat conservation.

The grading of particular sites is agreed by negotiation between the bat conservation organisations and either the National Caving Association (NCA) or the National Association of Mining History Organisations (NAMHO) in co-operation with their member groups. In many cases a more detailed statement on access control will be available from these organisations. Access control does not necessarily mean access is prohibited. Significant populations would have to be recorded before any access restrictions would be requested. Incidental observations of bats can be made without infringing the Wildlife and Countryside Act and reports are welcomed by the nature conservation organisations.

Grade 1 (fewer than 10 sites)

Sites used by bats throughout the year for hibernation and breeding. Access controlled throughout the year. Visits by prior arrangement with the key holder, in agreement with the relevant national or regional caving organisations or NAMHO, normally during spring or autumn.

Examples: Swan Hill Quarry, Shropshire (used by up to 80 lesser horseshoe bats throughout the year); Rock Farm Cave, Devon (used by several hundred greater horseshoe bats throughout the year).

Grade 2 (fewer than 100 sites)

Sites used by large or locally significant numbers of bats during the winter (normally 1 November to 30 April, but extended in a few cases) where seasonal access control is considered desirable or is already in effect. Control over activities such as blasting may also be required.

Grade 2a: sites already gated or grilled.

Unrestricted access by arrangement with the key holder during the summer or restricted access by agreement between the key holder, NAMHO or NCA or other relevant caving body during the winter. This agreement may cover activities such as blasting.

Examples: Agen Allwedd, Powys (used by more than 200 lesser horseshoe bats during the winter. Access controlled by a management committee that takes account of the bat interest. Blasting banned during the winter [1 October to 20 May]); Hangman's Wood Deneholes, Essex (used by up to 70 Natterer's, Daubenton's and long-eared bats. Recent restriction on visiting during the winter has significantly increased the number of bats).

Grade 2b: sites without protection.

Unrestricted access during the summer but winter visits and blasting should be avoided unless agreed with NCA / NAMHO.
Examples: West Llangynog Slate Mine, Powys (used by more than 50 lesser horseshoe bats); Ettington, Warwickshire (used regularly by the rare barbastelle bat as well as small numbers of Natterer's, Daubenton's and long-eared bats); Sandford Hill, Mendip, Somerset (various cave and mine sites used by greater horseshoe bats).

Grade 3 (many sites)

Sites known to be used by small numbers of bats during the winter. No formal access control but proceed with caution and follow the conservation code. Avoid winter visits if practical. Report numbers of bats seen.

Examples: Eglwys Faen, Powys (small numbers of lesser horseshoe, whiskered and Daubenton's bats); Gnomeys, Godstone, Surrey (used by small numbers of Natterer's, Daubenton's, whiskered, Brandt's and long-eared bats).

Grade 4 (many sites)

Sites not known to be used by bats or with only occasional records. Follow the conservation code and report any bat sightings.

Source: Bats Underground/BCT, pers. com.

11

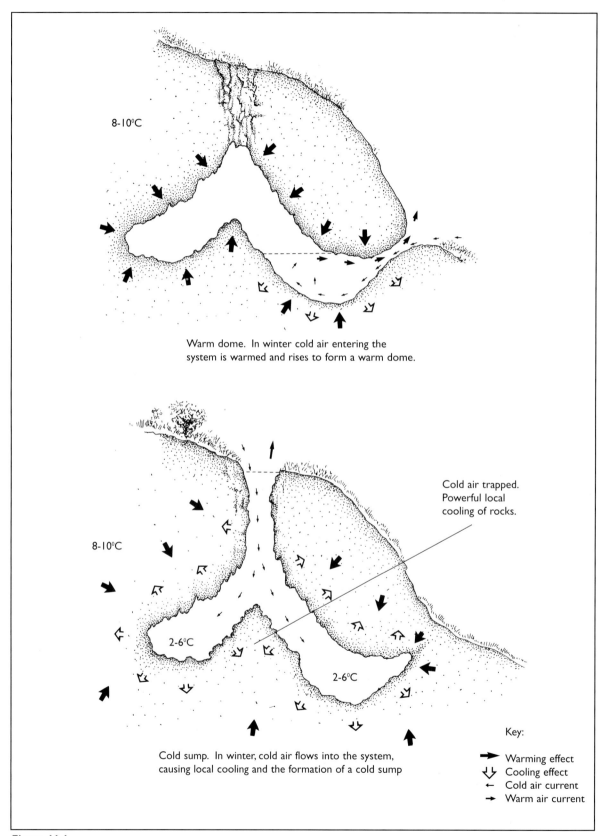

8-10°C

Warm dome. In winter cold air entering the
system is warmed and rises to form a warm dome.

Cold air trapped.
Powerful local
cooling of rocks.

8-10°C

2-6°C

2-6°C

Key:

→ Warming effect
↓ Cooling effect
← Cold air current
→ Warm air current

Cold sump. In winter, cold air flows into the system,
causing local cooling and the formation of a cold sump

Figure 11.1
(Continued)

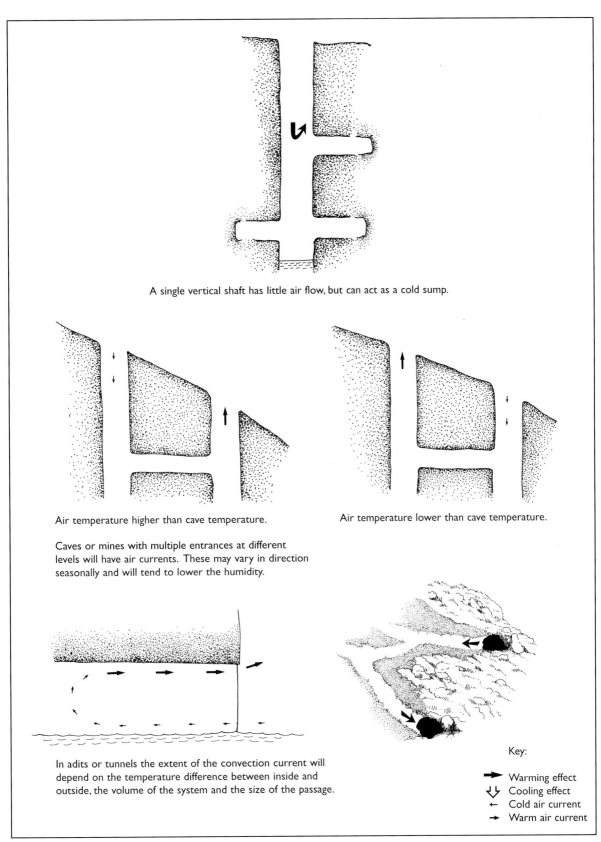

A single vertical shaft has little air flow, but can act as a cold sump.

Air temperature higher than cave temperature.

Air temperature lower than cave temperature.

Caves or mines with multiple entrances at different levels will have air currents. These may vary in direction seasonally and will tend to lower the humidity.

In adits or tunnels the extent of the convection current will depend on the temperature difference between inside and outside, the volume of the system and the size of the passage.

Key:
→ Warming effect
⤵ Cooling effect
← Cold air current
→ Warm air current

Figure 11.1
(Continued)

11.1.2 Grilles

The most frequently required conservation measure for caves and mines is protection against excessive disturbance. This is generally achieved by fitting a grille, which permits the free passage of bats but not people, although other measures such as security fencing may be appropriate in a few cases. If a grille is to be fitted, it is important to monitor bat numbers before and after fitting to check for any beneficial or adverse effects.

Grilles must be carefully planned if they are to be successful and a number of points must be taken into account.

- The SNCO must be consulted if the site is already used by bats. Grilles have the potential to damage bat roosts if not correctly designed and fitted, so advice must be sought on this. TheSNCOs also wish to keep records of all bat sites and all grilling works. Grilles can be expensive items and the SNCO may be able to grant-aid the cost of grilling known bat hibernacula and suggest other sources of funding.

- The species using a site should be identified before a grille is installed. Summer, as well as winter, use should be taken into account. Grilles should not be installed at times when disturbance is likely to result, e.g. during hibernation.

- Permission must be sought from the landowner and any tenants. A management agreement will help to set out responsibilities and any arrangements that have been made for access. Many owners will welcome the installation and maintenance of a grille, because this will help to ease fears about safety and discourage trespass. Many conservation and wildlife trusts have experience of such agreements and they may be willing to help.

- If the site is used by cavers, mine historians or similar groups, suitable arrangements for access by these groups must be negotiated before any work begins. Failure to do so will severely upset relations with responsible caving groups and may also lead to repeated damage or to destruction of the grille.

- The grille must be of appropriate design and construction (Figure 11.2). The bar spacing is one of the most important variables, because some bats, particularly horseshoes, are known to be reluctant to fly through narrow gaps. An air space of 150 mm between horizontals is recommended for greater horseshoe bats, but this may be large enough to allow children through and a slightly narrower spacing may be appropriate for sites used only by other species; a 130 mm gap seems to be a reasonable compromise. Vertical supports should be more widely spaced, although too wide a spacing will make the grille vulnerable to vandalism because the bars can be forced apart more easily. The exact spacing can be chosen to suit the size of the grille but should be in the range of 450–750 mm, with greater horseshoes being given the larger spacing. All grilles should be constructed to permit access for authorised persons and for safety. For small entrances, it may be most convenient to have the whole grille hinged and fitted on a subframe. This is particularly appropriate when doorways have to be grilled, as the subframe, hinges and lock can be concealed behind the door frame. Larger grilles will need to be fixed permanently in position and fitted with a door of at least 500 x 500 mm. This can be either hinged or sliding, depending on the circumstances. If hinges are fitted, these should be of robust construction or concealed so that they cannot easily be hacksawed through.

- It is generally agreed that the lock should be the weakest part of the grille so that a determined intruder may be tempted to break this relatively cheap and replaceable component rather than the grille itself. However, it should not be made too vulnerable and should be fitted so that it cannot easily be cut or levered off, although if the lock becomes seized or someone fills it with epoxy resin it needs to be accessible for replacement.

- The construction material should be chosen to suit the vulnerability of the site and the finance available (Figure 11.3). For sites where there is a low risk of vandalism, mild steel may be an appropriate material. This is cheap but is not resistant to cutting and rusts rather quickly. Its main advantage is that the grille can be cut and fitted in situ and welded with portable equipment. For sites at higher risk or where the grille is to be prefabricated, some form of toughened steel should be used for those parts of the grille that are most at risk. Reinforcing rod of 20 mm diameter is readily available and provides reasonable resistance to rust and to hacksaws. Tougher steels are available, but these are generally expensive and can be difficult to cut and weld. For particularly high-risk sites, a grille

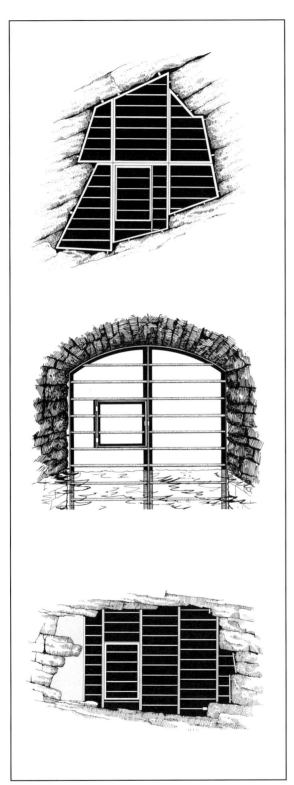

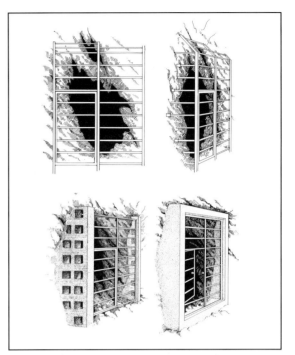

Figure 11.2b
Bat grilles. For vertical rock faces the grille can be made larger than the entrance and pinned to the wall. Irregular vertical surfaces may need a cage with side arms cut to length on site. Blockwork or shuttered concrete provide useful ways of squaring up entrances and stabilising soft or unstable strata.

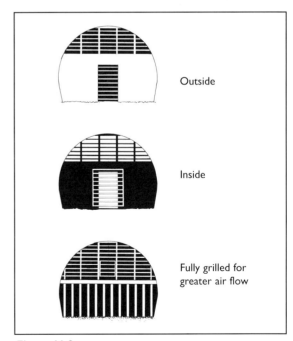

Outside

Inside

Fully grilled for greater air flow

Figure 11.2a
Bat grilles. Grilles for large or irregular entrances are best constructed in sections and bolted or welded together on site. Bars can be extended beyond the frame to fill awkward corners, but long unsupported bars will be a weak point in the grille.

Figure 11.2c
Tunnels, such as railway tunnels, with brick or block end walls, can have a grille fitted to the inside of the wall so that only the bars are visible. Full grilles can incorporate a lower section of vertical bars, which are hard to climb.

11

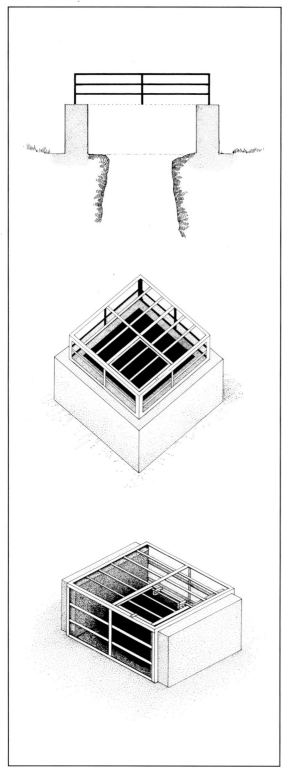

Figure II.2d
Bat grilles. Vertical shafts usually require stabilisation of the edges. Grilles should be fitted above ground level so they are not inadvertently walked on by people or animals. At least one vertical grille face about 50cm high should be provided so that bats do not have to fly vertically upwards through the grille.

based on the roller principle may be suitable. The main grille is made from 30–35 mm diameter steel tube, welded in the usual way, and hardened steel rods are then inserted into the tubes and left loose. If any attempt is made to hacksaw through the combination, the rod will simply revolve rather than being cut. Small and medium-sized grilles can generally be prefabricated out of a mixture of rod and angle and then trimmed to size, if necessary, on site. Large grilles may need to be prefabricated in sections and then bolted or welded together as they are fitted.

- It is often advantageous to protect grilles against rust. This is preferably done by galvanising at the time of manufacture (a hot-dip process) or by coating the grille with an anti-rust preparation such as 'Norusto' or 'Nutrarust'. Epoxy resin paints may also be used, but paints with a persistent smell, such as bitumen, should be avoided.

- By careful design and construction it is possible to make a grille that is extremely strong and resistant to damage. However, it must be remembered that no grille can be proof against powerful welding or cutting equipment and that a prolonged and determined attack will eventually breach any grille. Repair costs are likely to be proportional to the cost of the original grille. It is best to site the grille where it is visible from outside the cave or mine so that potential vandals are deterred.

- The grille must be fitted so that it does not impede air flow into the site. It is generally inadvisable to fit the grille into the narrowest part of an entrance, where it could critically affect air flow. If the narrowest point is the only logical place to put the grille, for example in a doorway, care must be taken to keep the obstruction to a minimum, particularly at floor and roof level.

- The grille must be securely fitted into solid rock, if available (Figure 11.4). It is no use fitting a carefully constructed grille, only to have it dug round or pulled out. A common method of fitting is to drill a series of holes around the entrance and cement in steel rods, which are then welded to the main grille. This is not always a convenient method because it requires the use of on-site welding equipment of adequate power and it is rarely possible to weld large-section high-carbon steel with a portable welder. An alternative is to fit the grille with lugs or a rim of steel angle and then pin it to the wall with rock-bolts. The heads of the bolts can then be rounded off or welded to the frame for additional security. Hard rock sites need only relatively short bolts, but sites in chalk or other soft strata may need long auger-type bolts screwed up to 900 mm into the rock. Sites with unstable or awkwardly shaped entrances may need a concrete or block surround to be built in place before a grille can be fitted. In very poor ground conditions, it may be preferable to create a new site close by rather than try to grille a system that would soon collapse anyway.

- In most cases, the base of the grille can be set into a trench cut into the floor of the site, which is then back-filled with concrete. Care must be taken that the original floor-line is preserved so

that air flow is not impeded. The trench should be a minimum of 300 mm deep, otherwise intruders may tunnel underneath. In soft earth or clay, it may help to hammer rods vertically into the earth at the bottom of the trench and set their tops into the concrete. At smaller entrances it might be better to use a door with small (letter-box) type access.

- The grille must be inspected regularly and maintained when necessary. A strongly made grille in a low-risk area is unlikely to need repair for many years but should be inspected regularly. In high-risk areas, the prompt repair of any damage will eventually discourage intruders who discover that they have to work hard to gain access at every visit.

An ice-house

The properties that made ice-houses so valuable in times before the invention of the refrigerator now make many of them suitable as bat hibernacula. The bats in an area near Maidstone were given a hand in being able to make better use of an ice house by English Nature and the local bat group. Firstly, the building was made secure against vandalism by fitting and strengthening the door with metal plates. However, this did not make the place immediately attractive

to bats and it was not until fine plastic mesh was attached to one side of the door, across the top and down the other side, that hibernating bats were found to be using the site. It is surmised that the mesh allows the bats to land and grip the mesh. They are then able to crawl up and over the top of the door and into the ice house.

Source: English Nature/Kent Bat Group

Railway Tunnel Enhancement

Disused railway tunnels can be valuable bat hibernation sites. The Wiltshire Bat Group has been managing a project that has increased the value of one such site. Hibernating bats were found in a tunnel during an initial survey in 1993 but conditions were less than ideal, with internal winter temperatures being similar to those outside. In 1994 the ends of the tunnel were sealed and bat access grilles were installed. This succeeded in reducing air movement, maintaining a relatively stable temperature of around 8°C, and increasing relative humidity from 80 to 95%.

During the summers of 1994 and 1995 wood was attached to the tunnel walls in order to create crevices suitable for hibernating bats.

The value of all of the hard work carried out is indicated by the increase in the number of bats using the site.

Hibernating bat populations have been surveyed three times each winter. At the end of 1993, prior to the construction of the end walls, a maximum of 41 bats was recorded. By the winter of 1996/97 this number had increased to 82 and by 2001/02 the maximum count was 168. More than 90% of the bats have been Natterer's bats. Other species found include brown long-eared, Daubenton's, whiskered/Brandt's and, occasionally, the rare barbastelle. Over 30% of hibernating bats are found to be using the crevices formed by the attachment of wood to the tunnel walls.

This successful project has suffered several problems. The end walls have twice been vandalised and damaged once by subsidence after heavy rain. On each occasion has repairs have been carried out.

Source: Wiltshire Bat Group

11.1.3 Creative conservation and site management

Many subterranean sites are potential bat hibernacula but are unsuitable for one reason or

another or are suitable for improvement, as measured by the numbers of bats recorded hibernating there. Protection from disturbance has already been dealt with, but other measures that may be taken include the following.

Manipulation of air-flow and temperature

Largely static cave or mine systems with little air movement are often too warm for most species and can be improved by the creation of additional entrances or air vents, so as to increase the proportion of the system subject to a dynamic air flow. The aim is to achieve an internal temperature of 0–6°C in January during frosty weather. If such manipulations are attempted, the numbers and positions of hibernating bats must be monitored carefully to try to gauge the success of the project. In contrast, tunnels that are open at both ends fluctuate too much in temperature and are too dry for bats. They can be improved by fitting partial barriers at the ends or in the middle of the tunnel (Figure 11.5). The resulting decrease in air flow allows the temperature to rise towards that in a similar static system. Simple straight adits or tunnels with a relatively high passage and entrance are often very suitable for bats because, although there is no through draught, the relative stability of the cave temperature in the tunnel can give rise to convection currents and a dynamic air flow (see Figure 11.1). Such currents can be prevented by mounds of rock or earth at the entrance, and it may be advantageous to clear these.

Reopening of blocked sites

Many subterranean sites have become unavailable to bats either through deliberate blockage or through collapse. These include caves, mines, tunnels, grottoes, ice-houses, lime-kilns and cellars. The reopening of such sites can lead to their rediscovery by bats and re-establishment as hibernacula. Before such work is undertaken, the permission of the landowner must be sought and it may be necessary to enter into an agreement over the long-term protection of the site. Immediate grilling is usually a condition of reopening what might be regarded as a dangerous place.

Provision of additional roosting points

Although bats can hang on to surprisingly smooth surfaces, many species prefer to roost in cracks or crevices. Some sorts of artificial tunnels or natural caves are lacking in these, and the provision of additional places can sometimes increase the attractiveness of the site to bats. Bats will roost in almost any sort of crevice, and successful devices have ranged from planks of wood leant against the walls to loose piles of bricks, bat-bricks or building blocks.

Provision of new hibernacula

Some areas of the country have very little in the way of underground sites. Others have tunnels in soft or dangerous strata. Both could provide suitable sites for artificial hibernacula. The positioning of new sites and the design of the structures are fundamental to their success and some suggestions are given in Figures 11.6 and 11.7. A specific example, the conversion of a pill-box, is illustrated in Figure 11.8 and many of the techniques used here can be applied to other types of hibernaculum.

It should be remembered that the majority of hibernacula in the UK are man-made, mostly as the products of former mining activities, and that their use by bats may take many years to develop. Site protection of a new hibernaculum is vital from the start, both from the point of view of the responsibility of the owner of the land and to limit site disturbance.

A design life of 100 years should be envisaged and professional assistance should be sought at all stages. The costs incurred in building new hibernacula are high, but funds from mandatory or voluntary mitigation works and suchlike are available from time to time.

Cave construction

About two dozen purpose-built bat caves have been constructed in the UK, many of them being of concrete pipe construction with added brickwork. The success rate (occupancy rate) has so far been poor, although their use will almost certainly increase over time. Creating the precise environmental requirements (particularly with regard to humidity) for bats in a purpose-built roost site is difficult, particularly when so little is known about what those requirements are. Over time, as our understanding of the needs of different species improves, it is likely that designs will reflect better the needs of bats and consequently be more successful.

The Bat Conservation Trust holds information about many of the projects undertaken to date and some of the projects have been reviewed in Bat News. Eurobats is currently reviewing measures taken for the preservation, protection, enhancement and creation of underground sites in order to produce further guidance on successful practices.

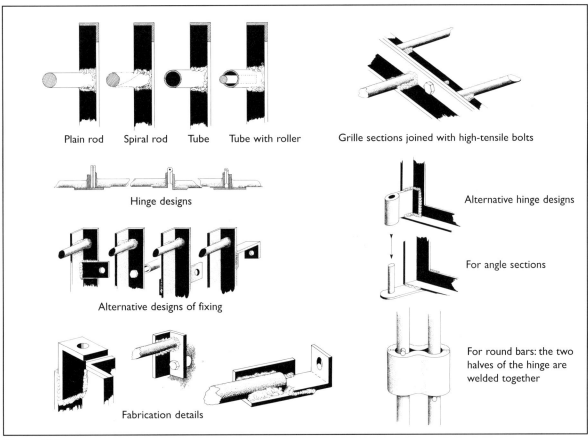

Figure 11.3
Constructing grilles. The choice of materials and method of
fabrication are often determined by what is available locally
and the vulnerability of the site being grilled. A grille that
looks strong can deter vandalism.

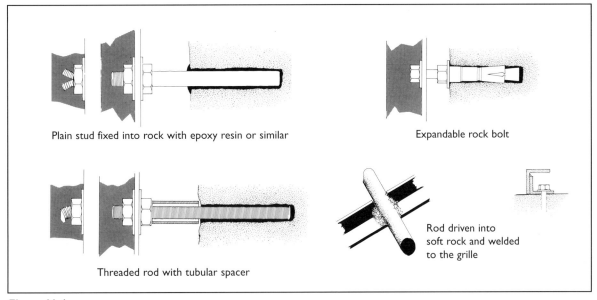

Figure 11.4
Alternative methods of fixing grilles in position.

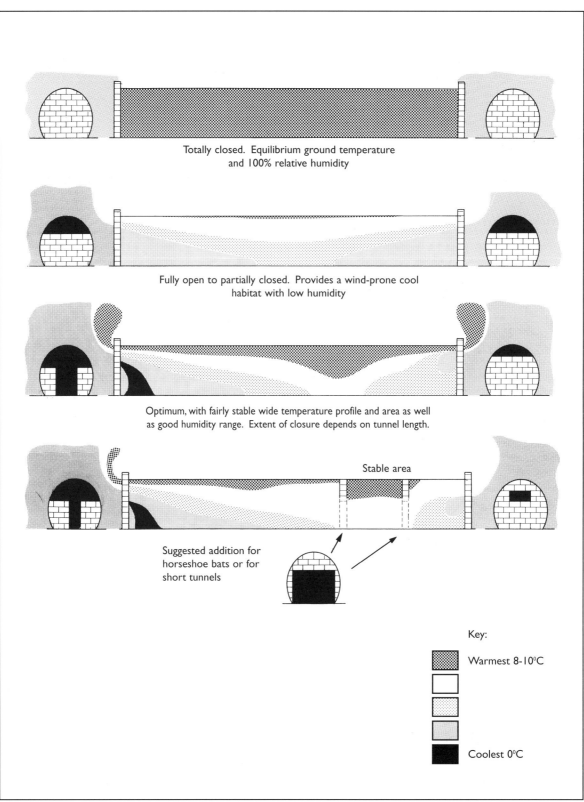

Totally closed. Equilibrium ground temperature
and 100% relative humidity

Fully open to partially closed. Provides a wind-prone cool
habitat with low humidity

Optimum, with fairly stable wide temperature profile and area as well
as good humidity range. Extent of closure depends on tunnel length.

Stable area

Suggested addition for
horseshoe bats or for
short tunnels

Key:

Warmest 8-10°C

Coolest 0°C

Figure 11.5
Creating bat hibernacula from tunnels. Air flow, temperature
and humidity can be controlled by the design of the end-walls.
Winter temperatures and air flows are shown.

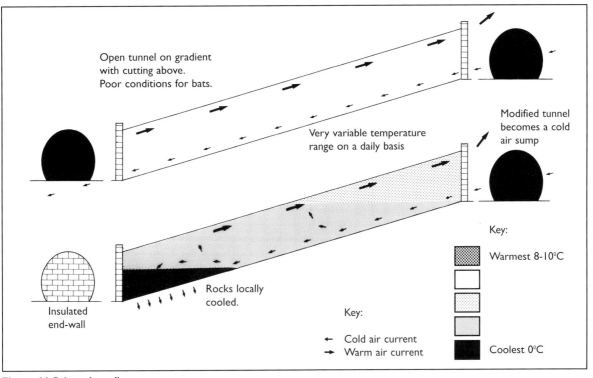

Open tunnel on gradient with cutting above. Poor conditions for bats.

Modified tunnel becomes a cold air sump

Very variable temperature range on a daily basis

Rocks locally cooled.

Insulated end-wall

Key:

← Cold air current
→ Warm air current

Key:

Warmest 8-10°C

Coolest 0°C

Figure 11.5 (continued)

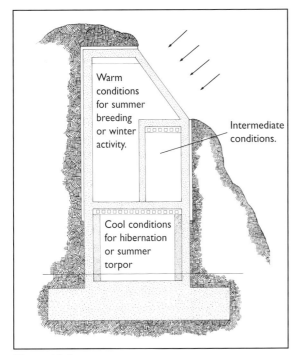

Warm conditions for summer breeding or winter activity.

Intermediate conditions.

Cool conditions for hibernation or summer torpor

Figure 11.6
Artificial roost site. A wide range of environmental conditions have been provided by using the cooling effect of the ground at the bottom and the warming effect of the sun at the top. Where such a structure can be placed over the entrance to an adit or shaft, convection currents will greatly aid the development of the warm conditions.

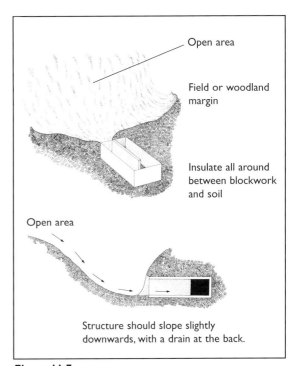

Open area

Field or woodland margin

Insulate all around between blockwork and soil

Open area

Structure should slope slightly downwards, with a drain at the back.

Figure 11.7
Creating an artificial hibernaculum. Constructing this tunnel at the base of the slope will allow cold air to flow into the site, resulting in temperatures lower than the local rocks (8-10°C). The inner end of the tunnel will be the warmest area.

11

Converting a pillbox for bats

The standard hexagonal pillbox, most common in the south-east of England, can be converted quickly cheaply and easily to a hibernaculum and occasional summer roost for bats (Figure 11.8a). The choice of box for conversion needs some thought; because one of the main threats is disturbance, boxes near to houses, roads or footpaths should be a lower priority than remote boxes on private land. Unconverted sites are often already in use as summer night or feeding roosts, although not normally as day roosts. This means a converted box may be readily adopted, even in its first year.

Step 1 The first requirement is to stabilise the interior temperature, humidity and light levels. Cut 100 mm medium-density concrete blocks in half and, from the inside, cement one into each of the firing slits at its narrowest point (Figure 11.8b).

Step 2 Three-quarters of a similar block is now cemented into the outside, widest, part of each firing slit. Leave a 200 mm by 20 mm gap at the bottom of the cement layer. You have created a hollow between the inner and outer blocks with bat access to the outside.

Step 3 Next, air flow into the building needs to be controlled. Two walls built of 200–250 mm concrete blocks will do this. The first wall should be flush with the outside of the box, up to two-thirds of the height of the entrance. The second wall, supported on a lintel, should extend two thirds of the way down from the roof at the innermost point of the entrance passage. The lintel can be supported on two columns of bricks (Figure 11.8c).

Step 4 The major part of the conversion is complete, but bats like cracks and holes to hide in. You must create these well out of the reach of rats and foxes. Nail wooden boards (Figure 11.8d) to walls, leaving 15–20 mm narrow gaps between wall and board. The inner shelf of each firing slit can also be built up leaving 20-mm gaps. Tiles can also be nailed to battens on the walls and ceiling to provide further roosting crevices (Figure 11.8e). The more crevices, the greater the possibility that bats will move in.

Step 5 If a security grille is needed, this can be fitted where the entrance passage is closed by the new wall. The grille should be constructed as described in this chapter, using the recommended bar spacing.

The conversion is now complete (Figure 11.8f).

Source: Frank Greenaway/Surrey Wildlife Trust

Bat Conservation Code

Caves and mines, their formations, artefacts and fauna, are all part of our national heritage. All visitors to underground sites should strive to maintain these sites for current and future generations.

Always follow the safety and conservation codes published by the caving and mining history organisations and liase with local groups over access and safety requirements.

Remember also that bats need your help to survive the winter. Most hibernating bats are very difficult to see – many squeeze into cracks and crevices and only the two horseshoe bats normally hang free. Just because you cannot see them does not mean they are not there. Remember the grading system and seek advice about any activity that might affect bats.

Those visiting known bat sites for purposes such as recreation, are asked to observe the voluntary conservation code and respect any special restrictions that have been placed on particularly important bat sites. Because disturbance can be so damaging, only a limited number of people are licensed to disturb or handle hibernating bats in underground sites and licences are issued only after training has been given. Such licences are issued for controlled, carefully considered basic survey and monitoring and occasionally for scientific research.

Contact with bats

- Do not handle bats (unless licensed). Also beware of dislodging bats from their roosting position particularly when you are moving through low passages.
- Do not photograph roosting bats. Flashguns can be very disturbing.
- Do not warm up hibernating bats. This can arouse them. Try not to linger in confined spaces as even your body heat is sufficient to cause arousal.
- Do not shine bright lights on bats. Both the light and the heat can trigger arousal.
- Do not use carbide lamps in bat roosts. Carbide lamps are particularly undesirable because of the heat and fumes.
- Do not smoke or make excessive noise underground. Any strong stimulus can arouse bats.
- Do not take large parties into bat roosts in winter. Rescue practices should also be avoided when bats are present.
- Do seek advice before blasting or digging. Explosives can cause problems both from the blast itself and from the subsequent fumes. In known bat sites blasting should be limited to the summer or to areas not known to be used by bats.
- Digging operations may alter the microclimate of bat roosts.

Source: Bats Underground/BCT

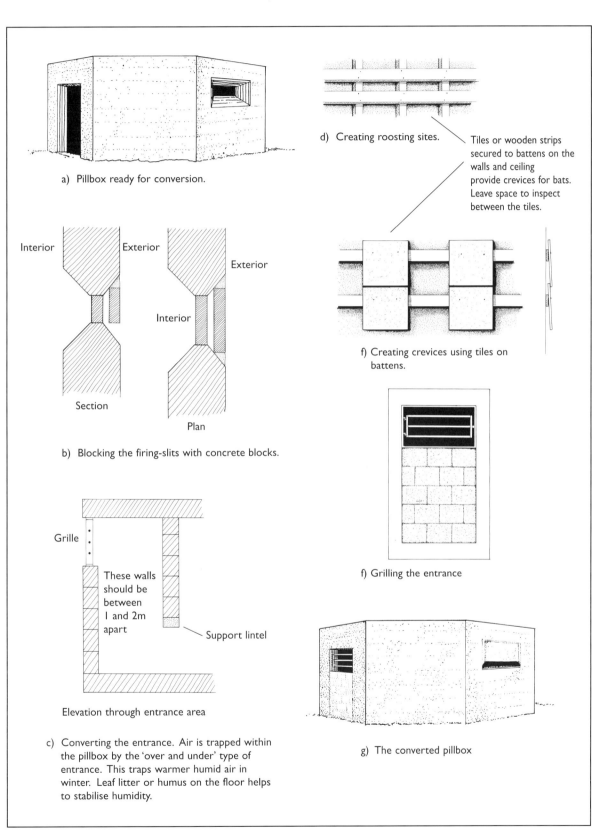

a) Pillbox ready for conversion.

Interior   Exterior

Exterior

Interior

Section

Plan

b) Blocking the firing-slits with concrete blocks.

Grille

These walls should be between 1 and 2m apart

Support lintel

Elevation through entrance area

c) Converting the entrance. Air is trapped within the pillbox by the 'over and under' type of entrance. This traps warmer humid air in winter. Leaf litter or humus on the floor helps to stabilise humidity.

d) Creating roosting sites.

Tiles or wooden strips secured to battens on the walls and ceiling provide crevices for bats. Leave space to inspect between the tiles.

f) Creating crevices using tiles on battens.

f) Grilling the entrance

g) The converted pillbox

Figure 11.8
Pillbox conversion for bat use. Many of the design details illustrated could be adapted to other situations.

11.2 Bats and trees

11.2.1 Hollow trees

Most of our bats are woodland animals. Hollow trees are used by a wide variety of species, for both summer and winter roosting, and bats will also roost in crevices in otherwise sound trees. Noctules and pipistrelles are most frequently associated with tree roosts, but many other species have been recorded using them. Naturally, these are the species that have also been found in bat boxes.

The major threat to tree roosts is the destruction of the site. Reports are received every year of bats, usually noctules, being discovered in trees that have been cut down or in boughs that have been removed. Invariably, the workmen are unaware of the presence of the bats until it is too late to save the roost. The most that can be done in such cases is to rescue the bats and release them nearby the same evening if they are fit and well. Attempts could also be made to provide an alternative roost nearby. Either a large bat box or a hollow limb from the felled tree could be used.

If bats are known to use a tree habitually, steps should be taken to ensure that the tree is not destroyed either deliberately or inadvertently.

11.2.2 The value of trees

All the species of bats in Britain are to some extent dependent on trees; for some just as a source of insect food, for others to provide roost sites as well. Horseshoe bats are in the first category, but noctules and Bechstein's bats use trees almost exclusively for roosting.

As a source of insect food

Native tree species are host to numerous insects and when the trees are felled this source is denied them. Not only are trees used as part of the life cycle of the insects, but they also provide shelter, so swarms can build up and the trees act as foci for them. Both standing and fallen dead wood are also sources of insect food for the bats: they should not be cleared away.

Roost sites

Bats may use any crack or hole in a tree as a roost site. Such sites are provided by woodpecker holes, hollows caused by rot and natural ageing and cracks from wind damage and lightning strikes. They may sometimes be found behind loose bark or ivy. Birds, other mammals, and insects such as bees all compete for these sites. Bats are least able to defend their roosts so can only use suitable sites when other animals have finished with them. Holes may be used as gathering sites in spring, maternity roosts in summer and mating places in autumn. Bats will hibernate in such sites if they are deep enough and buffered from temperature changes outside. Summer sites can be in more exposed places that are warmed by the sun.

11.2.3 Recognition of roost sites

It is not easy to find bat roosts in trees. Roosts occur in trees of all ages, sizes and types, but mature beech, oak and ash seem to be favoured. Signs to look for include:
* woodpecker holes, natural cracks and rot holes in trunks or branches that have a black streak below them where bat droppings have oozed out;
* smooth edges with dark marks at the entrance where the bats have rubbed against the wood and left natural body oils;
* droppings under the access point, although these are not easy to find among leaf litter, and are usually washed off the trunk by rain;
* chattering coming from the tree in summer – it is possible to hear some bats such as noctules either when it is hot or when they are about to emerge;
* bats swarming around the site on their return at dawn;
* bats present at the roost seen either emerging or by viewing tree holes using a mirror on a rod with a light or sophisticated probe such as a fibrascope or endoscope.

Hibernation sites are even more difficult to find because the bats leave no signs. The surest way to confirm the presence of bats is to wait for their emergence at dusk during the active season.

11.2.4 Management of trees

Bat workers should make all those involved in tree management aware of the needs of bats and the damage that can be done by felling and lopping of old branches. Although trees that are used by bats are protected by legislation, they are sometimes considered dangerous and so it is assumed that they should be felled.

Such action should be discouraged if at all possible, but may be unavoidable when the tree is near to a public place. Advice on how to make such trees safe rather than fell them can be obtained from the Bat Conservation Trust (The BCT leaflet 'Bats and Trees' gives guidance on the management of trees for bats); see also Cowan (2003).

If there is no option other than felling, the tree should be checked carefully for signs of bats. If they are found then the SNCOs must be asked for advice and felling should be delayed until the bats have gone or been removed. Once felled, the roost section should be cut out and strapped to a nearby, sound tree in a similar situation to its original position. If the bats are in the trunk then it is possible that the tree will be safe when reduced to the trunk alone. Try to persuade the owners to leave the trunk standing. Often a tree will become safe if the canopy is reduced or it is pollarded. If bats are present then it would be better to carry out this operation when the bats have left (again negotiate with SNCOs). If bats are in a crack of a branch kept open by stress, care must be taken when cutting so that the crack does not close and crush the bats. Holes may contain bats so care must be taken not to cut into the holes or directly above them. Tree management is best carried out in spring or autumn if bats are to be disturbed as little as possible because this would coincide with the least vulnerable parts of their life cycle. Woodland management should also include management of wide rides with diverse flora to encourage insect diversity.

11.2.5 Liaison with authorities

It is important that bat workers have good working relationships with various bodies involved with trees and woodlands, both public and private. In this way bats are more likely to be considered when tree management work is undertaken. Contacts with planning departments, highway authorities, wildlife trusts, tree wardens and estate managers are all important.

Informal agreements

Voluntary agreement by the landowner or tenant is often an appropriate way of protecting tree roosts. It is most important to ensure that all personnel engaged on woodland management or tree surgery work are made aware of the importance of the roost.

Wildlife and Countryside Act 1981 & Conservation (Natural Habitats &c.) Regulations 1994

Trees that are known to be bat roosts fall within the scope of this legislation, and the SNCO must be consulted before anything is done which would affect the bats or their roost. Deliberate damage or destruction is illegal, but the roost may be destroyed if this is 'the incidental result of a lawful operation and could not reasonably have been avoided' (section 10[3][c]). There could therefore be problems in preventing the destruction of roost trees as part of commercial forestry operations, or if there were a genuine danger of the tree falling down. However, the requirement to consult the SNCO does mean that there is at least an opportunity to put forward proposals to save the site. If clearance for building or development is proposed, the destruction of the roost would need to be covered by a Habitats Regulations licence from the appropriate government department.

Tree Preservation Orders

Tree Preservation Orders (TPOs) are a mechanism whereby local Councils can protect individual trees or groups of trees, particularly for their amenity value. An Order confers some protection on the trees that are specified and the permission of the Council is required before they can be pruned or felled. There seems no reason why known bat roosts should not be covered by a TPO, although trees which are in a dangerous condition may be exempt from the provisions of the Order. TPOs are almost invariably administered through the Planning Department of the District, Borough or City Council, many of which have a Tree or Woodland Officer. When first applied, the Order will run for an interim period of 6 months, during which time objections may be lodged by the landowner or other interested parties. If these are not forthcoming or are not upheld, the Order is confirmed and becomes permanent.

There appears to be no restriction on who can propose trees as candidates for a TPO, although clearly applications from responsible organisations are more likely to succeed. Advice on procedures may be sought from the SNCO or by a direct approach to the local Council.

11

The Hedgerow Regulations (1997)

These regulations protect important hedgerows in England & Wales. Under these regulations no landowner may remove a hedge without permission from the local planning authority. Many criteria are used to decide if a particular hedge is 'important'. One of these criteria is the presence of a species protected under Schedule 5 of the Wildlife and Countryside Act, e.g. all bats. A bat roost occurring within a tree in a hedgerow or a validated record of a roost within the hedgerow in the 5 years prior to the date of any application to remove the hedge would automatically result in the protection of the hedge. While the roost itself is protected under the Wildlife and Countryside Act, the protection of the hedgerow would be important in order to maintain cover and feeding habitat for bats using the roost.

11.2.6 Bat boxes

Bat boxes of many different designs can be erected on trees and buildings to provide roosting opportunities. Boxes are most commonly made of untreated softwoods, but increasingly boxes made of 'woodcrete' (a mixture of wood shavings and cement) are proving to be successful in attracting bats, having the advantages of better thermal insulation and resistance to rot and damage by woodpeckers and squirrels.

The most common design of bat box is that described in Stebbings & Walsh (1991) but a vast array of alternative designs have been field-tested with varying degrees of success. The Bat Conservation Trust publishes a leaflet covering the design and siting of boxes.

Correct siting of bat boxes is important to increase the chances of occupancy. Boxes should be at least 4 metres from the ground and species such as the noctule *Nyctalus noctula* are more likely to be attracted to boxes placed at 5 or 6 metres above ground. As a general rule boxes should be sited with the front facing SW to SE, which will ensure that the box warms up during the day. Boxes facing other aspects may be used and a common practice is to site three boxes on a single tree, all with different aspects, giving bats a choice of roost sites with different environmental conditions.

Occupancy rates of boxes vary, with many factors such as type of box, geographic location, season

and weather conditions influencing a particular bat's choice of roost site. Some bat box schemes in the UK return a 10 % occupancy rate, others 40% and in rare cases 70% or more. Occupancy does not imply long-term usage. Many boxes are used for short periods by a small number of bats. Occasionally boxes are used as maternity sites and impressive numbers of bats (40+) can be found in a single box. Current research suggests that boxes painted black to absorb more solar radiation enhance the internal temperature of the box and therefore make the box more attractive to bats.

Boxes can be erected almost anywhere with some chance of success but results will be significantly better if some thought is given to location. It is also important to make the job of checking the boxes a simple process. Erect boxes where there is easy vehicular access and create a location map of where the numbered boxes are sited. Avoid exposed sites.

Bat boxes should not be seen as an alternative to natural roosting sites such as tree-holes. Bat workers should encourage tree-planting as a long-term solution to lack of natural roost sites. However, boxes are an important resource to bats and have obvious value in conifer plantations, for example they can soon attract bats when sited along rides. They are essentially summer roost sites, standard boxes lacking the required insulating properties to make them suitable as hibernation sites.

Checking bat boxes is also a useful way of introducing potential bat workers to bats. It is simpler than clambering around in a roof space and offers the opportunity for all those participating in the box survey to see a bat with minimal disturbance.

When checking a bat box there are a few important rules to remember:
- Safety is paramount – climbing ladders on uneven ground is risky and the guidelines listed in Chapter 2 of this manual should be adhered to. Safety related to handling bats is also covered in Chapter 2.
- Before opening the box place an empty cloth bag in the exit hole or you will find that half the bats escape.
- Open the box carefully, to ensure that no bats (particularly their feet) are at risk of being trapped by the lid.
- If removing a bat for identification, sexing etc. have a cloth bag to hand with a tie to ensure

that it does not escape from the bag.

- When returning a bat to a box it is generally safer for the bat and easier for the bat worker to encourage the bat back into the box through the base slit rather than placing into the box through the open lid and then closing it.
- Beware of other animals, such as hornet and wasps, which also use bat boxes.

11.3 Bats in bridges

11.3.1 Roosting requirements for bats in bridges

Many bridges have suitable roost crevices for bats offering safety, stable temperature conditions, high humidity, nearby drinking water and feeding areas, and access to linear habitat features used for commuting. The cool, stable conditions found in many bridge crevices are ideal for bats of both sexes roosting in spring and autumn, and for males in summer, when bats may wish to enter daily torpor. Nursery roosts in bridges are presumably heated by the sun due to a southerly aspect or close proximity to the road surface, by the clustering of large numbers of females, or a combination of the two. Bridges with deep crevices may also offer good hibernation sites if they are sufficiently isolated from external temperature fluctuations. Partially blocked arches appear to be particularly suitable as hibernacula. A typical arched bridge design is illustrated in Appendix 1.

All bridges can provide suitable night roosts for resting, eating large prey or socialising. Male pipistrelle bats have used bridges as mating stations (Rydell *et al.*, 1994; Russ, 1995).

A high proportion of stone bridges are suitable for bats, with a smaller proportion of brick, concrete and steel bridges being suitable. The majority of bat roosts occur in crevices in stonework of bridges spanning watercourses. However, roosting sites have been recorded from a wide variety of bridge types.

Bats have been found roosting in gaps between stonework and brickwork; in expansion and construction joints; in drainage holes and pipes; in steelwork and occasionally within large enclosed voids within bridges. A range of crevice sizes are used from 100–1500 mm depth and 13–40 mm width. Daubenton's and Natterer's bats most often use crevices 30–400 mm wide and 300–500 mm deep.

Most bat roosts occur in bridges of at least 1m in height and they have been encountered in sites of up to 460 m altitude. In areas of broad-leaved woodland or slow flowing water there is a greater likelihood of bats using bridges.

Even though a number of bridges have been identified as nursery sites, the majority of bats do not appear to rear their young in bridges. Many bats move to bridges in late August. The highest occupancy of bridges generally occurs in September, although a few sites are used in deep winter.

11.3.2 Maintaining and creating roosts in bridges

Maintaining roosts

Bat roosting sites (crevices/holes) can and have been lost during maintenance and strengthening works on bridges. Engineers have been hesitant to retain voids for fear of creating weaknesses or water entry points and lack of knowledge about the importance of bridges for bats.

Holes in stonework and concrete are infilled by pointing (with concrete mortar), spraying (with gunite or shotcrete concrete) or pressure injection (with cementitous grout). Any of these processes may fill roost crevices and prevent access to other cavities within the bridge. More major works may cause even greater amounts of disturbance and potential death of bats.

Determining the presence of roost sites within a bridge is not always easy, particularly during the winter when there is likely to be little bat activity. Frequently, bridges may be too high or otherwise inaccessible to determine if crevices and holes are being used. However, knowledge of use of bridges by bats within a given area is useful particularly when you know that engineering works are proposed.

Bridges have to be inspected regularly and engineers carrying out the inspection may have the necessary equipment in place such as ladders, scaffolding or a hoist to enable an assessment of likely bat use within the structure. Engineers may also have access to specialised equipment such as fibrescopes which allow optical observation within deep crevices.

It is important to establish a working relationship with council engineering and/or highways

11

departments in cases such as those above but there is also much that can be achieved by bat workers alone. The Conservation of Bats in Bridges Project (Billington & Norman, 1997), found that the greatest occupation of bridges by bats was in the period September–October when dispersed maternit colonies, non-breeding groups and harems may be present along with males using sites as mating stations. However, bats may use bridges at almost any time of year and it is important that timing of maintenance works take into account bat activity at each specific site.

Creating roosts

Where bat roosts in bridges are lost due to demolition, re-building or engineering constraints, new bat roosting sites should be created within the structures, duplicating the original crevice dimensions. Engineers have often suggested fitting a bat box to structures after the works have been completed, but to date no bat box has been confirmed to re-create the same thermal capacity, conductivity and microclimate conditions that would be found deep inside a bridge. Bat boxes are useful in their own right but should not be seen as replacements for a lost bridge roost.

Crevice-width selection by bat species encountered in the Cumbria survey (Billington & Norman, 1997), suggests that any artificial roosting sites should contain a variety of crevice widths (13–70 mm) and depths (350–>1000 mm) for summer roosts, and deeper for winter hibernation sites. Bats generally avoid wider crevices, but they can occasionally roost in open situations on the walls of enclosed voids, for example. Where opportunities arise to incorporate bat roosting crevices into sites during repairs, rebuilds or construction of new sites these should be taken up. If possible, roosting sites should be incorporated into bridge spans because this is where 75% of bat roosts were found in bridges in Cumbria. Otherwise they should be sited as high as possible in the abutment walls. Some examples of bat roosting sites and roost creation techniques are shown in Figure 11.9.

Few ready made artificial roost units are available for use. A bat roost unit consisting of a hollow cube with three open sides is available from Marshalls Clay Products. This is designed to be placed inside a structure and faced with bat access bricks, which have slits to allow bats into a void of 110 mm x 150 mm x 215 mm.

The z-z-z clay bat brick from The Norfolk Bat Group has proved successful in underground sites. Concrete bat boxes of various designs, including a multi-crevice concrete box (by Billington) have been widely used in the UK.

Case histories of bridge maintenance works

Barth Bridge
A single-arch stone bridge with low flood inverts. Major re-pointing and pressure grouting was scheduled for May 1995. Bat signs were discovered in September 1994. Scaffolding was erected 2 weeks ahead of works to take account of any bats present. A detailed survey was carried out using a fibrescope and several bat holes were identified and marked. A site meeting was held with the engineer. A further survey and exclusion (after removing one Daubenton's bat) was carried out at the beginning of June, but due to contractors not following instructions most of the holes were lost.

Rash Bridge
Double-arch stone bridge in which the main roosts of Daubenton's (12) and Natterer's (3) bats are situated in the northern arch. Major re-pointing and pressure grouting works were carried out in 1994 and 1995. Works were delayed after bats were found. A fibrescope survey was carried out from scaffolding on the southern arch. Several bat holes were marked and successfully retained, some more than 700 mm deep. Works were delayed on the northern arch until May 1995 (in case hibernating bats were present). Holes were surveyed with a fibrescope and marked. Problems arose because some of the bat holes extended upwards for almost 1 metre. English Nature contracted an independent engineer to produce a report on retaining deep crevices. Before works on the northern arch were carried out several bats had to be excluded. Daubenton's bats were observed at the bridge in 1995 but Natterer's bats do not seem to have returned.

Examples of roost creation within bridges

Figure 11.10a-g show examples of roost creation from various sites. Cambeck footbridge was a new bridge of steel and concrete deck over stone faced abutments. Roost crevices were incorporated into the abutments (Figure 11.10g/h). At Fort Augustus, Inverness, Forest Enterprise drew up a design for an artificial roost site for their Civil Engineers. The roost was built into a bridge abutment about 650 mm above water level. The roost cavity is approximately 450 mm cubed and has a layer of bricks on the outside face with access slits between the brickwork. Drainage holes of 6-mm diameter were incorporated into the wall. The interior was filled with loose rock (Figure 11.10e/f). No bat use has yet been confirmed.

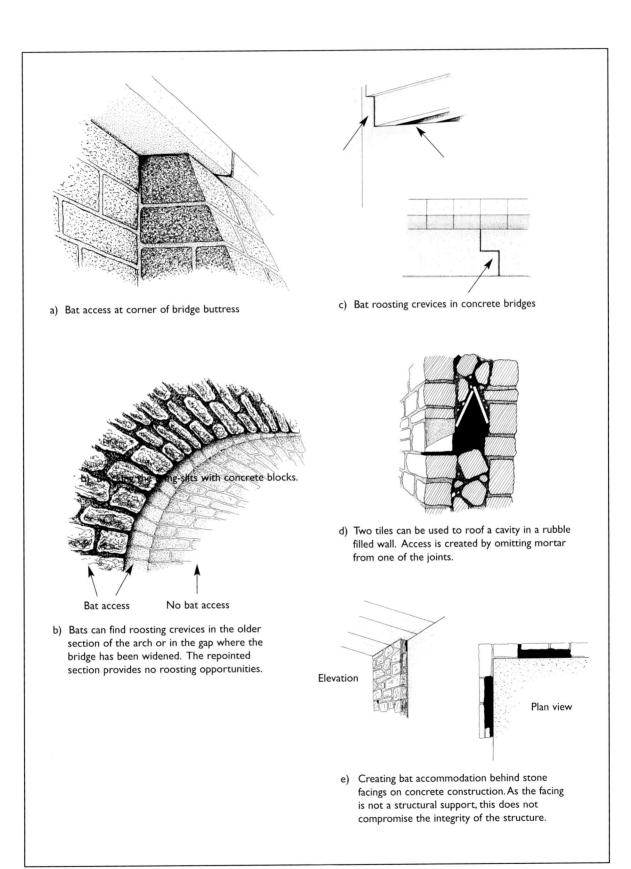

a) Bat access at corner of bridge buttress

c) Bat roosting crevices in concrete bridges

b) Bats can find roosting crevices in the older section of the arch or in the gap where the bridge has been widened. The repointed section provides no roosting opportunities.

Bat access   No bat access

d) Two tiles can be used to roof a cavity in a rubble filled wall. Access is created by omitting mortar from one of the joints.

Elevation

Plan view

e) Creating bat accommodation behind stone facings on concrete construction. As the facing is not a structural support, this does not compromise the integrity of the structure.

Figure 11.9
Bats in bridges

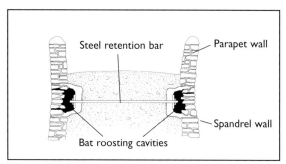

Figure 11.10a
Vertical cross-section of bat roosting cavities created during spandrel wall retention works (redrawn from Turner (1995)).

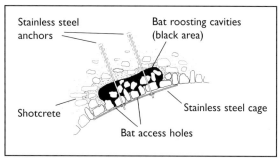

Figure 11.10b
Vertical cross-section of bat roosting cavities constructed by excavating into the underside of the archway (redrawn from Turner (1995)).

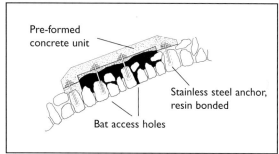

Figure 11.10c
Details of pre-formed roost unit fitted over arch stones during saddling works (redrawn from Turner (1995)).

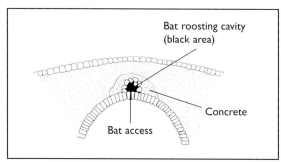

Figure 11.10d
Details of bat roosting cavity created at Garsdale Church Bridge during saddling works (designed by Billington & Donnison).

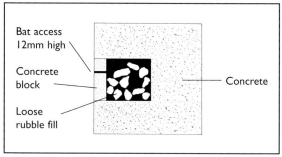

Figure 11.10e
Vertical section of bat roost built into a Forest Enterprise bridge abutment (redrawn from Whittaker (unpub.)).

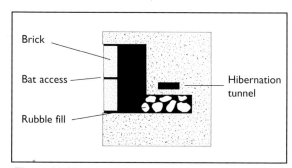

Figure 11.10f
Design modification of Figure 11.10e (redrawn from Whittaker (unpub.)).

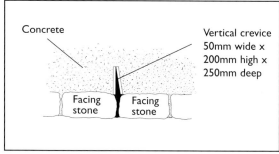

Figure 11.10g
Bat roosting crevice created during Cambeck footbridge construction (horizontal section through abutment).

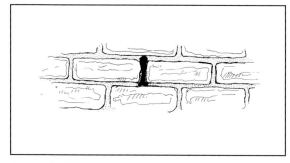

Figure 11.10h
External view of bat roost crevice shown in Figure 11.10g.

References and further reading

ANON. 1997. *Bats and trees: a guide to the management of trees*. The Bat Conservation Trust, London.

BILLINGTON, G.E. & NORMAN, G.M. 1997. *The conservation of bats in bridges project – a report on the survey and conservation of bat roosts in Cumbria*. COBIB/EN.

COWAN, A. 2003. *Trees and bats*. Arboricultural Association Guidance Note 1 (2nd edn). Arboricultural Association, Romsey. 64 pp. ISBN 0 900978 37 6.

GREENAWAY, F.R. 1990. *Converting a pill box*. Surrey Wildlife Trust, Dorking. 2 pp.

HIGHWAYS AGENCY. 1999. *Design Manual for Roads and Bridges, Vol 10, Environmental Design*. Section 1, The good roads guide – new roads Part 8. HA 80/99, Nature Conservation Management in Relation to Bats. Stationery Office, London. 36 pp. ISBN 0 11 552130 5.

HUTSON, A.M. 1995. Conservation of bats in the management of ancient monuments. *In: Managing Ancient Monuments: An Integrated Approach*, pp 71–78. Clwyd County Council, Clwyd. 238 pp. ISBN 0 900121 998.

HUTSON, A.M., MICKLEBURGH, S. & MITCHELL-JONES, A.J. 1995. *Bats underground: a conservation code*. 2nd edn. The Bat Conservation Trust, London. 6 pp. ISBN 0 872745 20 2.

MAYLE, B.A. 1990. *A biological basis for bat conservation in British woodlands – a review*. Mammal Review, **20(4)**, 159–195.

MAYLE, B.A. 1990. *Habitat management for woodland bats*. Research Information Note 165. Forestry Commission.

ROBERTS, G.M. & HUTSON, A.M. 1993. *Bat boxes: how to make them and where to put them*. The Bat Conservation Trust, London. 4 pp. ISBN 1 872745 18 0.

RUSS, J.M.R. 1995. *Bats, bridges and acoustic signalling*. Thesis, University of Aberdeen.

RYDELL, J., BUSHBY, A., COSGROVE, C.C. & RACEY, P.A. 1994. Habitat use by bats along rivers in North-east Scotland. *Folia Zoologica*, **43(4)**, 417–424.

STEBBINGS, R.E. & WALSH, S.T. 1991. *Bat boxes: a guide to the history, function, construction and use in the conservation of bats*. The Bat Conservation Trust, London. 25 pp. ISBN 1 872745 02 4.

TURNER, N. 1995. *Practical engineering and environmental problems associated with the strengthening of rubble filled masonry bridges inhabited by bats: including suggestions for measures compatible with the engineering solution and the preservation of bat roosts*. Unpublished report to English Nature.

WHITAKER, S. 1995. *Natural heritage interest of roads verges and bridges in Highland Region: a pilot study report to SNH North West Region*. Internal report. Scottish Natural Heritage, Inverness.

Daubenton's bat by a bridge. © Frank Greenaway

11

Greater mouse-eared bat. © Frank Greenaway

Appendix 1

Glossary of architectutral terms

Abutment	The end supports of a bridge or other structure
Aisle	Part of a church flanking the nave
Apse	Semicircular or polygonal end of a chancel or chapel
Architrave	Moulded frame surrounding door or window
Ashlar	Dressed stone with square edges
Balustrade	Series of small pillars supporting a handrail or coping
Bargeboards	Projecting boards on the sloping sides of the roof at the gable ends concealing the ends of the horizontal roof timbers
Barrel vault	Continuous plain semicircular or pointed arch
Battens	Horizontal timbers across the rafters to which the roof covering is fixed
Batter	A wall with an inclined face
Battlement (also crenellation)	Parapet with alternating indentations and raised portions
Bearing plate	Separates the main girder of a bridge from the impost of the abutment or pier
Bellcote	Turret in which the bells are found, usually at the west end of the church
Braces	Diagonal subsidiary timbers strengthening the frame of a roof and connecting a tie-beam with the wall below or a collar-beam with the rafters below
Bressumer	A large horizontal beam spanning a wide opening; the main horizontal beam in a timber-framed building
Buttress	A mass of masonry built against a wall to give added strength
Campanile	Isolated bell tower
Canopy	Decorated covering over pulpit, altar etc.
Castellated	Durmounted by battlements or turrets
Cavity wall	External wall built with two leaves, usually of brick or blockwork, separated by a gap or cavity 50 mm wide
Cellarium	Medieval Latin for a cellar or storeroom
Chancel	The east end of the church, where the altar is located; generally all that part of the church east of the crossing
Chancel arch	Arch at the west end of the chancel
Chantry chapel	Chapel attracted to or inside a church
Clerestory	Upper part of the walls of a church nave with windows above the roofs of the aisles; sometimes there is a narrow wall passage on the inside of the clerestory
Collar-beam	A horizontal beam connecting the rafters inside a roof; it is found higher up the slope of the roof than a tie-beam
Coom	The sloping part of the ceiling within an attic room
Coom space	The small triangular roof space below and behind a coom
Corbel	A projecting block, normally of stone, supporting a beam

Cornice	Any projecting ornamental moulding on the top of a building or in a room
Coursed rubble	Undressed stone laid in courses like bricks. The uneven gaps are packed with mortar
Cover flashing	A flashing that waterproofs a junction between, e.g. a roof pitch and a vertical surface such as a chimney
Coving	Concave moulding at the junction between wall and ceiling
Crenellation	See battlement
Crossing	Space where the nave, chancel and transepts of a church meet
Crowsteps	These perform a similar function to skews but are formed from smaller squarish blocks of stone, giving a stepped appearance to the top of the gable
Cupola	A small dome crowning a roof or turret
Cutwater	Additional footing added to a bridge pier at water level
Doorcase	The case lining a doorway, on which the door is hung
Dressings	Stonework in dressed blocks around doorways, windows and the corners of buildings
Dripstone	A projecting mould above an arch, doorway, window or other feature of a building
Eaves	The lowest part of a pitched roof, and its junction with the wall
Extrados	The upper curve of an arch
Facing	A dressed timber finishing piece, edging the face, e.g. a door hatching or opening
Fascia	Board on edge, running horizontally and fixed to the ends of the rafters; the guttering is screwed to this
Flashings	Strips of metal, usually lead, used on roofs to protect joints against damp
Fluting	Channelling running vertically up a column
Gable	The triangular upper portion of an end wall supporting a pitched roof
Gallery	Upper storey above an aisle, sometimes with arches looking into nave
Girder	A large longitudinal beam, frequently of steel
Haunches	Shoulders of an arch barrel between the arch spring and crown
Hip	The external angle formed by the meeting of two sloping roofs
Hipped roof	A roof with sloped rather than vertical ends
Hip rafters	The two ridge boards running in an inverted 'V' shape between the ridge and the eaves to form the hipped end of a roof
Impost	Upper stone course of a pier or abutment below the springing line, sometimes decorated with a moulded rim
Intrados	The inner curve of an arch
Jack rafters	Shortened rafters fastened between the eaves and the hip rafters
Jamb	Straight side of door, window or arch
Joists	Horizontal timbers to support ceilings, floors or both
Keystone	The central stone of a voussoir ring, sometimes larger than the rest

King-post	A vertical post standing on the collar- or tie-beam and reaching to the ridge to support it
Lintel	Single solid piece of concrete, steel, stone or timber built over an opening to support the wall above
Mansard roof	A ridged roof with the lower half of the ridge at a very steep angle
Mullion	A vertical division of a window or other opening, usually of stone
Narthex	Covered porch at main entrance to a church
Nave	Principal part of a church, seating the congregation, often flanked by one or two aisles
Nogging	Brick infill between timbers in a half-timbered building
Pantile	An 'S'-shaped roofing tile
Parapet wall	External wall of a building extended above the roof line and exposed on both sides
Parvis	Room over church porch, often for Sunday school
Pier	A solid masonry support; square or rectangular in section, unlike a column, which is circular
Portico	A roofed space forming the entrance of a house, church or temple; it is generally open or partly enclosed
Precast	Material (concrete) shaped in moulds before being built into a structure
Presbytery	The part of the church east of the choir
Pre-stressed	Concrete given tensile strength before exposure to loads
Pulpitum	A rood screen made of stone in a large church
Purlins	Continuous timbers running horizontally on the underside of the rafters just above the collar-beam (if present)
Puttock hole	Hole in wall into which beam or joist end fits
Queen-post	One of a pair of vertical posts located close to the ends of a tie-beam or collar-beam and connecting it to the rafters above
Quoins	Dressed stones at the outside angles of a building, often arranged so that their faces are alternately large and small
Rafter	Timber set at an angle to form a pitched roof and bearing on the wall-plate at the bottom and fastened to the ridge-board at the top
Rainwater head	A box-shaped structure at the top of a down pipe to collect water from a gutter
Reinforced	Concrete with steel bars incorporated
Reredos	Decorated structure behind and above an altar
Ridge-board	A horizontal board at the peak of a roof to which the rafters are attached
Rocaille	An outdoor artificial grotto decorated with stones or shells
Rood loft	Gallery provided for singers above the rood screen
Rood screen	Partition, usually of wood, between the nave and chancel of a church
Rood stairs	Stairs for reaching a rood loft
Sarking	Boarding or other covering under a slate roof
Shingles	Wooden tiles used to clad roofs, walls and spires

Skews	Large flat stones laid on the exposed top edges of a gable to finish the junction between wallhead and roof
Soffit	The underside of any architectural feature; the horizontal board under the eaves; the under surface of an arch
Spandrel	The courses of masonry over an arch ring, which extend up to the parapet and out to the abutments
Springing	The lowest point on an arch
Strapping	Timber framing on the inside face of a masonry wall, carrying the internal lining such as plasterboard
Stringcourse	A continuous projecting band in the surface of a wall
Strutting	Timber nailed between joists to prevent twisting
Tie-beam	A horizontal transverse beam connecting the ends of the rafters
Tilting fillet	A small triangular-sectioned timber running horizontally along on top of the sarking boards, just above the eaves, used to tilt up the bottom coarse of slates
Torching	Rough plasterwork, often incorporating horsehair, on the underside of slates or tiles
Transept	Transverse part of cross-shaped church
Truss	A number of timbers framed together to bridge a gap; modern roofs are often built with a trussed rafter construction
Tympanum	Space between the lintel over a door and the arch above it
Undercroft	Vaulted room, often underground beneath a church or chapel
Valley	The horizontal gutter at the base of the slopes of two parallel ridges or the gutter running from the ridge to the eaves at the internal angle formed when two ridges meet at right-angles
Vault	The roof curve of an arch
Verge	The exposed side edge of a roof, e.g. at a gable
Voussoir	The half circle of stones forming the outer edge of an arch
Wall-plate	A beam laid along the top of a wall to which the ends of the rafters are fixed
Weather-boarding	Horizontal boards overlapped to cover a timber-framed wall
Wind-braces	Short braces of timber, sometimes arched, fixed across the slope of the roof to strengthen it against wind
Wingwall	A continuation of the abutment side walls of a bridge

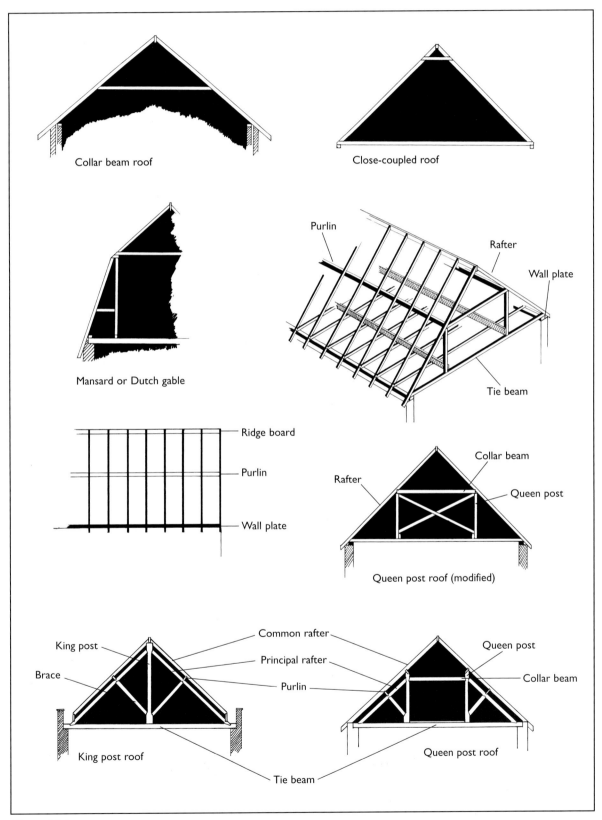

Figure A1.1
Roof types. Many variations are possible, but the basic
components, such as rafters and purlins, can usually be identified.

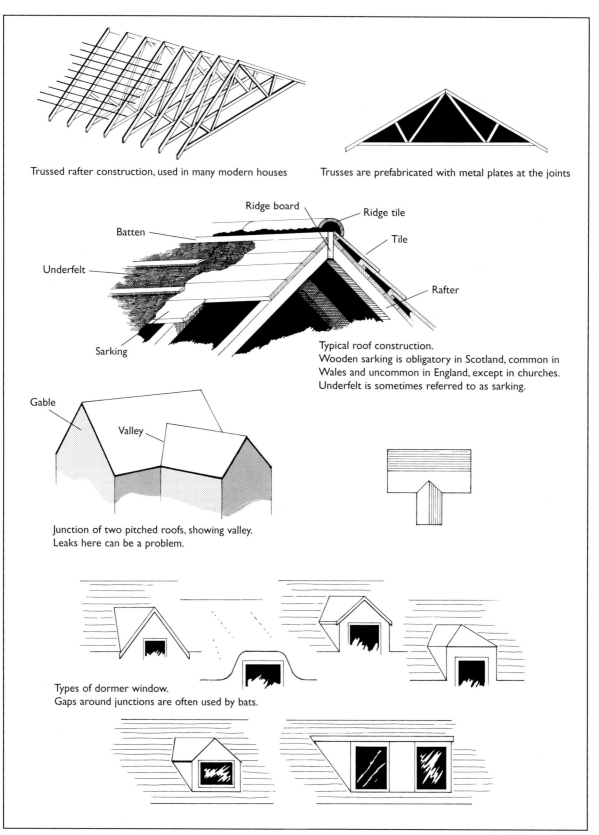

Trussed rafter construction, used in many modern houses

Trusses are prefabricated with metal plates at the joints

Ridge board

Ridge tile

Batten

Tile

Underfelt

Rafter

Sarking

Typical roof construction.
Wooden sarking is obligatory in Scotland, common in Wales and uncommon in England, except in churches. Underfelt is sometimes referred to as sarking.

Gable

Valley

Junction of two pitched roofs, showing valley.
Leaks here can be a problem.

Types of dormer window.
Gaps around junctions are often used by bats.

Figure A1.1
(continued)

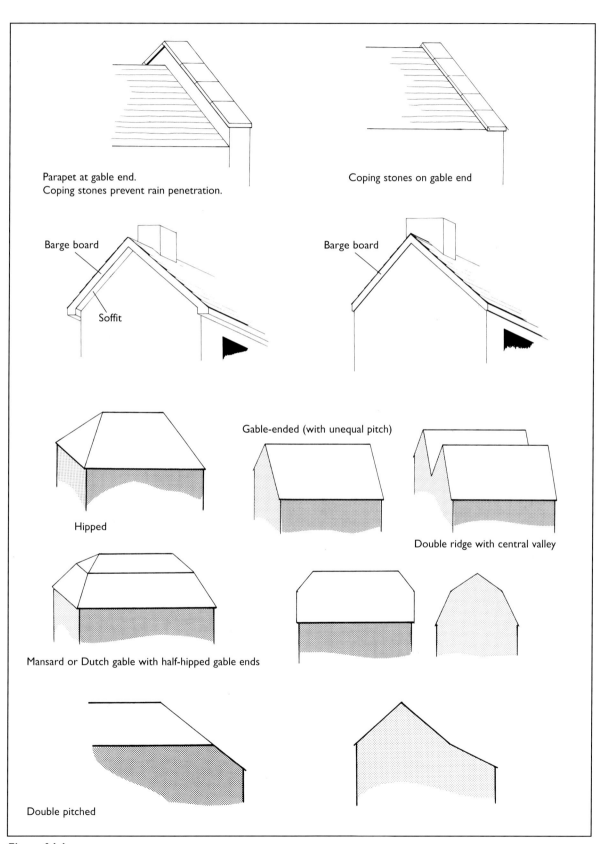

Parapet at gable end.
Coping stones prevent rain penetration.

Coping stones on gable end

Barge board

Soffit

Barge board

Gable-ended (with unequal pitch)

Hipped

Double ridge with central valley

Mansard or Dutch gable with half-hipped gable ends

Double pitched

Figure A1.1
(continued)

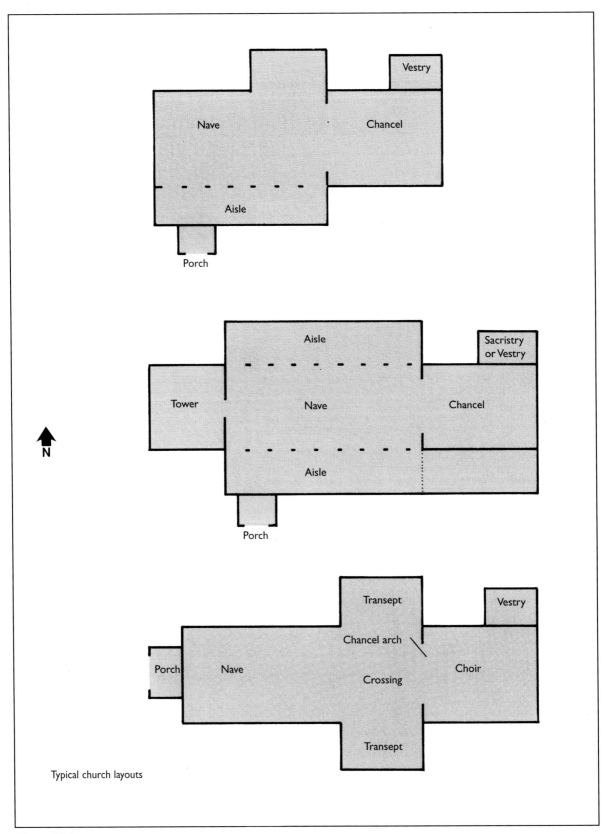

Typical church layouts

Figure A1.1
(continued)

Appendix 2

Glossary of caving and mining terms

Abseiling	Technique of sliding down a fixed rope in a controlled manner, usually using a special friction device (descender)
Adit	Horizontal or near horizontal tunnel in a mine with one end at the surface
Belay	Natural or artificial anchorage point for ropes or ladders
To belay	To attach to an anchorage point/to safeguard a person in transit by means of a lifeline
Belay belt	Waist belt suitable for attaching belaying rope to
Bolt	Device fitted into a drilled hole in the rock to make a belay point; may be an expansion device (spit or possibly Rawlbolt) or fixed with epoxy resin (ECO bolt)
Bridging	The situation where there is a void beneath an apparently solid floor within a mine (see false floor)
Carbide lamp	An acetylene gas lamp (unsuitable for use where bats are present or expected)
To cap	To seal off a shaft access
Cross cut	A level driven in barren rock, at an angle to a vein, for access or exploration
Day level	See adit
Deads	Waste rock associated with a mining operation, left inside a mine
Descender	Mechanical device used for abseiling
Dip	The angle of tilt of rock strata
Electron ladder	Modern form of flexible caving ladder with alloy rungs and steel wire sides; can be coiled
False floor	Usually of timber, often covered by deads and/or mud to give the impression of being solid
Fathom	Distance equivalent to six feet, often in old mine measurements
Fault	Fracture line in rock
Galena	Lead ore
Ginging	Stone or brick walling supporting loose ground around the top of a shaft; often unstable
Grille	Used to restrict access to a mine opening by humans, but not bats
Hanger	Re-usable attachments for bolts
Hanging wall	Wall or side overhanging a stope
Karabiner	Metal snap-link, usually oval, used for fastening ropes, ladders etc.
Krab	See karabiner
Level	Horizontal or near horizontal tunnel in a mine, usually driven from a shaft
Lifelining	Technique of securing the safety of a person in transit by means of a secure rope, kept taut by the lifeliner
Lode	A vein containing mineral ore
Mine	Place where mineral ore successfully extracted by use of tunnelling methods

Oldham lamp	Popular make of lead-acid powered cap lamp
Ore	Rock containing extractable mineral content
Pitch	Vertical ascent/descent
Prusiking	Technique used to climb up a fixed rope using mechanical gripping devices or special gripping knots
Rise	Underground shaft excavated upwards into the roof of a level or chamber
Run-in	A shaft or adit, which has been filled by fallen material but not systematically, hence there may be danger of bridging beneath apparently firm surface
Seam	See vein
Shaft	A vertical or near vertical penetration from the surface
Single rope techniques (SRT)	Those applied in the descent (abseil) or ascent (prusik) of a fixed rope on a pitch
Slide	A traverse fault
Sling	Webbing loop for main belay or improvised sit-harness
Sough	Drainage tunnel from a mine
Stalactite	Underground formation hanging from the roof
Stalagmite	Underground formation growing up from the floor
Static rope	A relatively inelastic rope, used for underground exploration purposes (not the same as climbing rope)
Stope	Cavity made by removal of ore; often a near vertical slit; if near horizontal may be called a flat
Sump (1)	A passage completely filled with water
Sump (2)	An underground shaft designed to collect water (for subsequent pumping)
Swl	Safe working load as stamped on underground equipment or specified for rope
Trial	Tunnel into the ground with the intention of extracting mineral ore but without success
Vein	A relatively narrow zone of rock geologically younger than its surroundings, often in a fissure or fault
Winze	A shaft dropping from the floor of a level

Appendix 3

Special forms

Bat Roost Visit Report Form

This was designed as a report form for volunteers or staff to complete after visiting a bat roost but can also be used as a record or survey card by Bat Groups.

Side 1: Roost details

1 **Name and address.**
The main entry here should be the address or location of the roost. This is usually straightforward for roosts in buildings, but for other roosts, such as mines, caves, ice-houses or trees, try to give a name (if appropriate) and a locality. Locality is usually the nearest place name on the Ordnance Survey map. If others are involved, for example builders or roofers, give addresses as appropriate and indicate who is the main contact.

2 **Grid reference.**
This is particularly important for non-building roosts but is required for all. Always try to give a reference with two letters and six figures (a six-figure reference - accurate to 100 m) but a four-figure reference is better than nothing.

3 **Roost type.**
The checklist will cover the majority of roosts, but use the space provided to add details if necessary or to describe unusual roosts.

4 **Age.**
For most buildings it should be possible to give some idea of age, even if it is to the nearest century. The newer a building is, the easier it should be to age it accurately.

5&6 Wall construction/roof covering.
These questions cover the most obvious physical characteristics of buildings that are likely to affect their use by bats. The checklists should cover most situations, but expand if necessary.

7 **Position of bat access point(s).**
This can be difficult to determine unless bats are seen emerging or droppings are found stuck to a wall. The checklist gives the most common possibilities but it will frequently be necessary to describe the access in more detail. The height above ground and facing direction (aspect) are important in characterising the sorts of places that bats prefer.

8 **Bats' roosting site(s).**
In roof voids or similar open areas, the roosting position can be determined by the presence of bats, by the position of accumulations of droppings or by staining or polishing on the woodwork. Bats roosting in enclosed areas, such as under gables, in caves, between felt and tiles, or in wall cavities, are more difficult to locate, but noise, droppings or proximity to entrance holes may give clues.

9 **Number of bats.**
Counts at emergence or possibly in the roost are most valuable, but even an estimate will give some idea of the size of the colony.

10 **Species.**
A specimen seen in the hand or at close quarters by an experienced observer is preferred, but identifications from droppings or bat detectors are worth recording, though these are not accepted by all recording schemes.

11 **Droppings.**
These can give information about the location and possibly the size of the colony, though the latter must be interpreted with caution.

12 **Other information.**
Any other relevant information should be given, perhaps from the owner of the building.

13 **Other visits.**
This is a space for surveyors to record other counts.

Side 2: Details of problems

14 **Description of problem.**
A brief description should be given of why advice about bats was sought and what the problems appear to be.

15 **Is there any threat to roost?**
This will follow on from 14. If the householder has been persuaded to take no action that would affect bats, note this here; otherwise make the nature of the threat clear.

16 **Attitude of owners.**
The conservation of bat roosts depends largely on the goodwill of owners and their attitude can be very important where maintenance or reinstatement of the roost may be suggested.

17 **Recommendations.**
Experienced volunteers will be able to suggest what advice should be given. This is very helpful to SNCO staff who have no first-hand knowledge of the situation. If there are special difficulties or complications, please note these here.

18 **Sketch.**
Even the most rudimentary sketch can be more helpful than a written description. Plan views of properties, with an indication of north, are probably easiest, but elevations can illustrate some problems better. Identify buildings clearly on large or complex properties.

19 **Names and dates.**
Please ensure that this section is always completed. The first part is useful in tracing the history of an enquiry; the second gives a contact if further information is required.

Bat roost visit report form

1 Name and address of roost and owner.
Give contact address if different.
If timber treatment firm or builder is
involved, give address.

For caves, mines etc, give name
and/ or locality.

_____

_____

_____

_____

_____

_____

2 Grid reference: (2letters, 6 figures)   Phone number(s):

3 Roost type: House/Church/Institution/Barn/Stables/Farm building/Ruin/Mine/Cave/Tunnel/Tree/Other(specify)

(Give further details)

4 Age:

5 Wall construction: Brick/Stone/Block/Wood/Other   Cladding: Wood/Tile/Slate/Other(specify)

Solid/cavity wall   Hanging tiles: Yes/No

6 Roof covering: Tile/Slate/Shingle/Stone/Thatch/Corrugated iron/Asbestos/Other(specify)

Lined with underfelt/Boards/Nothing/Other(specify)   Loft insulation: Present/Absent

7 Position of bat access point(s): Gable apex/Under soffit/Between tiles/Under flashing/Other(specify)

Height above ground: Facing direction (aspect):

8 Bats' roosting site(s): Under eaves/In roof apex/Under slates/Behind cladding/Other(specify)

9 Number if bats at date and time of visit:
Count or estimate?

10 Species: Indicate how identified and by whom

11 Droppings: If present, indicate quantity and distribution (depth and area)
(also on sketch overleaf)

Are droppings fresh or old?

12 Other Information: History of the colony/problem. Is use seasonal? etc.

13 Other visits: (dates and counts)

Circle choices: give further details if appropriate.

Summary and recommendations

14 **Description of problem:** Dropping/Intolerance/Fear/Smell/Noise/Bats in living area/Other

15 **Is there any threat to roost:** Exclusion/Timber treatment/Building work/Development/Destruction?

BCT survey?

16 **Attitude of owners:**

17 **Recommendations for action by the SNCO:**

18 **Sketch:**

19 **Request to visit received from:**   on:

Initial visit made by: on:

Biological Records Centre Single species card

The Biological Records Centre at the Centre for Ecology and Hydrology is the largest species recording centre in Britain. For bats, records should be submitted on the single species card illustrated.

Completion of the form is straightforward. Although the space for grid reference is ruled for four-figure references, six figures are preferred if possible. Locality should refer to the nearest place name on the Ordnance Survey map.

Nature of record should describe briefly how the identification was made so that the mammal recorder can judge whether the record is acceptable. Records based on droppings or bat detectors are not normally accepted.

Supplies of the cards are available free from Mr H. R. Arnold at BRC, CEH Monks Wood, Abbots Ripton, Huntingdon, Cambs PE28 2LS.
Website: http://www.brc.ac.uk/

MAMMALS	Species Pipistrellus pipistrellus				Year(s) 1998	Species no.
Recorder's name B. Wayne					Code no.	

Address: 'Horseshoes'
Hollotree Lane
Batsford, Gloucestershire

Grid reference					Vice county	Locality	Nature of record
100 Km	East		North				
SU	2 7	1	3 3	2		Horseshoe Hill, Hants	Seen in roost
SE	2	3	2	4		Batley, W. Yorks	In hand
SX	6 6	6	8 6	0		Batworthy, Devon	In hand
TA	3	1	2	8		Batty's Corner, Lincs.	In hand
SD	7 0	0	0 7	7		Duabhill, Greater Manchester	In hand
SJ	1	9	4	7		Horseshoe Pass, Clwyd	In hand

Please return to: **Biological Records Centre**
Monks Wood Experimental Station
Abbots Ripton, Huntingdon
PE17 2LS

RA 12

Appendix 4

The National Bat Monitoring Programme (NBMP)

The Bat Conservation Trust

Background

Measuring changes in bat populations is an important task for bat conservation. Only when we have precise information about the magnitude and direction of changes can we gain warning of threats to species, identify conservation priorities and advise on effective conservation action.

The National Bat Monitoring Programme began in 1996 and is run by The Bat Conservation Trust. The broad aim of the programme is to develop and implement long-term monitoring schemes for all species of bat resident in the UK. The programme, initially funded by DETR (now Defra) until 2000, now receives core funding from the JNCC and helps to fulfil the government's commitment to the Agreement on the Conservation of Populations of European Bats.

The programme relies on volunteer surveyors to collect data throughout the UK. Projects are designed to deliver population trend data, within defined confidence limits, using simple methods. Bat-detector training workshops are run throughout the summer to increase the skill's base of surveyors.

Monitoring Methods

Three main monitoring strategies are employed. with a number of projects run within each strategy. Some species are monitored on two projects.
* Summer colony counts
* Hibernation counts
* Bat-detector-based field projects

Bat species	SC	WH	F
Greater horseshoe		✓	
Lesser horseshoe	✓	✓	
Daubenton's		✓	✓
Natterer's	✓	✓	
Serotine	✓		✓
Noctule	✓		✓
Common pipistrelle	✓		✓
Soprano pipistrelle	✓		✓
Brown long-eared	✓	✓	

SC = summer colony counts   WH = winter hibernation counts
F = field counts using bat detectors

In addition, the Sunrise Survey project is a multi-species survey designed to find bat roosts.

Colony counts

Relevant species: lesser horseshoe, Natterer's, common pipistrelle, soprano pipistrelle, serotine and brown long-eared.

Two counts are needed in mid June. Complete counting packs, which contain protocols and recording sheets, are sent to volunteers. Householders playing host to colonies are an important source of potential counters. Involvement of roost owners is a positive conservation action because it highlights the importance of the colony as part of a national monitoring scheme.

For more difficult species, such as horseshoes and Natterer's, more experienced counters are needed. These species tend to emerge late in low light levels, often make repeated short flights before emerging and can use multiple exits. Groups of volunteers are needed to cover all potential exit points and bat detectors are recommended to help gauge activity and behaviour. Roosts of Natterer's bat are often found in trees, bridges, barns and churches, and successful counts require more effort than house-dwelling species.

Standardised instruction and recording sheets are produced for each survey.

Hibernation counts

Relevant species: Greater & lesser horseshoe, Daubenton's, Natterer's and brown long-eared bat.

Many hibernation sites have been visited regularly since the 1960s. Surveyors require a licence from the relevant SNCO before entering sites in winter. For the monitoring programme surveyors are asked to make two visits – one in the middle of January and the other in the middle of February. Standard recording sheets together with guidelines are sent to all hibernation licensees. Although the monitoring strategy is aimed at the five species named above, all bats encountered in sites are recorded. Surveyors can choose which sites to survey but it is important to stress for monitoring purposes that sites with few bats (or even sites of potential usage with no bats) are of equal importance to sites with large numbers of bats and should be visited where possible. The majority of hibernation sites in the UK contain few bats but if hundreds of these sites are monitored conclusions on population trends can be made.

Standardised instruction and recording sheets are produced and sent to all licensees.

Field counts

Relevant species: Daubenton's, common pipistrelle, soprano pipistrelle, serotine and noctule.

Monitoring bats at night in the field with bat detectors provides important information on the relative abundance and distribution of each species. A bat detector is required and some previous experience is necessary because surveyors are asked to distinguish species. No licence is required. Surveyors are assigned a 1-km square or 1-km waterway stretch, selected randomly (in proportion to different landscape types) and asked to walk a route on two evenings during July or August. They are requested to record bats while walking or to stop at points for a fixed period to record bat activity. Surveyors are asked to visit the square during the day to record some habitat details and to plan their route.

Standardised instruction and recording sheets are produced for each survey.

Sunrise Survey

Relevant species: All.

This survey is primarily aimed at new surveyors because no equipment or previous bat experience is required for participation. The objective of the survey is to identify roosts that can then be incorporated into the colony count project. Participants are asked to identify a potential bat structure (building, tree, bridge etc) or walk a 1-km transect in July, starting at 45 minutes before sunrise. Surveyors look for bats 'swarming' outside roost entrances to identify a site as a roost.

Feedback

All participants in the monitoring programme receive free copies of the programme's newsletter *Bat Monitoring Post*. This provides results from surveys once data has been collected and analysed, gives advance warnings of future surveys, and contains tips and feedback from the office and field surveyors.

Participation and experience required

The UK is fortunate in having over 90 local Bat Groups throughout the UK. Groups vary in size and activities, but all have a broad commitment to bat conservation and the majority of contributors to the monitoring programme are local Bat Group members. Some individual projects require little or no previous bat experience while others are restricted to experienced bat workers. The NBMP runs a number of training sessions in the use of bat detectors.

If you would like to participate in the National Bat Monitoring Programme please visit our website www.bats.org.uk or if you would like some more information please contact:

NBMP
The Bat Conservation Trust
15 Cloisters House
8 Battersea Park Road
London
SW8 4BG

Tel: 0207 627 2629
Fax: 0207 627 2628
E-mail: nbmp@bats.org.uk

Appendix 5

A selected bibliography

The following is a classified list of publications, which will enable anyone quickly to find their way around the world of bats. Nearly all have bibliographies or reference lists amounting to many hundreds of publications about bats.

Most of the books on this list are readily obtainable through libraries, and many are in print and may be purchased. A few may be difficult to obtain or out of print, in which case contact with university libraries or other specialist institutions will help.

Readers who are looking for recent titles or who wish for a comprehensive listing of books should review the Natural History Book Service website. The Bat Conservation Trust maintains a list of British books and leaflets on bats. For a longer listing of educational resources Bat Conservation International maintains a comprehensive list on its web site.

A   European bats – identification, biology, distribution and conservation

AHLEN, I. 1990. *Identification of bats in flight*. Swedish Society for Conservation of Nature and The Swedish Youth Association for Environmental Studies and Conservation. 50 pp. ISBN 91 558 50421.

ALLEN, P., FORSYTH, I., HALE, P. & ROGERS, S. 2000. Bats in Northern Ireland. *The Irish Naturalist's Journal*, Special Zoological Supplement. 33 pp. ISSN 0021 1311.

ALTRINGHAM, J.D. 1996. *Bats– Biology and Behaviour*. Oxford University Press, Oxford. 262 pp. ISBN 0 19 854075 2.

ALTRINGHAM, J.D. 2003. *British Bats*. New Naturalist Series 93, Harper Collins, London. 218 pp. ISBN 0 00 2201 40 2 (hb), 0 00 2201 47 X (pb).

BAAGØE, H.J. 2001. Danish Bats (Mammalia: Chiroptera): Atlas and analysis of distribution, occurrence and abundance. *Steenstrupia*, **26**(1), 1–117. ISSN 0375 2909.

BARATAUD, M. 1996 *Ballades dans l'inaudible - the inaudible world*. Sitelle, Mens. (Double CD, ref no 11706, plus 47-page booklet *The World of Bats*.)

BARRETT-HAMILTON, G.E.H. & HINTON, M.A.C. 1910–21. *A History of British Mammals*. Gurney and Jackson, London.

BRIGGS, B. & KING, D. 1998. *The Bat Detective*. Stag Electronics, Shoreham-by-Sea. ISBN 0 953242 60 9. (Field guide for bat detectors plus a CD of British bat calls).

CATTO, C. 1994. *Bat detector manual*. The Bat Conservation Trust, London. 34pp .

CORBET, G.B. 1978. *The Mammals of the Palaearctic Region: a taxonomic review*. British Museum (Natural History), London. 314 pp. ISBN 0 8014 1171 8. (& supplement 1984.)

CORBET, G.B. & HARRIS, S. 1991. *The Handbook of British Mammals*. Published for the Mammal Society by Blackwell Scientific Publications, Oxford. 588 pp. ISBN 0 632 01691 4.

ENTWISTLE, A.C., HARRIS, S., HUTSON, A.M., RACEY, P.A., WALSH, A., GIBSON, S.D., HEPBURN, I. & JOHNSTON, J. 2002. *Habitat Management for Bats*. JNCC, Peterborough. 47 pp. ISBN 1 86107 528 6.

GREENAWAY, F. & HUTSON, A.M. 1990. *A Field Guide to British Bats*. Bruce Coleman, London. 52 pp. (Available only from The Bat Conservation Trust.) ISBN 1 872842 003.

HARBUSCH, C., ENGEL, E. & PIR, J.B. 2002. Die Fledermause Luxemburgs. *Ferrantia, Travaux Scientifiques du Musee National d'Histoire Naturelle Luxembourg*, **33**, 1–149. ISSN 1682 5519.

HARRIS, S., MORRIS, P.A., WRAY, S. & YALDEN, D. 1995. *A review of British mammals: population estimates and conservation status of British mammals other than cetaceans*. JNCC, Peterborough. 168 pp. ISBN 1 873701 68 3.

HOWARD, R.W. 1995. *Auritus - a natural history of the brown long-eared bat*. William Sessions Ltd, York. 154 pp. ISBN 1 85072 168 8.

HUTSON, A.M. 1987. *Bats in Houses*. The Bat Conservation Trust, London. 32 pp. ISBN 1 872745 10 5.

HUTSON, A.M. 1993. *Action Plan for Conservation of Bats in the United Kingdom*. The Bat Conservation Trust, London. 49 pp. ISBN 1 872745 16 4.

JONES, K. & WALSH, A. 2001. *A Guide to British Bats*. AIDGAP, Field Studies Council & Mammal Society, Shrewsbury & London. 8 pp.

KAPTEYN, K. (ed.). 1993. *Proceedings of the First European Bat Detector Workshop*. Netherlands Bat Research Foundation, Wageningen. 128 pp. ISBN 90 9006435 4.

KRAPP, F. (ed.). 2001. *Handbuch der Saugetiere Europas*, Band 4: Fledertiere, Tiel I: Chiroptera 1: Rhinolophidae, Vespertilionidae I. AULA-Verlag, Wiesbaden. 603 pp. ISBN 3 89104 638 3. [In German.] First of two volumes with detailed species accounts of the bat fauna of Europe.

LIMPENS, H., MOSTERT, K. & BONGERS, W. (eds). 1997. *Atlas van de Nederlandse vleermiuzen*. KNNV Uitgeverij, Utrecht. 260 pp. ISBN 90 5011 091 6.

MCDONALD, D.W. & TATTERSALL, F. 2001. *Britain's Mammals: the Challenge for Conservation*. People's Trust for Endangered Species, London. 295 pp. ISBN 0 9540043 1 0. (With annual supplements.)

MITCHELL-JONES, A.J., AMORI, G., BOGDANOWICZ, W., KRYSTUFEK, B., REIJNDERS, P.J.H., SPITZENBERGER, F., STUBBE, M., THISSEN, J.B.M., VOHRALIK, V. & ZIMA, J. 1999. *The Atlas of European Mammals*. Poyser Natural History/Academic Press, London. 484 pp. ISBN 0 85661 1301.

OHLENDORF, B. (compiler). 1997. *On the Situation of the Rhinolophidae in Europe*. Arbeitskreis Fledermause Sachsen-Anhalt e.v., Stecklenberg. 182 pp. ISBN 3 89689 999 6.

O'SULLIVAN, P. 1994. Bats in Ireland. *Irish Naturalists' Journal* (Special Zoological Supplement). 21 pp. ISBN 0021 1311.

PAVLINOV, I.Ia., KRUSKOP, S.V., VARSHAVSKII, A.A. & BORISENKO, A.V. 2002. *Mammals of Russia: keys-distribution*. Zoologicheskii Musei M.G.U., Moscow IZD-VO KMK. 298 pp. [in Russian.] ISBN 5 87317 094 0.

RAMSEY, D. (ed.). 1994. *Nature conservation in environmental assessment*. English Nature, Peterborough. 50 pp. ISBN 1 85716 135 1.

RANSOME, R. 1980. *The Greater Horseshoe Bat*. Blandford Press, Poole. ISBN 0 7137 0986 3.

RANSOME, R. 1990. *The Natural History of Hibernating Bats*. Christopher Helm, Kent. 235 pp. ISBN 0 7470 2802 8.

RANSOME, R.D. 1996. The management of feeding areas for greater horseshoe bats. *English Nature Research Report No.174. 74 pp.* ISSN 0967 876X.

RANSOME, R.D. & HUTSON, A.M. 2000. *Action Plan for the Conservation of the Greater Horseshoe Bat in Europe* (Rhinolophus ferrumequinum). Council of Europe, Nature and Environment 109. 53 pp. ISBN 92 871 4359 5.

RICHARDSON, P.W. 1985. *Bats*. Whittet Books, London. ISBN 0 905483 41 3.

RICHARDSON, P.W. (compiler). 2000. *Distribution Atlas of Bats in Britain and Ireland*. London, The Bat Conservation Trust, 43 pp.

ROBERTSON, J. 1990. *The Complete Bat*. Chatto & Windus, London. 165 pp. ISBN 0 7011 3500 X.

RUSS, J. 1999. *The Bats of Britain and Ireland; echolocation calls, sound analysis, and species identification*. Bishops Castle, Alana Ecology Ltd. 103 pp. ISBN 0 9536049 0 X.

SARGENT, G. 1995. *The bats in churches project*. The Bat Conservation Trust, London. 122 pp. ISBN 1 872745 19 9.

SCHOBER, W. & GRIMMBERGER, E. 1998. *Die Fledermause Europas*. 2nd edn. Kosmos Verlag, Stuttgart, 267 pp. ISBN 3 440 07597 4. [In German.] Other editions in English, e.g. *Bats of Britain and Europe*. 1993. Hamlyn, London. 224 pp. ISBN 0 600 57965 4.

SCHOFIELD, H.W. & MITCHELL-JONES, A.J. 2003. *The Bats of Britain and Ireland*. 2nd edn. The Vincent Wildlife Trust, Ledbury. 32 pp. ISBN 0 946081 48 4.

SHIEL, C., MCANEY, C., SULLIVAN, C & FAIRLEY, J. 1997. *Identification of Arthropod Fragments in Bat Droppings*. Occasional Publications No.17. Mammal Society, London. 56 pp . ISBN 0 906282 33 0.

SIMPSON & BROWN ARCHITECTS. 1996. *The Design and Construction of Bat Boxes in Houses*. Scottish Natural Heritage, Perth. 32 pp. ISBN 1 853972061.

STEBBINGS, R.E. 2003. *Which Bat is it?* Mammal Society, London. ISBN 0 906282 19 5. 3nd edn.

STEBBINGS, R.E & GRIFFITH, F. 1986. *Distribution and Status of Bats in Europe*. NERC. 133 pp. ISBN 0 904282 94 5.

STEBBINGS, R.E. 1988. *Conservation of European Bats*. Christopher Helm, London. 246pp. ISBN 0 7470 3013 8.

STEBBINGS, R.E. 1992. *Bats*. Mammal Society, London. 32 pp. ISBN 0 906282 18 7.

STEBBINGS, R.E. 1992. *The Greywell Tunnel*. English Nature. 32 pp. ISBN 1 85716 103 3.

STEBBINGS, R.E. & WALSH, S.T. 1991. *Bat Boxes, 3rd edn*. The Bat Conservation Trust, London. 24 pp. ISBN 1 872745 02 4.

SWIFT, S. M. 1998. *Long-eared Bats*. T & A. D. Poyser, London. 182 pp. ISBN 0 85661 108 5.

TUPINIER, Y. 1997. *European Bats: Their World of Sound*. Editions Sitelle, Mens.

VAUGHAN, N. 1997. The diets of British bats. *Mammal Review*, **27**(2), 77–94. ISSN 0305 1838.

WALSH, A., CATTO, C., HUTSON, A., RACEY, P., RICHARDSON, P. & LANGTON, S. 2001. *The UK's National Bat Monitoring Programme, Final Report 2001*. London, Department for Environment, Food and Rural Affairs. 155 pp.

YALDEN, D.W. 1985. *The Identification of British Bats*. Occasional Publication No.5. Mammal Society, London. ISBN 0906 282 25 X.

B Bats worldwide – general accounts of biology and natural history

ALLEN, G.M. 1939. *Bats*. Harvard University Press, Cambridge, Mass. Reprinted 1962 by Dover Publications Inc, New York, and Constable & Co Ltd, London.

BARNARD, S.M. 1997. *Bats in Captivity*. Wild Ones Animal Books, Springville, CA. 194 pp. ISBN 1 886013 02 0.

BAILLIE, J. & GROOMBRIDGE, B. 1996. *1996 IUCN Red List of Threatened Animals*. IUCN, Gland. 368 pp. ISBN 2 8317 0335 2. (see www.redlist.org for updates.)

BARLOW, K. 1999. *Expedition Field Techniques – Bats*. Expedition Advisory Centre/Royal Geographical Society, London. 69 pp. ISBN 0 907649 82 3.

BRASS, D.A. 1984. *Rabies in Bats: Natural History and Public Health Implications*. Livia Press, Connecticut. 335 pp. ISBN 0 9637045 1 6.

CORBET, G.B. & HILL, J.E. 1991. *A World List of Mammalian Species*. British Museum (Natural History), London. 254 pp. ISBN 0 565 00988 5.

COUFFER, J. 1992. *Bat Bombs – World War II's Other Secret Weapon*. University of Texan Press, Texas. 252 pp.

CRIGHTON, E.G. & KRUTZSCH P.H. (eds). 2000. *Reproductive Biology of Bats*. Academic Press, London/San Diego. 510 pp. ISBN 0 12 195670 9.

FENTON, M.B. 1992. *Bats*. Facts on File, New York/Oxford. 207 pp. ISBN 1098 7654 321.

FINDLEY, J.S. 1993. *Bats: A Community Perspective*. Cambridge Studies in Ecology, Cambridge University Press. 167 pp. ISBN 0 521 380054 5.

GREENHALL, A.M. & SCHMIDT, U. 1988. *Natural History of Vampire Bats*. CRC Press, Florida. 246 pp.

GRIFFIN, D.R. 1986 (reprint). *Listening in the Dark.*

Cornell University Press, Ithaca/London. 415 pp.

HILL, J.E. & SMITH, J.D. 1984. *Bats: A Natural History*. British Museum (Natural History), London. ISBN 0 565 00877 3.

HUTSON, A.M. 2000. *Bats*. Colin Baxter Photography Ltd, World Life Library, Granton-on-Spey. 72 pp. ISBN 1 900455 67 6.

HUTSON, A.M., MICKLEBURGH, S.P. & RACEY, P.A. (compilers). 2001. *Microchiropteran Bats: Global Status Survey and Conservation Action Plan*. IUCN/SSC Chiroptera Specialist Group, IUCN, Gland/Cambridge. 258 pp. ISBN 2 8317 0595 9.

KUNZ, T.H. (ed.). 1982. *Ecology of Bats*. Plenum Press, New York & London. ISBN 0 306 40950X.

KUNZ, T.H. (ed.). 1988. *Ecological and Behavioral Methods for the Study of Bats*. Smithsonian Institution Press, Washington DC/London. 533 pp. ISBN 0 87474 411 3.

KUNZ, T.H. & FENTON, M.B. 2003. *Bat Ecology*. University of Chicago Press. 784 pp. ISBN 0226462064.

LOLLAR, A. & SCHMIDT-FRENCH, B. 2002. *Captive Care and Medical Reference for the Rehabilitation of Insectivorous Bats*. Bat World Publications, Texas. 340 pp. ISBN 0 9638248 3 X.

MICKLEBURGH, S.P., HUTSON, A.M. & RACEY, P.A.1992. *Old World Fruit Bats - An Action Plan for their Conservation*.International Union for Conservation of Nature and Natural Resources, Gland, Switzerland. 252 pp. ISBN 2 8317 0055 8.

NEUWEILER, G. 2000. *The Biology of Bats*. Oxford University Press, New York/Oxford. 310 pp. ISBN 0 19 509951 6.

NOWACK, R.M. 1994. *Walker's Bats of the World*. John Hopkins University, Baltimore & London. 287 pp. ISBN 0 8018 4986 1.

POPPER, A.N. & FAY, R.R. 1995. *Hearing by Bats*. Springer Handbook of Auditory Research, Springer-Verlag, New York/Berlin/Heidelberg. 515 pp. ISBN 0 387 97844 5.

RICHARDSON, P. 2002. *Bats*. London, The Natural History Museum. 111 pp. ISBN 0 565 09167 0.

RICHARZ, K. & LIMBRUNNER, A. 1993. *The World of Bats*. TFH Publications, Waterlooville. 192 pp. ISBN 0 86622 540 4.

SCHOBER, W. 1984. *The Lives of Bats*. Croom Helm, London. 200 pp. ISBN 0 7099 2389 9.

TUTTLE, M.D & HENSLEY, D.L. 1993. *Bat House Builder's Handbook*. Bat Conservation International. 32 pp. ISBN 0 9638248 0 5.

WILSON, D.E. 1997. *Bats in Question – the Smithsonian Answer Book*. Smithsonian Institution Press, Washington. 168 pp. ISBN 1 56098 783 3 (hbk), 1 56098 739 1 (pbk).

WILSON, D.E. & REEDER, D.M. 1993. *Mammal Species of the World; a Taxonomic and Geographic Reference*. Smithsonian Institution Press, Washington. [revised edition in press 2004.]

WIMSATT, W.A. (ed.). 1970. (vol 1 & 2); 1971 (vol 3). *Biology of Bats*. Academic Press, London. Vol 1: ISBN 0 12 758001 8, Vol 2: ISBN 0 12 758002 6, Vol 3: ISBN 0 12 758003 4.

YALDEN, D.W. & MORRIS, P.A. 1975. *The Lives of Bats*. David and Charles, Newton Abbott. ISBN 0 7153 6799 4. [Out of print.]

C Children's Books

CANNON, J. 1995. *Stellaluna*. David Bennett Books. ISBN 1 85602 156 4.

DAVIES, N. 2001. *Bat Loves the Night*. Walker Books. ISBN 0 7445 2887 9 hb (pb published 2002, ISBN 0 7445 9402 2).

GREENAWAY, F. 1991. *Amazing Bats*. Dorling Kindersley, London. 29 pp. ISBN 0 86318 649 1. [Out of print.]

HAFFNER, M. & STUTZ H.P.B. 1989. *A Family of Bats*. Adams & Charles Black, London. 31 pp. ISBN 0 7136 3127 9. [Out of print.]

JULIVERT, M.A. 1996. *The Fascinating World of Bats*. Ward Lock. 31 pp. ISBN 0 7063 7551 3.

SOWLER, S. 1993. *A Fruit Bat called Angelica*. Adelphi Press, London. 21 pp. ISBN 1 85654 135 5.

THOMPSON, S. 1989. *Bats in the Garden*. School Garden Company, Lincs. 35 pp. ISBN 1 85116 803 6.

THOMPSON, S. 1995. *Starfile on Bats*. SGC Books, Lincs. 18 pp. ISBN 1 85116 840 0.

THOMPSON, S. 1997. *Bats in Scotland (Investigations for 5-14 year olds)*. The Bat Conservation Trust, London. ISBN 1 872745 23 7. [Resource pack, available only from The BCT office.]

THOMPSON, S. 1998. *Exploring the World of Bats*. The Bat Conservation Trust, London. [Incorporating Bats in Scotland and additional material related to the rest of the UK, with National Curriculum notes. Resource pack. Available only from The BCT office.]

THOMPSON, S. & RICHARDSON, P. 1993. *Bat Conservation Project Book*. Hodder & Stoughton, Kent. 32 pp. ISBN 0 340 57256 6. (Now only available from The Bat Conservation Trust).

D Journals, magazines and newsletters

In addition to those listed many county bat groups produce regular or annual reports and newsletters.

Acta Chiropterologica (ISSN 1508 1109)
Museum and Institute of Zoology PAS
Wilcza 64
00-679 Warsawa
Poland
E-mail: wieslawb@miiz.waw.pl
Twice-yearly international journal of papers in English

Bats
Bat Conservation International
PO Box 162603
Austin
Texas 78716
USA
E-mail: pubs@batcon.org
Quarterly newsletter of BCI.

Bat Care News
Bryan and Maggie Brown
West Yorkshire Bat Hospital
10 North Avenue
Otley
West Yorkshire
LS21 1AJ
Tel: 01943 466101
E-mail: kbg91@dial.pipex.com
A quarterly magazine on bat care.

Bat News ISSN 0269 8501
The Young Bat Worker
The Bat Conservation Trust
15 Cloisters House
8 Battersea Park Road
London
SW8 4BG
The official publications of the Bat Conservation Trust

Bat Research News
G. Roy Horst, Publisher
Bat Research News
P.O. Box 5068
Potsdam, NY 13676-5068
E-mail: horstgr@potsdam.edu

Eurobat Chat
UNEP/Eurobats Secretariat
United Nations Premises
Martin-Luther-King-Str. 8
53175 Bonn
Germany
E-mail: chat@eurobats.org
Newsletter of the Agreement on the Conservation
of Populations of European Bats

Myotis ISSN 0580 3896
Dr R Hutterer
Zoologisches Forschungsinstitut & Museum
Alexander Koenig
Adenaueralle 150-164
D-5300 Bonn1
Germany
An annual journal with papers in English and
German

Nyctalus ISSN 0138 2276
Dr Joachim Haensal
Nyctalus
Brascheweg 7
D-10318 Berlin – Karlshorst
Germany
A twice-yearly journal with papers mainly in
German with English summaries

Plecotus et al.
E.I. Kozhurina
A.N.Severtsov Institute of Ecology and Evolution
Leninsky Prospect 33
Moscow 119071
Russia
E-mail: kefa@orc.ru
Annual journal with papers in Russian with English
summary

Scottish Bats
South East Scotland Bat Groups
9 Brunswick Street
Edinburgh
EH7 5JB
A journal with papers on bats in Scotland. See
http://www.scotbats.org.uk/

Vespertilio ISSN 1213 6123
Czech Bat Conservation Trust
c/o Petr Benda
Department of Zoology
National Museum Praha
Vaclavska nam. 68
CZ-115 79 Praha 1
Czech Republic
E-mail: petr.benda@nm.cz

Bat Protection Group of Slovakia,
c/o Marcel Uhrin,
Administration of National Park Muranska planina,
J. Kral'a 12,
SK – 05001 Revuca,
Slovakia.
E-mail: uhrin@sopsr.sk

Annual journal of papers in Czech/Slovak

Barbastelle bat. © Frank Greenaway

Appendix 6

Useful names and addresses

Statutory nature conservation organisations

SNCO responsibilities include licensing for activities identified in Chapter 1.

Countryside Council for Wales
Maes-y-ffynnon
Ffordd Penrhos
Bangor
Gwynedd LL57 2DW
Tel: 01248 385500
Fax: 01248 355782
E-mail: enquiries@ccw.gov.uk
Web site: http://www.ccw.gov.uk

The statutory nature conservation organisation for Wales. CCW has five area offices and a number of local offices.

English Nature
Northminster House
Peterborough PE1 1UA
Tel: 01733 455000
Fax: 01733 568834
E-mail: enquiries@english-nature.org.uk
Web site: http://www.english-nature.org.uk

Statutory nature conservation organisation for England. Administrative headquarters, including specialist support teams. English Nature also has 21 local offices. Consult your local telephone directory for details.

The Environment and Heritage Service
Commonwealth House
35 Castle Street
Belfast BT1 1 GU, Northern Ireland
Tel: 028 9025 1477
Fax: 028 9054 6660
E-mail: ehs@nics.gov.uk
Web site: http://www.doeni.gov.uk

An agency of the Department of Environment (Northern Ireland), which takes the lead in the implementation of the government's environmental strategies and policies in Northern Ireland. Its responsibilities include all relevant licensing.

Scottish Natural Heritage
12 Hope Terrace
Edinburgh EH9 2AS
Tel: 0131 447 4784
Fax: 0131 446 2277
Web site: www.snh.org.uk

Scottish Natural Heritage
17 Rubislaw Terrace
Aberdeen AB10 1XE
Tel: 01224 642863
Fax: 01224 643347

Statutory nature conservation organisation for Scotland. In addition to the above, SNH has 35 local offices. Headquarters will move to Inverness in 2005.

Other Government bodies

For the following bodies, responsibilities include licensing for certain activities identified in Chapter 1. For Northern Ireland, see under SNCOs.

Department for Environment, Food and Rural Affairs
European Wildlife Division
Temple Quay House
2 The Square
Temple Quay
Bristol BS1 6EB
Tel: 0117 372 8291
Fax: 0117 372 8182
E-mail: species@defra.gsi.gov.uk
Web site: http://www.defra.gov.uk/wildlife-countryside/ewd/

Scottish Executive
Species Team
Countryside and Natural Heritage Unit
Environment and Rural Affairs Department
Victoria Quay
Edinburgh EH6 6QQ
Tel: 0131 244 7140
Fax: 0131 244 4071
Web site: www.scotland.gov.uk

Welsh Assembly
Nature Conservation Branch
Countryside Division
Welsh Assembly Government
Cathays Park Cardiff CF10 3NQ
Tel: 02920 823363
Fax: 02920 801353
E-mail: countryside.licensing@wales.gsi.gov.uk
Web site: http://www.wales.gov.uk

Non Governmental Organisations

The Bat Conservation Trust
15 Cloisters House
8 Battersea Park Road
London SW8 4BG
Tel: 08451 300228
Fax: 020 7627 2628
E-mail: enquiries@bats.org.uk
Web site: http://www.bats.org.uk

The national organisation for bat conservation, which provides guidance and support for all local bat groups.

Bat Conservation International
PO Box 162603
Austin, Texas
78716-2603
United States of America
Tel: (512) 327 9721
Fax: (512) 327 9724
E-mail: batinfo@batcon.org
Web site: http://www.batcon.org/

Fauna and Flora International
Great Eastern House
Tenison Road
Cambridge CB1 2TT
Tel: 01223 571000
Fax: 01223 461481
E-mail: info@fauna-flora.org
Web site: www.fauna-flora.org

A charitable organisation whose mission is to safeguard the future of endangered species of animals and plants world-wide.

The Mammal Society
2b Inworth Street
London SW11 3EP
Tel: 020 7350 2200
Fax: 020 7350 2211
E-mail: enquiries@mammal.org.uk
Web site: http://www.mammal.org.uk

The national society for all amateurs and professionals with an interest in the study of mammals.

National Association of Mining History Organisations
c/o Peak District Mining Museum
The Pavilion

South Parade
Matlock Bath
Derbyshire DE4 3NR
Tel: 01629 583834
E-mail: wes@wtaylor44.fsnet.co.uk
Web site: http://www.namho.org/

The umbrella organisation for mine research groups. The Association publishes a useful code of conduct and can provide lists of local groups.

National Caving Association
Monomark House
27 Old Gloucester Street
London WC1N 3XX
E-mail: nca@nca.org.uk
Web site: http://www.nca.org.uk/

The umbrella organisation for caving and cave research groups and clubs. The NCA can provide guidance about underground surveys and lists of local clubs and interest groups.

The National Trust
Estates Department
33 Sheep Street
Cirencester
Gloucestershire GL7 1RQ
Tel: 01285 651818
Fax: 01285 657935
Web site: http://www.nationaltrust.org.uk/

The department dealing with advice on nature conservation on National Trust properties.

People's Trust for Endangered Species
15 Cloisters House
8 Battersea Park Road
London SW8 4BG
Tel: 020 7498 4533
Fax: 020 7498 4459
Web site: http://www.ptes.org/

A charitable trust funding scientific research and practical work in the field with the aim to protect creatures in the wild that are threatened with extinction, including bats. Administers Mammals Trust UK.

Subterranea Britannica
c/o Highcroft Cottages
London Road
Swanley

Kent BR8 8DB
Tel: 01322 408081
E-mail: nick@swanley1.freeserve.co.uk
Web site: www.subbrit.org.uk

National organisation with a specialist interest in
artificial underground sites. Has a range of local
member interest groups.

The Vincent Wildlife Trust
3 & 4 Bronsil Courtyard
Eastnor
Ledbury
Herefordshire HR8 1EP
Tel: 01531 636441
Fax: 01531 636442
E-mail: vwt@vwt.org.uk
Web site: www.vwt.org.uk

A private charitable trust, which provides assistance
to a wide range of conservation organisations as
well as employing its own field staff who carry out
research, monitoring and wardening work
(including bats).

The Wildlife Trusts
The Kiln
Waterside
Mather Road
Newark
Notts NG24 1WT
Tel: 01636 677711
Fax: 01636 670001
E-mail: info@wild-trusts.cix.co.uk
Web site: http://www.wildlifetrusts.org/

The national association of the local Wildlife
Trusts.

Equipment suppliers

General
Alana Ecology Ltd
The Old Primary School
Church Street. Bishop's Castle
Shropshire SY9 5AE
Tel: 01588 630173
Fax: 01588 630176
E-mail: sales@alanaecology.com
Web site: www.alanaecology.com

Supplies a wide range of field and lab equipment,
including items in most of the following categories.

Envisage
The Old Brickyard
Kiln Lane
Swindon SN2 2NP
Tel: 01793 538822

Supplies a wide range of field and lab equipment,
including items in most of the following categories.

Bat detectors

Alana Ecology Ltd
(see opposite)

David J. Bale
3 Suffolk Street
Cheltenham
Gloucestershire GL50 2DH
Tel: 01242 570123
Fax: 01242 570123
E-mail: courtpan@gxn.co.uk

Supplies the Tranquility and ECO Tranquility bat
detectors with a time expansion facility.

Envisage
(see above)

Supplied Duet and Batbox detectors

Magenta Electronics Ltd
135 Hunter Street
Burton-on-Trent
Staffordshire DE14 2ST
Tel: 01283 565435
Fax: 01283 546932
E-mail: Magenta_Electronics@compuserve.com
Web site: http://ourworld.compuserve.com/home-
pages/Magenta_Electronics

Supply a bat detector as a kit or assembled.

Pettersson Elektronik AB
Tallbackswagen 51
S -756 45 Uppsala
Sweden
Tel: +46 1830 3880
Fax: +46 1830 3840
E-mail: info@batsound.com
Web site: http://www.batsound.com/

Suppliers of professional bat detectors and sound
analysis software. Sole agent for UK & Ireland:

Alana Ecology Ltd (see p.158).

Skye Instruments Ltd
Unit 21
Ddole Enterprise Park
Llandrindod Wells
Powys LD1 6DF
Tel: 01597 824811
Fax: 01597 824812
E-mail: skyemail@skyeinstruments.com
Web site: http://www.skyeinstruments.com/

Stag Electronics
120 High Street
Steyning
West Sussex BN44 3RD
Tel: 01903 816298 / 07000 228269
Fax: 01903 816298
E-mail: info@batbox.com
Web site:www.batbox.com

Ultrasound Advice
23 Aberdeen Road
London N5 2UG
Tel: 020 7359 1718
Fax: 020 7359 3650
E-mail: sales@ultrasoundadvice.co.uk
Web site: http://www.ultrasoundadvice.co.uk/

Caving equipment

Bat Products
6 Tucker Street
Wells
Somerset BA5 2DZ
Tel: 01749 676771
Fax: 01749 676771

Bernies Cafe and Caving Supplies
4 Main Street
Ingleton
Carnforth LA6 3EB
Tel: 01524 241802
Fax: 01524 242439
Web site: www.berniescafe.co.uk

Caving Supplies Ltd
19 London Road
Buxton
Derbyshire SK17 9PA
Tel: 01298 71707
Fax: 01298 72463

E-mail: sales@caving-supplies.co.uk
Web site: http://www.caving-supplies.co.uk/

Inglesport
The Square
Ingleton
via Carnforth LA 6 3EB
Tel: 01524 241146
Fax: 01524 242035
E-mail: info@inglesport.co.uk
Web site: www.inglesport.co.uk

The above supply a full range of underground exploration equipment associated with caving including the Oldham T3 head torch, which is powered by a rechargeable lead-acid battery.

Hand nets

Alana Ecology Ltd
(see p.158)

Marris House Nets
54 Richmond Park Avenue
Bournemouth
Dorset BH8 9DR
Tel: 01202 515238
Fax: 01202 511252

Ian Forsyth
24 Malone Park
Belfast BT9 6NJ
Tel: 02890 665534
Fax: 02890 668442
E-mail: forsyth.i@btopenworld.com

Supplier of hand net and frame for catching bats emerging from roosts in buildings.

Watkins and Doncaster
Conghurst Lane
Four Throws
Hawkhurst
Kent TN18 5DZ
Tel: 01580 753133
Fax: 01580 754054
E-mail: sales@watdon.com
Web site: www.watdon.com

Supply a range of hand nets and other equipment for naturalists.

APPENDIX 6 160

Optical equipment (including night vision)

Alana Ecology Ltd (see p.158)

Gadgets.co.uk
6 Greenhill Crescent
Watford Business Park
Watford
Herts WD18 8RF
Tel: 0870 0806666
Fax: 0870 0805555
E-mail: sales@gadgets.co.uk
Web site: www.gadgets.co.uk
Supplies include a few cheaper night-vision scopes.

In Focus
The Wildfowl and Wetland Trust
London Wetland Centre
Queen Elizabeth Walk
Barnes
London SW13 9WT
Tel: 020 8409 4433
Fax: 020 8409 4441
Web site: www.at-infocus.co.uk

Good range of binoculars, etc. Eight shops
nationally. Will discuss night-vision equipment.

Ringing and marking

Alana Ecology Ltd (see p.158)

Biotrack Ltd
52 Furzebrook Road
Wareham
Dorset BH20 5AX
Tel: 01929 552992
Fax: 01929 554948
E-mail: info@biotrack.co.uk
Web site: www.biotrack.co.uk

Supplies radio tags.

Holohil Systems Ltd
112 John Cavanagh Road
Carp. Ontario
Canada K0A 1L0
Tel: +613 839 0676
Fax: +613 839 0675
E-mail: info@holohil.com
Web site: www.holohil.com

Supplies radio tags.

Labtrac Ltd
PO Box 19. Uckfield
East Sussex TN22 3TF
Tel: 01825 791069
Fax: 01825 791006
E-mail: sales@avidplc.com
Web site: www.avidplc.com

Supplies AVID microchip equipment (PIT tags).

Mariner Radar
Bridleway
Wood Lane
Campsheath
Oulton
Lowestoft
Suffolk NR32 5DN
Tel: 01502 567195
Email: sales@mariner-radar.com

Supplies receivers and antennae.

Porzana Limited
Elms Farm
Pett Lane
Icklesham
East Sussex TN36 4AH
Tel: 01797 226374
Fax: 01797 226374
E-mail: porzana@wetlandtrust.org

Supplies bat rings in alloy and incoloy metal.
UK batrings also available from

The Mammal Society
28 Inworth Street
London SW11 3EP
Tel: 020 7350 2200
Fax: 020 7350 2211
E-mail: enquiries@mammal.org.uk
Web site: www.mammal.org.uk

Telonics
932 Impala Avenue
Mesa. Arizona 85204-6699
USA
Tel: +480 892 4444
Fax: + 480 892 9139
E-mail: info@telonics.com
Web Site: www.telonics.com

Supplies receivers and antennae.

Titley Electronics
PO Box 19
Ballina
New South Wales 2478
Australia
Tel/Fax: +61 2 66866617
E-mail: titley@nor.com.au
Web site: www.titley.com.au

Supplies radio tags.

Other field equipment

Alana Ecology Ltd
(see p.158)

British Trust for Ornithology
Ringing Office
The Nunnery
Thetford
Norfolk IP24 2PU
Tel: 01842 750050
Fax: 01842 750030
E-mail: ringing.sales@bto.org
Web site: www.bto.org

Suppliers of bird ringing equipment, including aluminium section poles, spring balances, calipers, end-stop rulers, 'bird' bags and mist nets.

Electromail
PO Box 33
Corby
Northants NN17 9EL
Tel: 01536 204555
Fax: 01536 405555
Web site: http://rswww.com

A sister company of RS components, which deals with small orders and non-account customers. Suppliers of dial calipers, tally counters and digital thermometers.

Bat boxes and bat bricks

Alana Ecology Ltd
(see p.158)

Supply a range of Schwegler woodcrete bat boxes and traditional wooden bat boxes.

Envisage
(see p.158)

Supply a range of Schwegler woodcrete bat boxes and traditional wooden bat boxes.

Jacobi Jayne & Co
Wealden Forest Park
Herne Common
Canterbury
Kent CT6 7LQ
Tel: 01227 714314
Fax: 01227 719235
E-mail: enquiries@jacobijayne.com
Web site: www.jacobijayne.com

Supplies the full range of Schwegler woodcrete boxes.

C. J. Wild Bird Foods Ltd
The Rea
Upton Magna
Shrewsbury. Shropshire SY4 4UR
Tel: 0800 731 2820
Fax: 01743 709504
E-mail: orders@birdfood.co.uk
Web site: www.birdfood.co.uk

Supplies some bat boxes and other items relevant to bats.

Marshalls Clay Products
Howley Park
Quarry Lane
Woodkirk. Dewsbury
West Yorkshire WF12 7JJ
Tel: 01132 203535
Fax: 01132 203555
Web site: http://www.marshalls.co.uk

Manufacture and supply a bat access brick and bat roost unit.

Norfolk Bat Group
The Barn Cottage
Wheelers Lane
Seething
Norfolk NR15 1EJ
Tel: 01508 550784
Fax: 01508 550850
E-mail: john.golds@paston.co.uk
Web site: http://www.norfolk-bat-group.org.uk

Supplies the BAT-zzz-BRICK for hibernation sites.

Mealworms

Live Foods Direct Ltd
Houghton Road
North Anston Trading Estate
Sheffield S25 4JJ
Tel: 01909 518888
Fax: 01909 568666
E-mail: sales@livefoodsdirect.co.uk
Web site: www.livefoodsdirect.co.uk

Books, videos, stickers, novelties

Bat Bazaar
c/o Alana Ecology (see p.158)
Web site: www.batsnet.org/acatalog
Bat books, tapes, slides, jewellery, novelties, etc.
for sale to individuals and to bat groups for resale.

The Bat Conservation Trust
15 Cloisters House
8 Battersea Park Road
London SW8 4BG
Tel: 020 7627 2629
Fax: 020 7627 2628
Web site: www.bats.org.uk

The Mammal Society
(see p.157)

Natural History Book Service
2-3 Wills Road
Totnes. Devon TQ9 5XN
Tel: 01803 865913
Fax: 01803 865280
E-mail: nhbs@nhbs.co.uk
Web site: http://www.nhbs.com

A leading supplier of British and foreign books on
natural history.

Speleobooks
PO Box 10
Schoharie
New York 12157-0010
USA
Tel: +518 295 7978
Fax: +518 295 7981
E-mail: speleobooks@speleobooks.com
Web site: www.speleobooks.com

Wide range of bat and cave books, videos, posters,
stickers, novelties, etc.

Whiskered bat in flight. © Frank Greenaway

Appendix 7

Bat workers' training syllabus

This syllabus is to be used as a checklist for both the trainee bat worker (conservation and scientific licences) and the trainer.

Legal protection: Wildlife and Countryside Act 1981 & Conservation (Natural Habitats &c.) Regulations 1994 or equivalent

Basic protection

Bats are protected against intentional killing, injuring or taking. Their roosts are protected against damage, destruction or obstruction, and it is also an offence to deliberately disturb bats. There are variations in protection across the UK.

Limits to protection

Protection of both bats and their roosts is not absolute and in some situations is very weak.

Dwelling houses

In all parts of a dwelling house it remains illegal to kill, injure or take bats but their roosts may be obstructed, damaged or destroyed provided that the SNCO has been notified and allowed time to advise on how this may best be done. This requirement for consultation does not apply in the living area of the house. The existence of this defence means that householders do not have to have bats roosting in their house if they clearly do not want them, but they are not allowed to kill or injure them and they should consult the SNCO about the best way of getting rid of them.

Lawful operations

Bats may be killed or injured or their roosts damaged or destroyed provided that this is the 'incidental result of a lawful operation and could not reasonably have been avoided'. However, the SNCO should be consulted about the interpretation of this defence before any action is taken and will provide advice on how any adverse effects on the bats may reasonably be avoided.

Circumstances requiring consultation

It is important that this is clearly understood. The SNCO should be consulted about any proposed deliberate action against bats or their roosts in dwelling houses or about any operation that will incidentally but foreseeably affect bats or their roosts wherever these may be.

Limitations of advice by volunteers

The law requires that the SNCO is notified and allowed time to provide advice. Volunteers can assist the SNCO in providing the best possible advice but they must either refrain from giving advice themselves or explain that action should not be taken until the advice has been confirmed by the SNCO.

Licensing

Licensable activities

Most activities that are prohibited in the Act or Regulations are licensable in one way or another. The SNCO is the licensing authority for activities carried out for scientific, conservation or educational purposes (including marking and photography). The appropriate government department (see Appendix 6) is the licensing authority for preventing the spread of disease, preventing serious damage, preserving public health or public safety or other imperative reasons of overriding public interest.

Licences are not required for the exclusion of bats from dwelling houses or for anything which is covered by the 'lawful operation' defence. The only requirement is that the SNCO is notified and allowed a reasonable time to advise.

SNCO licences

The SNCOs provide a number of general types of licence, the most important of which are conservation (roost visitor), scientific (survey and monitoring), research and marking, and training. Endorsements can be added to any of these licences to permit a wide range of other activities.

Licence applications should normally be on the standard forms provided and the application should be endorsed by a licensed trainer once the trainee has reached the required standard. If a trainer is not available, the names of two referees will be acceptable as a second choice.

Licences normally restrict the licensee to work in a limited area, usually one or more counties. This is intended to prevent any friction between neighbouring bat workers and to cut down on the possibility of a number of people visiting the same roosts independently. However, even within a county, it is important that local bat workers liaise informally with each other in order to avoid misunderstandings and repeat visits to sites.

Other licences

Government departments issue licences under the Habitats Regulations for preventing the spread of disease, preventing serious damage, preserving public health or public safety or other imperative reasons of overriding public interest. The latter reason is the most common and these are often referred to as 'development licences' because they are most frequently issued to permit damage or destruction of bat roosts or disturbance of bats during development works. Applications must fit the purpose of 'overriding public interest' and also pass tests of 'no satisfactory alternative' and 'no adverse impact of favourable conservation status'.

Bat biology and ecology

Basic biology
Taxonomy
Relationships with other mammals
Characteristics of families
Trainees should be aware that bats form a very distinctive zoological order and that the two families represented in Britain are quite distinctive.

Physical adaptations for flight
Physiological specialisations
The ability of bats to enter and arouse from daily torpor and seasonal hibernation is an extremely important feature of the order, and an understanding of this is vital when considering their life histories, sensitivity to disturbance, etc.

Senses

Trainees should be aware of the importance of sight and hearing to bats and should be able to give a simple account of the way in which their echolocation system operates.

Basic ecology

Importance in ecosystems
Life histories
Lifespan
Breeding
Food and feeding
Seasonality

Social behaviour

Colony formation and composition
Mating systems and behaviour

Maternal behaviour
Juvenile behaviour

Habitat selection

Roosting
Range of roost sites
Seasonal changes in site selection

Feeding

Range of feeding habits
Diurnal rhythms in feeding behaviour
It is important that trainees have a good understanding of the lives of bats so that they are able to deal convincingly with questions put to them by householders. The level of competence will obviously improve with experience, but everyone should at the very least have read one or two of the currently available books on bats and have discussed all the headings listed with his or her trainer.

Bat conservation

Threats to bats

It is very important that bat workers should be able to answer convincingly the very common question, 'Why are bats protected?'.

Historical evidence

Some of our best evidence about the declines in bat numbers over the last century comes from studies of former and current distributions. The greater horseshoe bat is the best-studied example. Other evidence comes from the works of Victorian naturalists who recorded bats as apparently being much more common than today.

Current threats

Habitat change/loss
This is probably the single most important factor that has affected bat populations in the last 100 years. The intensification of agriculture, loss of woodlands and draining of wetlands have all had their effect, both in reducing the number of insects available to bats and in reducing the availability of roost sites.

Loss of hibernacula
Loss of summer roost sites

Effects of modern farming
Loss of insects

Pesticides

Remedial timber treatment
This has probably been implicated in population declines, because many of the treatment fluids in use until recently could kill bats, even some time after treatment. Modern treatments are much less toxic, but roosts should not be treated when bats are present.

Agricultural pesticides
These can affect bats either directly, by accumulation through the food chain, or indirectly, by reducing the numbers of insects available to the bats at critical times of the year.

Persecution and intolerance
Many colonies have been, and probably continue to be, lost through direct persecution.

Sensitivity of bats to disturbance
Training for all levels of licence should cover this section, because the guidelines are applicable to a wide range of circumstances.

In winter
Every time a bat hibernaculum is entered by a party of surveyors a proportion of the bats will invariably be disturbed and begin to arouse. If the survey is by a single careful person, the proportion arousing may be very low, and conversely a large careless party may arouse many of the bats. Repeated disturbance of individuals can reduce their survival by forcing them to use food reserves, which they may not replace easily.

Hibernating bats should, therefore, not be disturbed unnecessarily and should not be handled without a good reason for doing so. Areas known to be used by hibernating bats should not be repeatedly visited unless as part of an intensive survey or research project (which would need a survey or research licence). Further guidance on the frequency of visits is given in the section on survey work.

In summer
Excessive disturbance of breeding colonies can cause mothers to abandon their young or young to become separated from their mothers and so should be avoided. Some species seem more sensitive to

disturbance than others. Horseshoe bats are alert most of the time and will normally fly when approached to within 3 or 4 metres. Other species are more approachable and some, such as pipistrelles, can normally be picked up quite easily because they are most reluctant to fly.

Public relations

Site visits

Site visits are probably the major area of interest of all Bat Groups. Training for such visits is largely a matter of experience and trainees should accompany their trainer on at least half a dozen visits before being considered for their own licence. Training under the following headings should consist of both discussions and practical experience and the trainer should be confident that the trainee will be able to deal competently and sympathetically with householders before endorsing a roost visitor licence application.

Safety

Ensuring that visits are carried out safely is an important aspect of training and time must be spent ensuring that the trainee is aware of the main safety issues. These are: personal safety on the visit; safe working practices when using ladders or other access equipment; potential hazards in buildings, particularly in roofs; and safety when handling bats. Trainees should be encouraged to undertake risk assessment as a matter of course when arranging visits. The SNCOs will have their own safety requirements for visits carried out at their request and these should always be adhered to.

Visits to householders who have discovered bats
Arranging the visit
Analysing the situation
Persuasion and education
Sensitivity to fears and phobias
Practical help and limits to advice
Follow-up action
Further visits
Recording and reporting
Consultation/liaison with the SNCO

Visits to buildings requiring works that may affect bats
Arranging the visit
Analysing the situation

Inspecting the site
Collecting relevant information
Follow-up action
Completion of report
Suggestions for advice
Liaison with the SNCO

Presenting bats to the public

Giving talks
Trainers should check that those who are prepared to give talks about bats have a good understanding of bat biology and are not going to spread 'misinformation' about bats.

Dealing with the media
Not all Bat Group members will need to deal with the media but all should be told of the basic rules.

Practical methods

Health and safety in bat work

Health and first aid
Trainees should be aware of necessary disease precautions, especially against rabies.

Travel, and night or lone working
Trainees should be aware of simple precautions to minimise any personal risk.

Safety in and around buildings
Visits to locate or inspect bat roosts may involve access to parts of buildings that present particular safety hazards. Trainees must understand the importance of being properly equipped for such work and with the concept of risk assessment.

Safety underground
Visits to caves and mines require particular attention to equipment and safe methods of working. Trainees should be familiar with the safety code in Chapter 2.

Safety at tree roosts
Safety at public events

Handling and examining bats

Handling
All trainees for a handling licence (who should have received pre-exposure rabies vaccination) must be able to handle bats safely and comfortably.

This will necessarily involve practical experience, which could, perhaps, start with captive animals but must also include handling wild bats. Points to emphasise are that bats should be handled only for a good reason and when this can be done safely, that handlers should avoid being bitten and take appropriate action if they are, that bats should not be kept for longer than necessary and that bats should always be released close to the point of capture. Trainees will vary in their ability to handle bats, but, as a guideline, they should have handled wild bats on at least five occasions and should preferably have handled more than one species.

Identification
For roost visitor licences, trainees should be confident about identifying the common species in their area and should be familiar in theory, if not in practice, with the features that identify all British species. It is important to emphasise that all bats must be examined carefully before reaching a conclusion, because otherwise mistakes will be made. All trainees should be familiar with one of the published keys on British bats.

Trainees for survey licences should be able readily to identify a wider range of bats in a variety of situations.

Examining
Trainees should be able to handle bats for examination and should be able to sex bats and measure the forearm length. It is advantageous if trainees can distinguish juveniles, but this is not a requirement of the training scheme. It is neither necessary nor desirable that trainees are able to take a wide range of measurements, because these are required only for specialist projects.

Catching bats
Trainees for roost visitor licences need to be trained how to catch bats safely in roosts and at roost entrances. Trainees for survey licences who wish to carry out specialist research projects may need training in techniques of catching bats in the open or in large numbers at roosts, but this should not be generally encouraged.

Inside roosts
In some circumstances bats may simply be picked up carefully within roosts (assuming that there is a need to catch one) or, if likely to fly, they may be caught by placing a hand-net gently over them.

Bats should not be caught in flight or swiped at with a hand-net.

At roost entrances

The approved technique is to hold a hand-net directly below the roost entrance so that an emerging bat falls straight into it as it drops from the roost entrance. The bat can then be carefully extracted from the net. Emphasis should be placed on the need to keep the net still and the undesirability of disturbing the colony so that emergence is disrupted. This is a straightforward technique and trainees should be competent after perhaps five attempts. Cone-trapping is a specialised research technique and should not be used to catch small numbers of bats for identification.

In the open

All methods of catching bats in the open have the potential to harm bats if used carelessly. The most common methods are harp-trapping or mist-netting and licences for this will only be given to applicants who have received appropriate training and agree to follow SNCO guidelines.

Survey work

The majority of applicants for licences require a conservation (roost visitor) licence so that they can visit householders and disturb or handle bats associated with buildings. A small proportion of applicants will wish to extend their interest to survey work for bats and bat roosts and may require a licence to disturb or handle bats in hibernacula or to catch bats in the open.

Hibernacula

Safety

Working safely in underground sites such as caves, mines, ice-houses or tunnels requires a good understanding of the potential hazards and the basic safety rules that must always be observed. Good safety advice is provided by the various caving and mine history organisations.

Frequency of survey

The dangers of excessive disturbance have already been covered in a previous section because of their general applicability.

The acceptable frequency of survey will vary with the configuration of the site, the number of bats involved and the purpose of the survey. It is

impossible to give hard and fast rules but the following paragraphs give some guidance.

For intensive short-term (a few years) surveys to establish patterns of usage, a visit every 3 or 4 weeks by a careful individual or small party would probably be acceptable. Maximum party size should be related to the size of the hibernaculum and the density of bats.

Long-term surveys should normally require only one or two visits per winter, preferably at a time when the maximum number of bats is present. Again, party size should be related to the size of the hibernaculum and the density of bats.

Casual unplanned visits 'to see the bats' should be avoided, however strong the temptation. If you do wish to take trainees to see hibernating bats, try to arrange that they accompany you on planned survey trips and assist with counting the bats.

It should rarely be necessary to handle hibernating bats, because the great majority can be identified by close inspection. Horseshoe bats need be handled only as part of a research project.

Liaison

Although one individual or group may limit their visits to a site in a sensible way, it is clearly essential that there is not some other individual or group also visiting the same site and thus doubling the number of visits. Liaison between workers within an area is extremely important and should be given emphasis during training.

Summer roosts

Frequency of survey

Most of the remarks about winter surveys apply equally to summer surveys if visits inside the roost are necessary. However, most summer surveys should involve counting the bats as they emerge from the roost at dusk, with, perhaps, a few inspections inside to check on the agreement between internal counts and emergence counts. Provided that common-sense precautions are taken, there need be no limit placed on the number of emergence counts that are made.

If the species cannot be identified by careful inspection within the roost (horseshoe bats can normally be identified in this way), it will be acceptable to hand-net a bat as it emerges. Do not net more than a few bats, because this is unnecessary.

Training checklist	Tick
Legal protection: Wildlife and Countryside Act 1981 & Conservation (Natural Habitats &c.) Regulations 1994 or equivalent.	
Basic protection	
Limits to protection	
Dwelling houses	
Lawful operations	
Circumstances requiring consultation	
Limitations of advice by volunteers	
Licensing	
Licensable activities	
SNCO licences	
Other licences	
Bat biology and ecology	
Basic biology	
Taxonomy	
Relationships with other mammals	
Characteristics of families	
Physical adaptations for flight	
Physiological specialisations	
Senses	
Basic ecology	
Importance in ecosystems	
Life histories	
Lifespan	
Breeding	
Food and feeding	
Seasonality	
Social behaviour	
Colony formation and composition	
Mating systems and behaviour	
Maternal behaviour	
Juvenile behaviour	
Habitat selection	
Roosting	
Range of roost sites	
Seasonal changes in site selection	
Feeding	
Range of feeding habits	

Training checklist (continued)	Tick
Diurnal rhythms in feeding behaviour	
Bat conservation	
Threats to bats	
Historical evidence	
Current threats	
Habitat change/loss	
Loss of hibernacula	
Loss of summer roost sites	
Effects of modern farming	
Loss of insects	
Pesticides	
Remedial timber treatment	
Agricultural pesticides	
Persecution and intolerance	
Sensitivity of bats to disturbance	
In winter	
In summer	
Public relations	
Site visits	
Safety	
Visits to householders who have discovered bats	
Arranging the visit	
Analysing the situation	
Persuasion and education	
Sensitivity to fears and phobias	
Practical help and limits to advice	
Follow-up action	
Further visits	
Recording and reporting	
Consultation/liaison with the SNCO	
Visits to buildings requiring works which may affect bats	
Arranging the visit	
Analysing the situation	
Inspecting the site	
Collecting relevant information	
Follow-up action	
Completion of report	
Suggestions for advice	

Training checklist (continued)	Tick
Liaison with the SNCO	
Presenting bats to the public	
Giving talks	
Dealing with the media	
Practical methods	
Health and safety in bat work	
Health and first aid	
Travel and night or lone working	
Safety in and around building	
Safety underground	
Safety at tree roosts	
Safety at public events	
Handling and examining bats	
Handling	
Identification	
Examining	
Catching bats	
Inside roosts	
At roost entrances	
In the open	
Survey work	
Hibernacula	
Safety	
Frequency of survey	
Liaison	
Summer roosts	
Frequency of survey	

Appendix 8

Model risk assessments relevant to bat survey work

Chapter 2 provides advice on safety preparations. These model risk assessments provide a standard means for assessing the risks in three situations:
• entry into disused mines;
• initial entry into derelict and dilapidated buildings and structures;
• entry into and work in confined spaces.

These models have been developed for use within the National Trust. They form a basis for specific local site assessments, carried out by managers at individual properties. The National Trust cannot accept any responsibility for any errors or omissions, where these models are used by other organisations.

Specific legal requirements may change and readers should make the necessary enquiries to ensure that they are aware of the latest legislation.

Model risk assessment for entry into disused mines

Work Activity	Entry into disused mines
Other relevant model risk assessments	Entry into confined spaces.
Physical hazards arising	Being struck by falling rock; Contact with rock and other obstructions (head injury); Asphyxiation from build-up of dangerous gases or lack of oxygen; Explosion from ignition of flammable gases; Falls from height from collapse of floor, or openings in floor; Drowning; Trips and falls on same level; Hypothermia, arising from long periods underground, or following trapping underground by flooding or rock falls.
Health hazards arising	Exposure to radon (only significant where extensive work underground is carried out).
Persons at risk	Countryside staff and others engaged in bat surveys, industrial archaeology, geological surveys. Visitors.
Principal organisational precautions	No person should go underground alone. Planning: Obtain plans of the mine workings in advance; Note weather conditions for at least 24 hours before going underground, particularly into caves or mine systems prone to flooding after heavy rain; The minimum size of party entering mine four persons (in the event of injury, one person should remain with the injured person, while two persons go for assistance). A minimum of two persons are required as back-up at the mine entrance; At least one person in the party should be experienced in the work; At least one person in the party underground should be a qualified first-aider; Hazards should be identified in advance; The capabilities of the members of the party should be taken into account; Monitoring for dangerous gases/lack of oxygen should take place where these are identified as potential hazards; Expert geological advice should be sought on the stability of strata in abandoned mines; Entry should only take place under a written permit-to-work system; Extra time should be allowed for the exit from the mine; Written emergency procedures should be prepared.

Model risk assessment for entry into disused mines (cont)

Principal physical precautions	**Equipment:** Gas monitoring equipment should be used to warn of the presence of dangerous gases; Vapour sealed electric headlamp units should be worn, and a spare lamp of different type carried by each person going underground; Lifelines (where required by the nature of the mine and length of the expedition); Ropes and harnesses may be required for access to parts of the mine; Survival bags (when a long period underground is contemplated) should be taken; Spare food and drink should be carried; Waterproof watches should be worn; First aid kits should be carried. **Protective clothing:** Safety helmets to BS EN 397 (formerly BS 5240) should be worn; Eye protection to BS 2092 should be worn if hammers and chisels are used for rock samples; Safety boots; The need for wet suits and/or waders should be considered; Adequate clothing should be worn for a cold, wet environment. **Exposure:** Exposure can occur very rapidly underground in the cold, wet conditions. If exposure is suspected, take the following action: find a dry location away from draughts; huddle together for warmth and cover the head and hands; place the exposed or injured person in the survival bag, ideally with another person; cover the head and hands; use ropes and other equipment for insulation from the floor; give some of the spare food; two persons should go for assistance, leaving the exposed person and one other together.
Specific legal requirements	Mines and Quarries Act 1954; Wildlife and Countryside Act 1981; Management and Administration of Safety and Health at Mines Regulations 1993.
Further guidance	HSE Approved Code of Practice L44 - "*The management and administration of safety and health at mines*"; Institute of Biology - "*Safety in biological fieldwork - guidance notes for codes of practice*"; Conservation Safety Manual (contained within NT Health and Safety Manual) – Section 3 - "*Safety in field work*". National Trust Bat Pack – "The conservation of bats and their legal status" (1996)

Date/NT Ref.5 February 1997.WRK 013

Model risk assessment for initial entry into derelict and dilapidated buildings and structures

Work activity	Initial entry into derelict and dilapidated buildings and structures
Explanatory note	This Model Risk Assessment (MRA) covers initial appraisal of and entry into a derelict or dilapidated building, to establish its general integrity, its structural stability, and the nature and extent of other hazards created by its current and former uses. A separate MRA covers detailed survey and initial work on such buildings.
Physical hazards arising	Falls from height, due to rot or damage to floors and structural members, and concealed and unprotected edges and openings; Fall of materials, due to the instability of the structure; Electric shock or burns from faulty electrical installations; Fire/explosion from ignition of gas leaking from cylinders or faulty/damaged installations; Oxygen deficiency or accumulations of poisonous gas in confined spaces; Injury from loose or projecting objects; Trips and slips; Unexploded ordnance; Waterlogged or flooded basements, pits or cellars; Assault in remote locations.
Health hazards arising	Exposure to chemical or similar contamination, arising from: - abandoned chemicals (spillage or in containers); - asbestos materials; - PCB's (polychlorinated biphenyls) in old oil-filled electrical equipment. Exposure to radioactive contamination. Biological hazards, e.g. leptospirosis (Weil's Disease), pathogens from leaking sewers, disease from decaying animals or accumulations of bird/bat droppings, contact with hypodermic syringes. Dust, e.g. from lead, arsenic in old paint.
Persons at risk	Batworkers, owners, tenants, consultants, contractors and unauthorised visitors.
Principal organisational precautions	Information should be collected from plans and other documents prior to the initial site appraisal; An initial appraisal should be carried out to identify structural defects and hazardous areas; Relevant information should be given to consultants and contractors before entry is allowed; At least 2 persons should be involved in the initial entry - notification should be given to another person of their whereabouts, and the duration of their visit.
Principal physical precautions	Barriers and signs: Unauthorised persons should be excluded from the site by physical barriers, at a sufficient distance from the building to allow for falling debris; Signs should be posted to warn of hazards to visitors and unauthorised persons. Equipment and protective clothing: Hard hats and steel toe-capped protective footwear should be worn at all times; Dust masks, eye protection, gloves and disposable suits may be required; A first-aid kit should be available; Other useful equipment might include: - flashlight or miner's-type headlight; - portable radio communication; - access inspection ladder; - rope or tape to mark the route; - stick (for exploration); - binoculars.
Specific legal requirements	Control of Lead at Work Regulations 1980; Ionising Radiations Regulations 1985; Asbestos at Work Regulations 1987; Control of Substances Hazardous to Health Regulations 1994.

Model risk assessment for initial entry into derelict and dilapidated buildings and structures (cont)

Further guidance	HSE booklet HS(G)58 - "Evaluation and inspection of buildings and structures" (1990); HSE booklet HS(G)66 - "Protection of workers and the general public during the development of contaminated land" (1991); HSE Guidance Note GS 5 (revised) - "Entry into confined spaces" (1995); HSE Approved Code of Practice L28 - "Work with asbestos insulation, asbestos coating and asbestos insulating board"; Department of the Environment booklet - "Asbestos materials in buildings"; HSE leaflet MS(A)19 - "PCBs and you "; NT Health Hazard Information Sheet No. 2 - "Weil's Disease": NT Bat Pack - "The conservation of bats and their legal status "; Suzy Lamplugh Trust pocket guide - "Personal Safety at work for you".

Date/NT Ref. 12 March 1996 WRK 006

Model risk assessment for entry into confined spaces

Work activity	Entry into and work in confined spaces
Explanatory note	The term "confined space" includes closed tanks, sewers, tunnels, caves, open manholes, trenches, pipes, pits, vats, flues, furnaces, silos, ducts, as well as other enclosed rooms and spaces, e.g. basements, ceiling voids, where there is inadequate natural ventilation.
Physical hazards arising	There are three principal hazards associated with confined spaces: 1. Flammable gases. Fire and explosion hazards can exist in confined spaces where gases such as LPG have accidentally leaked into the space, or where decaying matter and sewage have produced flammable gases such as methane. 2. Toxic gases. Toxic, harmful or corrosive fumes and vapours can exist in, or be generated by the work in a confined space - for example, some painting work, application of certain adhesives (e.g. when laying floor tiles), cleaning areas or objects using solvents, welding, fumes emitted when sludge and other residues are disturbed during cleaning tanks or pits, the use of LPG appliances, and petrol and diesel engine fumes. 3. Oxygen deficiency. Oxygen deficiency can occur naturally in confined spaces, for example where manholes, tunnels and trenches in chalk soil fill with carbon dioxide forcing out breathable air, or where rotting vegetation and rusting of metal in tanks can consume much of the oxygen and hence make the air unbreathable. Work activities in confined spaces can also reduce the oxygen level by replacing it with inert gas such as in pipe freezing operations in trenches or inert gas welding. Other hazards include: Drowning; Falls from height, and slips and trips; Falling objects; Contact with moving machinery; Oxygen enrichment.
Health hazards arising	Contact with biological hazards, such as leptospirosis (Weil's disease), tetanus and legionella; Heat stress; High levels of noise; Dust.
Persons at risk	Batworkers, owners, tenants, consultants, contractors and others having to enter confined spaces.

Model risk assessment for entry into confined spaces (cont)

Principal organisational precautions	Is it essential to enter the confined space? Can the work be carried out from outside? If not, the following system must be followed: 1. Recognition - all batworkers should be able to recognise a situation or work location which is a confined space. 2. Assessment - a full and comprehensive site risk assessment is essential before any work starts, for all confined space operations. 3. Preparation - consider the previous use of the space. Prevent ingress of liquids, gases and vapours from outside the confined space. Locking off and blanking off of supplies or services may be necessary. The confined space may need to be purged, cleaned or steamed before safe entry is possible. Forced ventilation may be required. 4. Test - if the condition of the atmosphere is unknown, it will usually be necessary to sample the atmosphere for flammable and toxic fumes, and oxygen level. This will be necessary to establish whether the space can be entered safely without breathing apparatus, or only entered with it. 5. Safeguards - rescue harnesses must be worn by all persons entering the confined space. A lifeline should be attached to the harness and the free end kept outside with the safety observer. The lifeline need not be attached if it presents a greater risk from entanglement, although it should be kept close by. 6. Permit-to-work certificate - the person in charge must complete a permit-to-work certificate, specifying what safety measures have been taken. The permit should specify any limitations to the work, and set the time by which the work must be completed and the confined space vacated. The should be properly cancelled on completion of the work. A sample layout of a permit is contained in HSE Guidance Note GS5. 7. Safety observer – no-one shall enter a confined space unless there is someone outside to keep watch throughout, and to communicate with those inside. In an emergency they must be able to summon help, hut under no circumstances enter the confined space. One person alone will not be able to pull out an unconscious person on a line and harness, unless a lifting device is available. 8. Rescue – emergency procedures should be established in advance. Is there a means of contacting the emergency services close at hand? Is there a trained first-aider close by? 9. Training - those persons overseeing the work, entering and working in the confined space and acting as a safety observer will need to be adequately trained. Training should cover rescue and emergency procedures and the use of emergency breathing apparatus and harnesses.
Principal physical precautions	Do not use petrol or diesel engines inside, or close to confined spaces; Avoid using substances that give off hazardous fumes or vapours; Do not carry out hot work in confined spaces; Do not use tools which can produce sparks; Never attempt to clear fumes or gases with pure oxygen; Do not rely on canister respirators in confined spaces (they can filter out contaminants in the atmosphere but will not replace deficient oxygen).
Specific legal requirements	Factories Act 1961 (Section 30); Construction (Health, Safety and Welfare) Regulations 1996.
Further guidance	HSE Guidance Note GS5 - "Entry into confined spaces" (1995); HSE Guidance Note GS15 - 'Cleaning and gas freeing of tanks containing flammable residues" (1985); HSE Construction Information Sheet No.15 - "Confined spaces"; HSE leaflet IND(G)198L – "Working with sewage "; HSC Consultation Document CD105 - "Proposals for replacement of the law for work in confined spaces".

HEALTH AND SAFETY LEGISLATION

Some of the key requirements of the health and safety legislation, which are appropriate for work with bats, are given below.

Health and Safety at Work etc Act 1974 requires:

- employers and self-employed workers to ensure they provide and maintain workplaces, equipment and systems of work that are, so far as is reasonably practicable, safe to workers and the public;

- employees to take care of their own and others' health and safety, and to co-operate with their employer or any other person to enable them to comply with health and safety duties;

- *A guide to the Health and Safety at Work etc Act 1974 (L1) gives further information.*

Control of Substances Hazardous to Health (COSHH) Regulations 2002 provide a framework of actions designed to control the risk from a range of hazardous substances including biological agents. These actions include:
- assess the risk;
- prevent the risk by substitution if possible;
- control the risks using appropriate measures, e.g. *work process, systems and engineering controls;*
- control exposure at source, e.g. *adequate ventilation systems and appropriate organisational measures;*
- control the working environment including general ventilation;
- maintain, examine and test control measures;
- provide suitable personal protective equipment (PPE) when adequate control of exposure cannot be achieved by other means;
- monitor exposure at the workplace;
- provide information, instruction and training for workers;
- make arrangements for health surveillance of workers where necessary;
- *COSHH: a brief guide to the regulations (INDG131 rev1); Control of Substances Hazardous to Health (4th edn). The Control of Substances Hazardous to Health Regulations*

2002. Approved Code of Practice and Guidance (L5); Health Surveillance under COSHH: guidance for employers; The management, design and operation of microbiological containment laboratories; and 5 steps to risk assessment (INDG163 rev1) give further information.

Management of Health and Safety at Work Regulations (MHSWR) 1999 require employers and self-employed workers to:

- identify the measures they need to take by carrying out risk assessments;
- institute safety management systems;
- appoint persons to assist in health and safety management;
- ensure co-ordination and co-operation where two or more employers or self-employer persons share a workplace;
- make emergency arrangements;
- provide information and relevant training for employees;
- *Successful health and safety management (HSG 65) gives further information.*

The Carriage of Dangerous Goods (Classification, Packaging and Labelling) Regulations 1996 require consigners to:

- classify the biological agent or substance containing the biological agent for transport according to the criteria laid down in the 'Approved Requirements';
- determine the packing group and package in accordance with the appropriate packing instruction;
- appoint a Dangerous Goods Safety Adviser if necessary;
- *Are you involved in the carriage of dangerous goods by road or rail?; Approved Carriage List: Information approved for the carriage of dangerous goods by road and rail other than explosives and radioactive material (ACL); European Agreement concerning the international carriage of dangerous goods by road (ADR); Approved Vehicle Requirements. Carriage of Dangerous Goods by Road Regulations 1996 (AVR); and Regulations Concerning the International Carriage of Dangerous Goods by Rail (RID) give further information.*

Other legal requirements also exist under a range of other specific health and safety legislation. These duties include reporting of Injuries, Diseases and Dangerous Occurrences Regulations and assessing other specific risks to workers (e.g. from manual handling and stress).

References

Legislation

Health and Safety at Work etc Act 1974.
SI1974/1439. The Stationery Office 1974.
ISBN 0 11 141439 X.

Management of Health and Safety at Work Regulations (MHSWR) 1999. SI1999/3242. The Stationery Office 1999. ISBN 0 11 0856252 2.

Control of Substances Hazardous to Health (COSHH) Regulations 2002. SI2002/2677. The Stationery Office 2002. ISBN 0 11 042919 2.

Reporting of Injuries, Diseases and Dangerous Occurrences Regulations (RIDDOR) 1995. SI1995/3163. The Stationery Office 1995. ISBN 01 1053 7523.

The Carriage of Dangerous Goods (Classification, Packaging and Labelling) Regulations 1994. SI1994/669. The Stationery Office 1994. ISBN 01 1043 6695.

The Data Protection Act 1998. The Stationery Office 1998. ISBN 0 10 542998 8.

2000/54/EC. Protection of workers from risks related to exposure of biological agents at work (seventh individual directive within the meaning of Article 16(1) of Directive 89/391/EEC). OJ L262. 17.10.2000.

Guidance

A Guide to the Health and Safety at Work etc Act 1974. (L1). HSE Books 1990. ISBN 0 7176 0441 1. (A priced publication.)

Successful health and safety management (HSG 65) 2nd edn. HSE Books 1997. ISBN 0 7176 2034 4. (A priced publication.)

COSHH: a brief guide to the regulations (INDG131 rev1). HSE Books 2002. (Free as single copies.)

Control of Substances Hazardous to Health. 4th edn. The Control of Substances Hazardous to Health Regulations 2002. Approved Code of Practice and Guidance (L5). HSE Books 2002. ISBN 0 7176 2534 6. (A priced publication.)

Health Surveillance under COSHH: guidance for employers. HSE Books 1990. ISBN 0 717604918. (A priced publication.)

5 steps to risk assessment. (INDG163 rev1). HSE Books 1998. (Free as single copies.)

Guide to the reporting of Injuries, Diseases and Dangerous Occurrences Regulations 1995 (L73). HSE Books 1998. ISBN 0 7176 1012 8.

Are you involved in the carriage of dangerous goods by road or rail? (INDG234) HSE Books 2000. ISBN 0 7176 1676 2. (A free leaflet.)

Approved Carriage List: Information approved for the carriage of dangerous goods by road and rail other than explosives and radioactive material (ACL) (L90). HSE Books, 3rd edn. ISBN 0 7176 1681 9. (A priced publication.)

European Agreement concerning the international carriage of dangerous goods by road (ADR). The Stationery Office. ISBN 0 11 941712 X.

Approved Vehicle Requirements. Carriage of Dangerous Goods by Road Regulations 1996 (AVR) (L89). HSE Books, 2nd edn. ISBN 0 7176 1680 0.

Regulations Concerning the International Carriage of Dangerous Goods by Rail (RID). The Stationery Office 1998. ISBN 0 11 552032 5.

Second supplement to 'Categorisation of biological agents according to hazard and categories of containment' (MISC 208). HSE Books 2000.

Consulting employees on health and safety: A guide to the law. (INDG 232). HSE Books 1999. ISBN 0 71761650. (Available in priced packs or can be downloaded for free from www.hsebooks.co.uk)

Appendix 9

Department for Environment, Food and Rural Affairs
Scottish Executive Environment and Rural Affairs Department
Welsh Assembly Government

Bat Samples
for Rabies Screening

Please complete a **seperate** form for each species submitted.

Name and address of person submitting the specimen

Postcode

Telephone No. (including
national dialling code)

**Name and address of FINDER
(if different to person submitting the specimen)**

Postcode

Telephone No. (including
national dialling code)

Specimen detail

Species	Sex	Age

Date and
time found   Ref.
No.

Date and
time of death

Cause of death

Location

Map reference

Cicumstances of finding:

For Laboratory Use Only

Letter No.

Sample No.

Date received:

————— **RESULT** —————

Symptoms:

General condition:

Give details of any biting or scratching incidents
involving humans or animals:

it is not normal to send a result; in the event of a positive
result the finder would be contacted immediately.

If there are special reasons for requiring a result
to be sent, tick this box ....

Signature

Date

Please send completed form and specimen(s) to:
Graham Parsons
Rabies Diagnostic Unit,
Veterinary Laboratories Agency
Woodham Lane, Addlestone, Surrey KT15 3NB
Telephone No. 01932 357645

Further enquiries please contact:
Dr A R Fooks,
Head of Rabies Research
and Diagnostic Unit
Telephone No. 01932 341111

Internal Use Only

Copies to:
(1) SVO Page Street
(2) Dr A R Fooks

BAT 1 (Rev. 10/01)